KNIGHT-CAPRON LIBRARY
LYNCHBURG COLLEGE
LYNCHBURG, VA. 24501

New Directions in African Fiction

Twayne's World Author Series

Bernth Lindfors, Editor
University of Texas at Austin

TWAS 869

New Directions in African Fiction

Derek Wright

Northern Territory University

Twayne Publishers
An Imprint of Simon & Schuster Macmillan
New York

Prentice Hall International
London • Mexico City • New Delhi • Singapore • Sydney • Toronto

Twayne's World Author Series No. 869

New Directions in African Fiction
Derek Wright

Copyright © 1997 by Twayne Publishers

All rights reserved. No part of this book may be reproduced or transmitted in any form or by any means, electronic or mechanical, including photocopying, recording, or by any information storage and retrieval system, without permission in writing from the Publisher.

Twayne Publishers
An Imprint of Simon & Schuster Macmillan
1633 Broadway
New York, NY 10019

Library of Congress Cataloging-in-Publication Data

Wright, Derek.
  New directions in African fiction / Derek Wright.
    p. cm. — (Twayne's world authors series ; TWAS 869)
  Includes bibliographical references (p.   ) and index.
  ISBN 0-8057-4556-4 (hardcover : alk. paper)
  1. African fiction (English)—History and criticism.   I. Title.
II. Series.
PR9344.W75   1997
823—dc21   97-20634
                                                         CIP

The paper used in this publication meets the minimum requirements of American National Standard for Information Sciences—Permanence of Paper for Printed Library Materials. ANSI Z39.48–1984. ∞ ™

10 9 8 7 6 5 4 3 2 1

Printed in the United States of America

For Penny

Contents

Preface ix
Acknowledgments xi
List of Abbreviations xiii

> *Chapter One*
> The Postcolonial Predicament, 1965–1970 1
>
> *Chapter Two*
> Lyric Fatalism and Mystic Utopianism: History as Myth and Ritual in Kofi Awoonor's *This Earth, My Brother* . . . and Wole Soyinka's *Season of Anomy* 23
>
> *Chapter Three*
> Orature Revisioned: Yambo Ouologuem's *Bound to Violence* and Ayi Kwei Armah's *Two Thousand Seasons* 42
>
> *Chapter Four*
> Orality and Dictatorship: Ngugi wa Thiong'o's *Matigari* and Nuruddin Farah's *Sweet and Sour Milk* 60
>
> *Chapter Five*
> The African in White South African Fiction: Landscape and Mythology in J. M. Coetzee's *Life and Times of Michael K* 80
>
> *Chapter Six*
> A Wounded Nation: Shimmer Chinodya's *Harvest of Thorns* and Zimbabwe's Legacies of Liberation 95
>
> *Chapter Seven*
> Regurgitating Colonialism: The Feminist Voice in Tsitsi Dangarembga's *Nervous Conditions* 108
>
> *Chapter Eight*
> Ethnic Voices: M. G. Vassanji's *The Gunny Sack* 123

Chapter Nine
Imagined and Other Worlds: Magic History in Kojo Laing's *Search Sweet Country* and Ben Okri's *The Famished Road*   140

Chapter Ten
Prospective: Into the Nineties   162

Notes and References   *181*
Selected Bibliography   *190*
Index   *199*

Preface

The present study charts significant developments in recent African fiction through the close examination of selected works in their historical contexts, taking as its starting point the crisis of postindependence disillusionment in the mid-1960s and concluding with experimental writing of the 1990s. Its range is broad, featuring a total of 21 novels by 15 authors from nine countries. Even so, the book is not intended as a comprehensive history of the African novel in the last quarter of the twentieth century and, except in the opening and concluding chapters, does not attempt any general survey of the field. This work, like my previous studies of Ayi Kwei Armah, Wole Soyinka, and Nuruddin Farah, is more about texts than trends. My aim has been to identify the intrinsic peculiarities and often unique qualities of individual works within the parameters of their own indigenous cultural discourse rather than to locate their position in some wider intellectual sequence or continental zeitgeist. Moreover, although it is more than just a random collection of essays, the book has no binding theoretical orientation and calls upon theories of literature and language only when the authors themselves—as in the case of Coetzee, Farah, Dangarembga, and Laing—appear to be cognizant of them.

A short work such as this demands drastic selection, although yardsticks need not be uniform. In my treatment of some regional literatures the accent has fallen largely, although not exclusively, upon innovation and invention. Thus the younger, contemporary generation of West African novelists has been represented by Ben Okri, 'Biyi Bandele-Thomas, and Kojo Laing rather than by Festus Iyayi and Ken Saro-Wiwa. This is because the former group seems to me to indicate a more genuinely new direction in African fiction and a movement away from the mainstream social realism. Even allowing for the work of Tutuola and Soyinka, social realism was the dominant mode of expression for this fiction up to the mid-1980s. In discussions of other areas of the continent, where national upheavals have had a more profound impact upon literature, history has been privileged over style: Thus postindependence Zimbabwe is represented by Shimmer Chinodya and Tsitsi Dangarembga, not by the more flamboyant Dambudzo Marechera.

Thanks are due to a number of people and institutions for aid in the composition and production of this book: to Bernth Lindfors for alerting me to material pertinent to the debate in the final chapter; to the Northern Territory University for a semester's sabbatical during which the work was completed; and to my undergraduate and postgraduate students of postcolonial literatures for their lively feedback on some of the ideas expressed within, most particularly my doctoral student Maggi Phillips for her valuable insights into Ben Okri's writing. Finally, I am grateful to the editors of *Commonwealth, Journal of Commonwealth Literature,* and *Modern Fiction Studies* for permission to reproduce material contained and presented in a different form in articles originally published by those journals.

Acknowledgments

I am grateful to the following publishers for permission to quote extracts from the works listed:

Heinemann Educational, a division of Reed Educational and Professional Publishing Ltd., for *This Earth, My Brother* ... (1972) by Kofi Awoonor; *Matigari* (1989) by Ngugi wa Thiong'o; *The Gunny Sack* (1989) by M. G. Vassanji; and *The Last Harmattan of Alusine Dunbar* (1990) by Syl Cheney-Coker.
Doubleday, a division of Bantam Doubleday Dell Publishing Group, Inc., for *This Earth, My Brother* ... by Kofi Awoonor, copyright © 1972 by Doubleday. Used by permission of Doubleday, a division of Bantam Doubleday Dell Publishing Group Inc.
East African Educational Publishers Ltd. for *Matigari* (1989) by Ngugi wa Thiong'o.
Cambridge University Press for *Myth, Literature and the African World* by Wole Soyinka, copyright © Cambridge University Press 1976. Reprinted with the permission of Cambridge University Press.
Baobab Books, a division of Academic Books Ltd., for *Harvest of Thorns* (1989) by Shimmer Chinodya.
The Women's Press Ltd. for *Nervous Conditions* (1988) by Tsitsi Dangarembga. By permission of The Women's Press Ltd.
Rogers, Coleridge and White Ltd. for *Sweet and Sour Milk* by Nuruddin Farah, copyright © Nuruddin Farah 1979. Reproduced by permission of the author c/o Rogers, Coleridge and White Ltd.
Penguin Books USA Inc. for *I Saw the Sky Catch Fire* by T. Obinkaram Echewa, copyright © 1992 by T. Obinkaram Echewa. Used by permission of Dutton Signet, a division of Penguin Books USA Inc.
Reed Consumer Books Ltd. for *Life and Times of Michael K* by J. M. Coetzee, first published by Secker and Warburg, copyright © J. M. Coetzee 1983; and for *Search Sweet Country* by B. Kojo Laing, first published by William Heinemann Ltd., copyright © B. Kojo Laing 1986.
David Godwin Associates and Phoenix House Publishers for *Astonishing the Gods* by Ben Okri, copyright © Ben Okri 1995.

Jonathan Cape Ltd., Random House UK Ltd., and David Godwin Associates for *The Famished Road* and *Songs of Enchantment* by Ben Okri, copyright © Ben Okri 1991, 1993.

Efforts to trace other copyright holders have not been successful; responses and relevant information will be welcome.

Abbreviations

ATG	*Astonishing the Gods*
BONYB	*The Beautyful Ones Are Not Yet Born*
BTV	*Bound to Violence*
FR	*The Famished Road*
GS	*The Gunny Sack*
HOT	*Harvest of Thorns*
ISSCF	*I Saw the Sky Catch Fire*
LHAD	*The Last Harmattan of Alusine Dunbar*
M	*Matigari*
MG	*Major Gentl and the Achimota Wars*
MK	*Life and Times of Michael K*
MLAW	*Myth, Literature and the African World*
MOP	*A Man of the People*
NC	*Nervous Conditions*
NLAE	*No Longer at Ease*
OR	*Osiris Rising*
S	*Sardines*
SOA	*Season of Anomy*
SOE	*Songs of Enchantment*
SSC	*Search Sweet Country*
SSM	*Sweet and Sour Milk*
TEMB	*This Earth, My Brother . . .*
TTS	*Two Thousand Seasons*

Chapter One

The Postcolonial Predicament, 1965–1970

Between 1956 and 1965 the whole of Africa, minus the southern states, French Djibouti, and the Portuguese territories of Angola, Mozambique, and Guinea-Bissau, achieved independence. All over the continent the new national leaders, in their inaugural addresses, thanked and praised their people for their support in united common struggles, stressing that the victory belonged to every one of them, and pledged their governments to economic self-reliance through indigenous control of resources, to the rehabilitation of African cultural identity, and to programs of detribalization, democratic modernization, and equal opportunity. In Ghana, Kwame Nkrumah confidently predicted that the slumbering giant of Africa would emerge as a major world power whose greatness would be "founded on hope, trust, friendship and directed to the good of all mankind,"[1] and it is to this populist euphoria that the character Teacher, in Ayi Kwei Armah's *The Beautyful Ones Are Not Yet Born* (1968), looks longingly back: "The promise was so beautiful.... [A]t last something good was being born.... There was something so good about the destroyed people waking up and wanting to make themselves whole again."[2]

During the period immediately preceding independence, African intellectuals at home and abroad idealized the embryonic nation-states, and the fiction of the period gave expression to an intense nationalistic fervor. In *The African* (1960), by the Sierra Leonian William Conton, the future political leader Kisimi Kamara devotes himself to an ideal of "strength and freedom through unity and the subordination to that ideal of all tribal loyalties."[3] In *One Man, One Wife* (1959) and *One Man, One Matchet* (1964) by the Nigerian T. M. Aluko, the protagonists attack provincialism and tribal chauvinism, and the youthful hero of Chinua Achebe's *No Longer at Ease* (1960), during his first year of overseas education, addresses a naïve nostalgic poem to the new nation-state, exhorting his "noble countrymen" to "walk in unity ... [f]orgetting region, tribe or speech, / But caring always each for each."[4] In

Nigerian fiction of the early 1960s, this idealism was colored by both international aspiration and local patriotism. In his *Beautiful Feathers* (1963), dedicated to the federation's first prime minister, Cyprian Ekwensi extols the virtues of a Nigerian Pan-Africanist movement, whereas the early novels of Flora Nwapa, Elechi Amadi, and John Munonye present warmly celebrative pictures of traditional African village life and values.

A decade later, few of the heady expectations of independence had even come close to being fulfilled. At its creation in 1957, Ghana was one of the richest tropical countries in the world, with large gold, timber, and bauxite resources, and bank reserves of £200 million. Nine years later, at Nkrumah's fall, the latter were down to £30 million, the national debt stood at £360 million, and the average wage was among the lowest in West Africa.[5] The leader's grandiose industrial and public utility projects were attended by increasingly riotous ministerial corruption and wealth-hoarding scandals, which were contained up to 1961 but eventually swamped the whole country. As the ruling elite became bitterly opposed to criticism from Ghanaian intellectuals, newspapers were shut down and opponents imprisoned without trial. Finally the nation's self-proclaimed "Osagyefo" (savior) rigged a referendum for a one-party state, set up special courts with no rights of appeal, and dismissed judges for giving inconvenient rulings. In neighboring Nigeria, the six-year period of civilian rule following independence (1960–1966) saw a series of makeshift, unstable coalition governments between the Islamic North and one of the main ethnic groups of West, East, or South, each marred by intensifying political violence, corrupt electioneering, intimidation, and assassination. As its three diverse nations proved to be equally incapable of living apart or together, the new state's fragile nationalism quickly foundered on the rocks of ethnic rivalry and institutionalized corruption, plunging the country into tribal genocide (1966) and civil war (1967–1970). Even Algeria, where freedom was violently won by militant struggle, was not exempt from the fate of sub-Saharan decolonization. After independence in 1962, faction fighting resulted in a succession of virtual dictatorships by privileged managerial cadres that left the mass of the Algerian population disenfranchised. As in Kenya, an opportunistic nationalist administration dissociated itself from the militants and excluded them from power, and the peasantry were dispersed into small landholders in a state capitalist system and took no further part in the direction of the revolution. Though the war stimulated political consciousness and fostered temporary equalities, it did not permanently dissolve social and religious divisions, and Ben Bella's limited, short-lived program for female emancipation had little effect on the patriarchal domination of women. Neither did anticolonial struggle produce a successfully decolonized nation. The crippling effect of the war left Algeria dependent upon heavily conditional French economic and technical aid and entrenched legal, educational, and bureaucratic systems. The French performed atomic tests in the Sahara, and Algeria continued to supply raw materials within the structure of an essentially colonial economy.

In other parts of Africa the situation was much the same. Between 1960 and 1968 there were 25 unconstitutional changes of government across the continent, 18 of them military coups, so that by the end of the decade almost every one of the pluralist parliamentary democracies hastily set up by the departing colonial powers had given way to one-party states or dictatorships (only in Tanzania, during the 1961 elections, was this brought about by democratic processes). In Kenya, Uganda, and Rwanda, as in Nigeria, intractable ethnic rivalries led to one group seizing power at the expense of others. In these and in other countries, the outcome was a succession of monolithic, nonegalitarian political and cultural structures, tailored to fit a single dominant interest: Islam, in the case of the Algerian revolution, and a moralistic Christianity and Catholicism in, respectively, the cases of Kenyan socialism and Tanzanian *Ujamaa* ("familyhood").

For the majority of the African population conditions did not improve after independence but deteriorated. In the absence of innovative husbandry, the exhaustion of cultivable lands caused a pauperized peasantry to drift to urban slums and shantytowns, swelling the ranks of the unemployed and precipitating social breakdowns that the new black power elites were not equipped to deal with. Thus, a decade after the colonial exodus, independence had not brought unity, social justice, peace, or prosperity to Africa; on the contrary, it had produced division and fragmentation, inequality and class elitism, political violence, and economic stagnation. It had, moreover, not weakened but strengthened Africa's dependency upon the ex-imperial European powers. Thus it was not unusual for national leaders like Senghor of Senegal and Houphouet-Boigny of the Ivory Coast to warn their people against the dire consequences of cutting political, economic, and cultural ties with the mother country.

The reasons for Africa's postindependence crisis and collapse are not hard to find. First, the colonial legacy proved to be more hindrance than help. The outgoing imperial powers had hurriedly patched over ethnic fissures with the artificial structure of the European nation-state, obscuring social infrastructures—army, civil service, unions—that were riddled with tribalism. In countries such as Nigeria they bequeathed national democratic systems to populations whose political horizons were entirely tribal and provincial and who had received no training in the alien practices of parliamentary politics and multiparty democracy. Most of Nigeria's and Ghana's ethnic societies, far from being democratic and egalitarian, were in fact strongly stratified, hierarchical, and monarchic (for example, the Yoruba, Hausa, Akan, and Ashanti), and these autocratic structures were reinforced by authoritarian colonial administrations.

Moreover, in the British colonies of West Africa, an important feature of the imperial legacy was the establishment of and admission to positions of influence, long before independence, of a propertied and prosperous indigenous bourgeoisie, a class that was not suddenly created in the panic rush of decolonization; for this group the ideals of social revolution, equalization of wealth, and equitable distribution of resources were neither possible nor desirable. In these purely administrative colonies, where there were no lands to seize from white settlers, the educated intellectuals were not forced to seek common cause with the masses, nor were they provoked into a united militant struggle by their common exclusion, but they were groomed as successors by the colonial regime and co-opted into the leadership. The national independence movements consolidated the power of the socially dominant middle class, with whom the colonial powers maintained a long-established political dialogue, and made possible the smooth transfer of power from a white to a black elite. In Nigeria and Ghana and in the former French colonies of Senegal and the Ivory Coast, national liberation was from the beginning a heavily class-colored concept, and the party elites, eager to profit from the spoils of decolonization, appealed not to ideology but chiefly to class interest and (particularly in Nigeria) to traditional ethnic, religious, and regional loyalties. More important, Europe had not only provided these new nations with their political ideals and forms but had also given them access to Western luxuries and material comforts. Subsequently, the West African bourgeoisie, keen to emulate its European prototype and frustrated by the restricted professional opportunities offered to it during the colonial period, was eager to wrest economic power from a foreign elite and transfer it to a native one, albeit under the cover of a populist nationalism. If the resentment of this class was aimed at colonial capitalism, it was only insofar as no indigenous class was fully profiting from it. Beneath the camouflage of nationalist rhetoric, the personal acquisitiveness of the new national leaders and the idea of political office as the main route to wealth and economic power were plainly visible. As James Booth has shown, the first regional leaders of the Nigerian federation each subscribed to a broad philanthropic capitalism; by their own admission they were motivated by unabashed personal ambition and self-aggrandizement and were untroubled by the concentration of vast wealth in a few hands.[6] In the early years of independence the elitist attitudes and class arrogance of these national political figures were expressed in Nigerian fiction, notably in the novels of T. M. Aluko, in which a superficial modern progressivism conceals an essentially reactionary vision and the strengthening of the power elite's rule over the ignorant and uneducated masses is vigorously advocated.

In all other respects, however, the African bourgeoisie proved to be a pale imitation of its European counterpart. In young independent nations initially obliged to use colonially created economic channels, this class was content merely to serve in a client role, as a neoimperial business agent in a transmission line between the nation and Western capitalism, protecting and profiting from the foreign investments of its British and French prototypes. Coupled with imperial technical aid and qualified by political conditions, such investments ensured that these economic channels quickly sank back into quasi-colonial lines. In his 1969 essay "A Mystification: African Independence Revalued," Ayi Kwei Armah noted that economic flow patterns and lines of commercial access, running from cash-crop area to imperial metropolis, changed little during the postindependence years. He also observed that terms of trade were still fixed chronically against the African farmer and miner and that postcolonial Africanization programs more often entailed the expansion, rather than the disappearance, of expatriate personnel.[7] In his analysis of neocolonial elites in *The Wretched of the Earth* (1961), Frantz Fanon characterized this client-bourgeoisie as an underdeveloped, unproductive, parasitical caste, a useless and diversionary excrescence; he alleged that it stifled the development of sound economic bases and mass culture and that it was completely lacking in the entrepreneurial energy and invention of its European model: "Here, the dynamic, pioneer aspect, the characteristics of the inventor and of the discoverer of new worlds which are found in all national bourgeoisies are lamentably absent. . . . [N]ot a single industry is set up in the country."[8]

A Ghanaian census shortly before the fall of Nkrumah revealed that only 7 percent of the country's wage earners were employed in manufacturing industries, compared with 40 percent in the public sector.[9] The taxi driver in Armah's *Beautyful Ones* comments on the unproductive consumption of a nation living beyond its means—"everybody is making things now except us. We Africans only buy expensive things" (*BONYB*, 140). In Armah's second novel, *Fragments* (1970), Ghanaians succumb to the idolatrous materialism of a cargo mentality, attributing to the white world godlike powers of invention and innovation that they are unwilling to develop themselves. In these novels the merely imitative, indolent governing bourgeois caste is seen as beginning at the end of its class career: Hence when they assume power, the national leaders are already moribund and decrepit, ready for the grave. When this class vanishes, wrote Fanon, "it will be seen that nothing new has happened since independence was proclaimed, and that everything must be started again from scratch" (*WOE*, 142). Armah's anonymous hero reflects at Nkrumah's fall that "in the life of the nation itself . . . nothing really new would happen" (*BONYB*, 162). Since local industry and commerce were insufficiently developed and indigenous capital resources too meager to supply the bourgeoisie's demands in its frantic, hedonistic scramble for Western luxury goods, it inevitably resorted to embezzling government-controlled municipal funds, pilfering as much as it could get away with from the public coffers. The process is symbolized by the bus conductor in *The Beautyful Ones* who steals money from passengers' fares on payday and by a cynical daubing in a latrine about the state groaning under the burden of private corruption: "Who Born Fool / Socialism-Chop Make I Chop / Contrey Broke" (*BONYB*, 124).

Traditional values were also implicated in this process of corruption, often lending a spurious legitimacy to evil modern practices and combining the worst of the old and the new. The novels by Achebe, Aluko, Armah, and Soyinka that are about contemporary 1960s West African society make it clear that bribery, nepotism, tribal favoritism, and discreet theft—not taking "enough for the owner to see," in the words of the narrator's father in Achebe's *A Man of the People* (1966)[10]—were integral components of a coherent system of patronage that successfully prevailed in traditional society. As Obi, the protagonist of Achebe's earlier novel, puts it, "Our people say that if you pay homage to the man at the top others will pay homage to you when it is your turn to be on top" (*NLAE*, 18). These local forms of influence and ingratiation proved to be dysfunctional above the village level, however, and dangerously inadequate in the context of an impersonal mass-democratic system. Translated to the larger scale of nation-state capitalism, the string-pulling patronage of traditional African life was perverted into a system of wholesale bribery that resulted in the corrupt advancement of vote-buying politicians (such as Chief Nanga in *A Man of the People*), at the expense of the public good. The much-abused extended family system worked in a similar way. This system was once the linchpin of the traditional community and acted as a bulwark against social discord by guaranteeing some share of prosperity for all. Now, however, it began to undermine the social body by turning against it the self-serving interests of a few powerful careerists and their families, in whose hands wealth and power were now concentrated. Consequently, both family and state ceased to be solidarities of reciprocal interests and became channels for manipulation and exploitation. Only those members of society who had a "big man" in the family were able to feed from the new prosperity, turning traditional group economics into a facade for parasitic dependence: As Baako puts it in Armah's *Fragments,* the family "gets rich, mainly at the expense of the community," whereas "the community has disappeared from the story."[11]

The novels of this group of writers abound with vestigial survivals from traditional life that either lose their value altogether in their transposition to contemporary contexts or function only in debased form. In Soyinka's *The Interpreters* (1965) the journalist Sagoe composes a satiric eulogy for his country's "orgiastic funerals"—"a man could spend his entire life just feasting on a dead man. And many did."[12] In Armah's *Beautyful Ones* the lengthy funeral rites of village custom become the pretext by which a corrupt urban clerk fraudulently extends his holidays. In these works traditional welcoming panegyrics are transformed, with a little modern ingenuity, into occasions for ostentatious pomp and display for wealthy returnees from overseas, and libation is seized as an excuse for bibulous indulgence. Sycophantic opportunism is camouflaged as traditional respect for elders, and kola nut offerings are perverted from honorable tokens of esteem and hospitality into shameless bribes. Ancient songs of praise are misused by toadying television producers and newspaper magnates, and folk myths are incorporated into neocolonial media propaganda.

Perhaps the greatest single obstacle to Africa's postcolonial progress, however, and the main reason why the new power elites proved unequal to the task of leadership and nation-building was the lack of any framing ideology, social vision, or body of principles with which to navigate the difficult years ahead. African nationalism was primarily a struggle *against* colonialism, not a movement *for* or *toward* anything, and its proponents had a better idea of what they wanted to remove than of what they wanted to replace it with. Few of the new leaders thought beyond the moment of independence to the kind of states they were creating or evolved any original ideas or directions for their construction. The greater part of nationalist rhetoric was a confusing mixture of self-advertisement and public altruism, capitalism and socialism, often failing to resolve itself into any ideological or intellectual position, and little was said about the specifics of social restructuring beyond vague ideas of modernization and detribalization. Fanon was convinced that the greatest danger threatening postcolonial Africa was this absence of ideology and that the only way to break the grip of Europe's influence and forestall the inevitable regression into intellectual dependency was to devise an original non-Western ideology. The few attempts to discover ideological alternatives, however, quickly ran aground. Impatience with both colonial capitalism and its Marxist countercreations, together with the obligation to be original and to refuse the loan of foreign conceptual tools, drove Africa's new political and intellectual leaders back upon all manner of dubiously derived African social, political, and cultural philosophies: Senghor's negritude, Nkrumah's African personality and "consciencism," Nyerere's Ujamaa, and Kaunda's humanism. In truth these experiments were neither "African" nor "Socialist," as vaunted, but variants on Western bourgeois hegemonies, and they led neither outward into a new stage of political history nor inward into traditional indigenous thought but only into deeper dependency upon the West.

Most prominent among these fabricated ideologies were the doctrines of Senghor, Nkrumah, and Nyerere, which to varying extents drew upon myths of a classless or "communalist" pretribal, precolonial Africa. By the mystification of the communalist-socialist syndrome, the new nationalist leaders used Africa's traditional social and political homogeneity to entrench dictatorships and to bolster the monolith of the one-party totalitarian state by stifling dissent and abolishing opposition parties. The African politician, says the satiric narrator of Achebe's *A Man of the People*, barricades himself in his government palace and then issues instructions through loudspeakers that "all argument should cease and the whole people speak with one voice and that any more dissent and argument outside the door of the shelter would subvert and bring down the whole house" (*MOP,* 37). Under the banner of rehabilitating a future national culture, Senghor and Nkrumah glorified Africa's past and revalorized its cultural heritage, but this racial introversion was essentially an obscurantist exercise, an opiate to divert attention from contemporary troubles and from their own failure to introduce any radical social changes that might alleviate suffering in the present. In place of a constructive political ideology, Africans were given nostalgic myths, high-sounding rhetoric, and personality cults. The masses were urged to forget their present miseries by remembering the heroic life of a charismatic leader and "father of the nation" and his role in the independence struggle. They were exhorted to identify his gains with their own, as if his personal interests and fortunes were synonymous with those of the entire people, his individual aggrandizement and privileged prosperity the properties of the nation.

Where did the writers stand in this situation? With the exception of isolated figures such as Ousmane Sembene of Senegal, all of the writers of the postindependence era were themselves members of the Western-educated bourgeois elite. During the years of the liberation struggles, African writers and intellectuals had tended to throw in their lot with the nationalist movements and join their popular fronts; like Achebe in *Things Fall Apart* (1958), they often reinterpreted their people's cultural heritage and helped to reestablish a sense of their tribal and African, as well as their national, identity. It gradually became clear to this group, however, that national independence was a limited and selective affair—that it meant liberation for the political and professional elites, including themselves, not for the majority of the population. At this point these artists and intellectuals became disaffected with and alienated from the new national administrations and were forced into painful reappraisals of their position and of the dilemmas and contradictions that beset them. As writers in largely illiterate communities, privileged in the midst of squalor and deprivation, they found themselves caught up, ideologically, in class values that were at variance with their own progressive and radical beliefs, their very Western literary forms the artistic equivalents of the foreign luxury goods with which the ruling elites cut themselves off from the people. Stranded between government power on the one side and the mass of the population on the other, they became increasingly marginalized, ineffectual, and threatened figures, reflected in their fictional self-portraits. The sensitive American-educated intellectuals of Armah's early novels endure traumas of isolation, breakdown, and madness, whereas the youthful idealist of Achebe's *No Longer at Ease* discovers that his European education gives him access not only to a comprehensive vision of service to the new nation-state but also to the corrupt consumerist privilege that his village expects and demands of him and that eventually lands him in prison. In *A Man of the*

People and *The Beautyful Ones* intellectuals are ridiculed, denounced, and expelled by corrupt and drunken party officials, while Soyinka's "interpreters" are outlawed by a mediocre bourgeois establishment consisting of petty snobs, social climbers, and political opportunists. Moreover, as the writers and intellectuals became more critical of government inertia and corruption, the regimes became hostile toward them, often—like Chief Nanga, the "man of the people" of Achebe's novel—camouflaging their philistinism and anti-intellectualism behind a facade of populist traditionalism. Increasingly, postindependence African writers who criticized their governments risked censorship, exile, imprisonment, or death.

Many novelists of the period looked beyond the confines of their own class comforts to a wider, more democratic social vision, seeking solidarities with peasants and urban proletariats that appeared to be sanctioned by the early nationalist rhetoric, and their protagonists give expression to this idealism. In Lenrie Peters's *The Second Round* (1965), Dr. Kawa returns from his overseas medical training committed to populist humanitarian ideals of public duty and service: "I want to see all men happy because it's the only way I can be happy."[13] In like manner, Achebe's Obi in *No Longer at Ease* and Odili in *A Man of the People* are initially inspired by high-minded idealism and public altruism in their disinterested devotion to the corporate body of the new state. Okolo, the protagonist of Gabriel Okara's *The Voice* (1964), and Baako, the expatriated intellectual hero of Armah's *Fragments*, each desire to place some meaningful social vision at the disposal of their communities. In each instance, however, the noble vision founders. Nauseated by urban decadence and corruption, Kawa is forced to a remote country practice where his skills are underused; Obi and Odili fall foul of the corrupting power of privilege and political nepotism, and the Okara and Armah heroes discover that the new communal faiths are a rootless, sterile materialism and self-seeking individualism that isolate communally minded spirits like themselves from the citizens that they intend to serve. The result, in the case of most of these characters, is bitter disappointment and despair, framed by the author's postcolonial disillusionment.

However, as Neil Lazarus has demonstrated in his detailed deconstruction of the mythology of independence, much of this authorial disillusionment derived from an initial misreading of the national liberation struggle. During Africa's first round of independence, Lazarus argues, many radical writers and intellectuals fell into the trap of mistaking political for social struggle, failing to see that nationalism and revolution were incompatible agendas. This resulted in an unwarranted messianic conflation of national freedom and social revolution in which the emancipatory significance of independence was grossly exaggerated.[14] There was a tendency among this group to romanticize the anticolonial resistance movements and to underestimate the dissension within them. Furthermore, they mistakenly ascribed, on the one hand, a coherent social vision to the first nationalist leaders and, on the other, a revolutionary consciousness to the awakening masses. The truth is that independence was never the staging area for revolution that the writers took it for. In light of the ramshackle political structures that the nationalist governments inherited from the colonial regimes, the inflated expectations of independence appear to have been unrealistic, and the position of Africa's radical intellectuals contradictory, from the very beginning.

Such misunderstandings, it appears, owed much to the influence on sub-Saharan political thought of the ideas of Frantz Fanon and his analysis of decolonization. Specifically, Fanon's intellectual disciples followed his misreading of the Algerian revolution, failing to see that it was a traditionalist struggle to recover a lost precolonial inheritance rooted in the Arab and Islamic past, not a battle for a new society. More generally, and most pertinently in the West African context, Fanon's followers dutifully despaired of bourgeois nationalism and clung to their mentor's vague, almost mystical, faith in "the upward thrust of the people" and "the leadership of the people . . . in defiance of the interests of the bourgeoisie" (*WOE*, 132). Subsequently, they proceeded to envisage the years of decolonization as driven by a popular insurrectionary impetus that issued not from a revolution prepared for by independence but from independence itself. Thus, in the flashback to the decolonizing years at the center of Armah's *Beautyful Ones*, Teacher misleadingly presents the Ghanaian masses as a messianic revolutionary force mobilized by Nkrumah's Convention People's Party (CPP). In fact, however, the CPP, although having a large membership, was never the popular mass party that it advertised itself as. As Lazarus observes, the problem with Fanon's messianic projections was that they made the setbacks of the postcolonial era seem incomprehensible (Lazarus, 17). Thus, when independence failed to live up to its early promise, it came in retrospect to be regarded as a gigantic swindle, a mystifying confidence trick, and its failure was accounted for, in the political melodrama of the period's fiction, in terms of conspiracy theory, sabotage, and the personal betrayals of parasitic leadership elites. "How long will Africa be cursed with its leaders?" asks the man in Armah's first novel, a text that, according to Lazarus, is not really a work of postcolonial disillusionment because it is still "illusioned"; in other words, the work—carved from the pain of unfulfilled promises—suffered from the misapprehension that the era of independence marked a revolutionary conjuncture in Africa. "Expecting too much in 1960, they [Armah's generation] became much too cynical in 1968; or much too despair-ridden, or too ready to cry betrayal" (Lazarus, 24).

Indeed, much African fiction of the postindependence 1960s answers to Lazarus's description. In these works the utopian rhetoric of the preindependence period and the first years of nationhood gives way to a mood of cynical disillusionment and weary defeatism and to a pervasive tone of privileged, fatalistic despair, generated somewhat gratuitously by a disappointed idealism that is as ill defined as it is unwarranted in its excess. Achebe's two novels of contemporary life, Armah's first two books, Soyinka's *Interpreters*, the Peters and Okara novels, and Kofi Awoonor's *This Earth, My Brother* . . . (1971), together with East African novels such as Robert Serumaga's *Return to the Shadows* (1969), are depressingly unilateral in vision, telling much the same story. In each book the first postcolonial civilian administrations career to a halt, the economy defunct and resources exhausted. As a result of government fraud, embezzlement, racketeering, and commercial malpractice perpetrated by a succession of brazen ministerial buffoons, drunken attorneys, crassly corrupt media moguls, and sinecure-holding bureaucrats, the state is bankrupt. The responses of the books' narrators to this avalanche of catastrophes is often feebly inadequate. In *A Man of the People* Odili falls back, fatalistically, on a bleak behavioral essentialism, claiming that "we ignore man's nature" if we expect the Nangas of the world to surrender their ill-gotten power and privileges and, after the assassination of a political idealist and friend, concludes cynically that, in a world without justice, "you died a good death if your life had inspired someone to come forward and shoot your murderer in the chest—without asking to be paid" (*MOP,* 149). In Awoonor's *This Earth, My Brother* . . . the lawyer protagonist Amamu has come to take for granted social injustice, the empty promises of politicians, and the practical impossibility and inevitable failure of revolution. Because Amamu regards these somber perceptions fatalistically—as part of the ordained scheme of things—the book's pessimism assumes almost metaphysical proportions.

Much the same is true of Armah's *Beautyful Ones,* in which corruption, imaged scatologically by the filth and waste of consumer materialism, is presented as an absolute and inescapable condition that can be removed only by recourse to more of itself, so that there is no morally pure way to procure even the necessities of life. In this novel voices, figures, and movements are graphically endowed with consumptive or excremental properties, and the anonymous hero, battling temptation in a putrescent world where dirt has replaced air, resigns himself wearily to the fact that "there was no more point in his continuing his efforts to keep the rot out of himself" (*BONYB*, 101). In the unnamed man's narrative the accelerated life of the Nkrumah regime shrinks satirically to the dimensions of the body's ingestion and evacuation circuit, indicating its brevity, degradation, and failed progress. As it careers to an exhausted standstill, its course littered with aborted projects, it is seen paradoxically to have left everything unchanged. At its fall the man ruefully observes: "Now another group of bellies will be bursting with the country's riches! . . . New people, new style, old dance" (*BONYB*, 157–58). The totalitarian cultural mentality of Armah's Ghanaians is much in keeping with his novel's totalistic, metaphoric vision. The mass psychology of materialism and the spongelike devolution of consumerist values from the nation's power centers results in what is effectively a single-class culture. Here the oppressed worship and emulate their oppressors, the popular will is indistinguishable from the will of the leaders, and the community is really a fraternity of fraud in which the guilty, like the bus conductor, invite their detectors to a share of their loot. In Teacher's flashback to the decolonizing years, "the people," to whom he originally looked as a source of revolutionary energy, appear merely to seesaw from a dismissive cynicism toward the old leaders to a collaborative cynicism toward the new ones, while anyone who does not join in the contemporary scramble for imported luxuries is outlawed. Honest men (like the man) are now redefined as criminals, fraud and collusion are "manly, heroic things," and the exposure of public theft is the work of "unpatriotic elements" and "saboteurs." Although much more extreme than Awoonor's and Achebe's, Armah's dystopian vision has its origin in the same disappointed idealism. To the extent that the man himself is beguiled by Teacher's dream of "moving a whole people forward" and continues to believe in a "future goodness," his vision is still implicated in the discredited utopian perspective of much postcolonial African writing; his despair, predicated on the failure of a nonexistent revolution, is born of the same deluded messianic hope. As Lazarus has cogently argued, *The Beautyful Ones* is itself conceived within an incurably optimistic revolutionary frame. Having committed itself to an unrealistic vision of political unity in the years of anticolonial struggle, it is then obliged to present Nkrumah's postcolonial policies as a betrayal of his earlier radicalism (Lazarus, 187).

The fiction of the 1960s, however, looked beyond the personal treacheries of leaders and the betrayal of nebulous popular idealism in its location of the blame for Africa's postcolonial political debacle. The intellectual heroes of the novels of Achebe, Aluko, Ngugi, and Soyinka and of Armah's second and third books pinpoint a number of targets. In addition to the corrupt privilege, greed, and economic parasitism of government elites, these include the naïveté and low political consciousness of the masses, which lowered their moral resistance to corruption and rendered them vulnerable to the cynicism of their middle class masters. Additional targets were overseas education programs that fed back into African societies more of what kept them stagnant, unproductive, and dependent. Also faulted were traditional prestige and patronage systems through which clans and extended families furthered their own narrow interests at the expense of the public good, enhancing their own status by encouraging their Western-educated protégés in habits of conspicuous consumption far beyond their means (both Obi, in *No Longer at Ease*, and Baako, in Armah's *Fragments*, are regarded by their kinship groups as investments that must be made to pay dividends).

Added to these factors were of course the intellectuals themselves, who were part of the problem they were analyzing—a contradiction that is most acutely evident in Soyinka's *Interpreters*. This novel focuses upon the revolt of five recently returned university graduates of the independence generation against brazen government corruption and power abuse, public fraud and press dishonesty, philistinism and academic hypocrisy. The group's reformist zeal is blocked at every turn, however, by monopoly interests and nepotistic influence that exclude them from real power. Quickly abandoning any attempt at practical action, they retreat into private quests, elitist cults of sensibility and taste, and a glib, self-gratifying satire that fails to penetrate the malaise of their muddled society. Unwilling to degrade themselves by participation in a corrupt public system, Soyinka's interpreters too easily allow themselves to be outmaneuvered by the mediocre bureaucrats, vulgar philistines, and servile academic hacks of the elite class of which they are themselves disaffected members and are content merely to unleash their negative satiric energies on the symptoms, rather than on the sources, of the disease—a malady in which they too are implicated. On the one occasion in the book when they venture beyond their class frontiers to "interpret" a member of the lower social order, their collective self-absorption leads indirectly to his death. The pursuits of Soyinka's privileged, ultrasophisticated intelligentsia are, finally, escapist opiates. Having given up trying to change their society, they merely "interpret" it.

The position of the twin narrators in Armah's second and third novels is not very different from that of Soyinka's collective protagonist, and insofar as the novelist appears to endorse their ideas, his own implied viewpoint is that of the safe, lonely eminence to which Western education has removed the alienated African intellectual. In *Fragments* and *Why Are We So Blest?* (1974), the two complex subjectivities who serve as the novels' interpretative consciousness (Baako and Juana, Modin and Solo) are opposed to a largely undifferentiated "community," unilaterally characterized by corrupt materialism, political cynicism, and spiritual paralysis. In Baako's cargo theories and abstract screenplays for Ghana television in *Fragments,* "the people" are conceived chiefly at the level of mythology and have only the remote, shadowy coherence of screen images, while in *Why Are We So Blest?* they are even further estranged, romantically intellectualized by Modin into oppressed "peripheral masses" awaiting the miracle of Promethean deliverance from enslavement to a "Western centre" and existing, primarily, to be saved. In these two novels the exclusive focus on the interpreting consciousnesses and the passage of most of the action through them not only affords them centrality but also gives the impression that they exist at a higher level of intensity and perception (in Baako's case, a chemical imbalance actually generates a "consciousness expansion effect"). The effect is to eclipse the subjects of the protagonists' tortured reflections by making their own spiritual traumas—which are finally the intellectual luxuries of a comfortable privileged elite—seem more interesting and important than the mass deprivation that they agonize about. Their task does not stop at critical awareness, however, for Armah, unlike Soyinka, appears to place the discovery of the communal will and, implicitly, society's salvation with the self-sacrificing heroism of these isolated, solitary individuals.

Following Fanon's vague faith, in *The Wretched of the Earth,* in alliances between the massed population and selected principled intellectuals who were in touch with "the upward thrust of the people," the novelist ventures into the same politically simplistic territory of lone heroic champions and "the masses"; thus in *Why Are We So Blest?* Modin, though knowing nothing of the lives of the latter, arrogates to himself the right to depict their collective unconscious will as "revolutionary." None of this is a significant advance on Teacher's fantasy of fraternity and gratuitous identification with an imagined "popular will" in the first novel, his nostalgia for the time "when the single mind was filled with the hopes of a whole people" (*BONYB*, 162). The truth in fact is that Armah's spiritually ailing interpreters, like Soyinka's, carry no common burden of suffering that they share with the oppressed community, only a weight of guilt-ridden privilege and remorse that distances them from it. Modin is an ironic Promethean and also that most ineffectual product of Western liberal education: the academic revolutionary who, without the practical skills and knowledge needed for participation in a proletarian struggle and already infiltrated by the values of the oppressor, actually hampers the revolutionary process. This cultural arrogance and unwitting complicity with class elitism are, moreover, faults from which Soyinka and Achebe have not been exempt in their critical statements: Witness Soyinka's description of the African writer as "the record of the mores and experience of his society and as the voice of vision in his own time," or Achebe's equally presumptuous statement that it is in the "question of education . . . [that] my aims and the deepest aspirations of my society meet."[15] This appropriation, by the artistic and intellectual elite, of the hypothetical aspirations of a "whole people" was but a variant on the nationalist leader's invitation to the populace to identify his personal gains as their own.

By the end of the decade African writers, writing about and for an elite from a position of self-absorbed privilege, had reached something of an impasse, and it was in *Why Are We So Blest?* that their dilemma received its most extreme expression—and ultimate exorcism. In this work the narrative's dislocated time schemes and multiple consciousnesses express not only the splintered life of the Europeanized African but also the "discrete beauty" of a despised European modernism. The narrator thus concludes that when the African writer, seduced by Western aestheticism, has to borrow the styles and narrative techniques of the former colonial oppressor to bewail the continuing oppression of the African race, then writing itself becomes an act of betrayal, fashioning interesting art (for a primarily white audience) out of defeated revolution, aesthetic success from political failure. *Why Are We So Blest?* was a milestone along Armah's chosen route out of the circle of Westernized privilege, an attempt to write himself through and clear of the dilemma of the radical African writer, and the direction of his writing had in fact been anticipated at the start of the previous decade by Fanon in his tripartite scheme for the decolonized writer. In *The Wretched of the Earth,* Fanon wrote that after the "assimilation phase," in which literature was dominated by the literary styles and techniques of the colonial master, came a second phase of disturbance and painful liberation in which the uprooted, expatriated writer tried to recross the gulf that had grown up between the author and the African community (in this category are *No Longer at Ease*, *The Second Round*, *Fragments*, and *Why Are We So Blest?*). In his third or "fighting phase," Fanon then specifically recommended as a way out of the neocolonial impasse a "literature of combat" that would enliven in modernized form "the stories, epics, and songs of the people" as they existed in the oral tradition (*WOE*, 193). In this militant phase the writer, eager to shed privilege and establish broad-based political and cultural solidarities, would seek out the functional potential of the traditional past for purposes of future reconstruction and in so doing would devise a revolutionary literature to address and awaken the people.

Clearly, Armah's experimental fourth novel, *Two Thousand Seasons* (1973), in which a pluralized, communal narrative voice draws upon the race memory for a mythologized history of the Akan people, was an attempt to follow Fanon's prescriptions, both generally, in its approximation of a more genuinely indigenous form and revolutionary focus, and specifically, in its view of history and its gestures toward broad-based populism through a simulated orature. In the sweep of this book's epic canvas, the dystopian history of the postcolonial period is seen not as an absolute, unchanging reality but as a temporary aberration and freak of historical circumstance. The "white road" of linear fragmentation ultimately proves to be merely part of an immense curve on the trajectory of a wider cosmic "cycle of regeneration" that the narrator calls the "Way." This very course is destined to carry Africa back along a circular path to its indigenous roots. Fortified by this recovered faith, the collective narrator is able to cast off despair and envisage the end of the neocolonial destruction of African culture. As I demonstrate in chapter 3, however, the perspective offered by *Two Thousand Seasons* is more mythological than historical and the community built around the developing African "Way" more hypothetical than actual. The author's reorientation of his earlier solitary visionaries toward group values and a communal worldview ostensibly gives his art a more democratic and authentically African flavor. In practice however the anonymous narrative "we" identifies not with the masses, except insofar as they are included in the ethnic spirit, but with small cadres of visionary intellectuals and exceptional individuals (called "creators," "makers," or "inspirers") who are envisaged as champions of the society's conscience and saviors of the race. In both this book and his later novel *The Healers*

(1979), Armah's populism is essentially ideological and theoretical, driven by polemic rather than by any interest in popular culture or concept of broad-based power; little is seen or heard in either book of the African people whose reunification the messianic seers speak so much of. These works, for all their vaunted egalitarian communalism, are still governed by a basically elitist dynamic and authoritarian ethic.

It was only at the end of the 1970s and in the early years of the 1980s, as the second round of anticolonial struggles and independence movements gathered intensity, that radical African writers were called upon to combat their practical ineffectuality at the social level by making a decisive break with middle-class intellectual culture. The writings and speeches of the new revolutionary leaders—Amilcar Cabral of Guinea-Bissau, Samora Machel of Mozambique, Agostinho Neto of Angola, and Robert Mugabe of Zimbabwe—posed crucial questions about the kind of independence their armed struggles were directed toward (questions never asked by the nationalist leaders of the 1950s). These principals called upon intellectuals and writers to commit themselves to the task of actually creating the conditions that would make revolution possible, as distinct from merely conceptualizing it. In the context of the violent struggles in Zimbabwe and the Portuguese colonies, this meant that the writer, in an act of class suicide, would establish solidarity with the masses by living among them, thus experiencing the material conditions of their lives and helping to ground the liberation struggle in popular culture. Meanwhile, in the first-round independent nations oppressed by neocolonial regimes, writers influenced by the new revolutionary leaders, notably Ngugi, rose to the new challenge; they investigated both their readership and the channels through which their work was produced and distributed, and they explored ways in which these might be democratized. In Ngugi's own case and in that of Nigeria's Ken Saro-Wiwa, the writer was to turn political activist, promoting popular culture by local publishing and media enterprises and forging alliances between urban workers, peasants, and intellectuals by organizing adult literacy drives, traveling workshop theater, and community development programs. In an attempt to reach a broader indigenous audience for their writing, standard English was abandoned, in Ngugi's case for his native Gikuyu and in Saro-Wiwa's for a version of the interethnic pidginized English spoken by the Ogoni traders and fishermen of Nigeria's Southeast. Under the influence of Ngugi and the new militant political leaders, the late 1970s and early 1980s saw the rise of a new proletarian social realism devoted to the deprived and dispossessed strata of African society. In the fiction of Kenya's Meja Mwangi, Senegal's Aminata Sow Fall, and Nigeria's Saro-Wiwa and Festus Iyayi, and in Ngugi's own *Petals of Blood* (1977) and *Devil on the Cross* (1980), even the most grimly depicted social horrors are shown to be alterable, and the urgent insistence on social change sounds through the writer's subversive anger.

The decade also saw a burgeoning of fiction by African women writers—Botswana's Bessie Head, Nigeria's Flora Nwapa and Buchi Emecheta, Ghana's Ama Ata Aidoo, and Senegal's Mariama Ba—which revealed that political emancipation had done little to erode continuing traditions of patriarchal dominance and female subservience and in which political imperatives to subordinate sexual freedom to issues of national liberation were vigorously resisted.

Social realist and feminist writing, however, were stages and milestones over a 25-year period that saw many different and developing fictional responses to Africa's deepening postindependence crisis. The writers gathered in the following chapters resorted to a variety of explanations, extenuations, and strategic resolutions. Kofi Awoonor, in *This Earth, My Brother* . . . , and Wole Soyinka, in *Season of Anomy* (1973), attempted to subsume their nations' seasons of corruption and catastrophe in broader, numinous mythic perspectives, albeit with much irony and little tempering of present despair, while Armah's enclosure of colonial and postcolonial interludes in African seasonal time in *Two Thousand Seasons* did much the same thing, only in a more positive and hopeful mood. On the other hand, the Malian writer Yambo Ouologuem, in his *Bound to Violence* (1971), took a more cynical and iconoclastic view of the workings of myth in African history. Whereas Armah's later fiction revealed a growing tendency to blame all Africa's woes upon Western interference and the betrayal of African communalist ideals by aberrant contemporary leaders, Ouologuem debunked altogether the notion of autochthonous egalitarian value structures. He preferred instead to present the African past as a continuum of indigenous colonialism and feudal despotism running from early Negro overlords to postindependence elites.

No less skeptical but more discriminating than Ouologuem was the Somali novelist Nuruddin Farah, who in a 1989 interview said of postcolonial corruption and materialism: "I am tired of hearing all these ills placed at the doorstep of the colonial powers. They are surely responsible for sabotaging the structures of African society, but we have been independent for however long now, and we are surely responsible for the things we have done."[16] Although it focuses on the Westernized "privilegentsia," Farah's 1979 novel, *Sweet and Sour Milk*, does not blame Western influence for Somalia's postcolonial turmoil. Instead it points to inveterate domestic and clan traditions that were not suited to the new democratic state but lent themselves more readily to authoritarian and dictatorial forms of government. "In *Sweet and Sour Milk*," Farah commented in the same interview, "the betrayal is within the family . . . [and] the Somali nation as a family, the betrayal is no longer that of colonialism, it is no longer from outside, but from within" (Jaggi, 186). Moreover, whereas Armah, in his two historical novels, and Ngugi, in his later *Matigari* (1986), used oral culture as a channel toward a broad-based egalitarian populism, Farah presents the oral tradition in an altogether more sinister light, as a ready tool for repressive surveillance techniques and political terror in a totalitarian state.

The South African J. M. Coetzee, in *Life and Times of Michael K* (1983), marks reflexively the limits of white moral and mythological power in a continuing colonial situation. Meanwhile, the Zimbabwean Tsitsi Dangarembga, in her revisitation of colonial Rhodesia of the 1960s in *Nervous Conditions* (1988), calls harrowingly to account the oppressive patriarchal traditions of the indigenous culture, though finally placing the bulk of the blame elsewhere. Returning from 1960s' London, her schoolgirl heroine Nyasha is caught not between modern and traditional African worlds (as is Achebe's Obi) or between the West and a vulgarly Westernized Africa (as is Armah's Baako). Rather, she is stranded between contemporary European culture and a half-Westernized colony that still exists at an earlier phase of Britishness. Furthermore, the cultural independence of the colony is most seriously hampered by the African elite's addiction to an evangelical, Victorian-style missionary Christianity. In *Harvest of Thorns* (1989), Shimmer Chinodya's novel of the Zimbabwean War of Independence, the culturally confused protagonist runs aimlessly away from this same "exaggerated Christianity" into the arms of the partisans. Chinodya's novel is also more broadly indicative of trends in 1980s' African writing insofar as his reconstructed 1960s' township, at once ideologically Westernized and disempowered by white colonialism, is an unashamedly contradictory, hybridized place. Here foreign and indigenous practices mingle in complicated and confusing ways, a phenomenon equally in evidence in the Dar-es-Salaam of M. G. Vassanji's *The Gunny Sack* (1989), where the cultural contradictions are reinforced by racial tensions. Vassanji's three generations of Tanzanian Asians hover confusedly between their Asian and African identities, the conflict between exclusivist and eclectic concepts of racial identity galvanizing them into new commitments and responsibilities. During recent years this trend toward diversification and heterogeneity has intensified, and the process of cultural interfusion has become ever more intricate, with the result that in the 1990s, African cultural identity and political liability are much more complex phenomena than they were in the 1960s.

Thirty and forty years after national liberation, the plight of independent Africa—civil war, famine, tribal genocide, military tyranny and terror—is as grim and desperate as ever, but the very extremity and protracted gravity of the situation have at least helped to clarify matters for the artist. As the colonial period retreats into the distant past, it is no longer tenable for African writers and intellectuals to go on blaming all of the continent's woes on Western imperialism or on the personal betrayals of reactionary neocolonial leaders. "We cannot simply blame leadership, because we can get rid of them if we want to," says Farah (Jaggi, 186). In addition, it is no longer fashionable to seek solutions in cultural decolonization and Africanization programs such as those recommended by Chinweizu and his associates in the 1970s.[17] Neither is it possible—or desirable—for the African novelist, two decades after Armah's *Two Thousand Seasons*, to engage in purist exercises in racial retrieval and nebulous mythologized ethnic histories, extricating African from Western cultural values, as an answer to or diversion from contemporary political evils. In his pioneering polemic *A Mask Dancing: Nigerian Novelists of the Eighties* (1992),[18] the Nigerian critic Adewale Maja-Pearce called on the contemporary Nigerian (and, by implication, the African) novelist to cease to erect simplistic, spurious dichotomies between indigenous "communalism" and Western "individualism." He also decried the creation of misleading distinctions between "traditional African" and "European" values in misguided attempts to rescue a notional precolonial African worldview from European influence. To counteract these fallacious concepts, he challenged writers to engage fully with the contemporary world, the complex heritage, and the English language (now as much a Nigerian and African language as Yoruba and Kiswahili) that had formed them. For Maja-Pearce, as for Soyinka, there is no such thing as "tradition" in the sense of a pristine, pre-European body of values. Traditional African societies, in order to survive the colonial onslaught and its aftermath, have always drawn upon their inner resources to adapt and change, and their cultures have never been petrified blocs of immaculate, immutable wisdom but mobile and dynamic entities continually in flux, invigorated and cumulatively redefined by new additions. And yet, argues Maja-Pearce, this very adaptability and the subsequent hybridization that ought to be celebrated are in fact denigrated by a modern African intelligentsia who continue to cling to the idea that they have somehow betrayed their heritage, which must therefore be constantly exhumed. The contemporary Nigerian intellectual, says the critic, establishes false oppositions to resist the interpenetration of old and new experience by projecting what is modern in the African reality into the category of "foreign," alienating it to the other side of some artificial border. In this pursuit of muddled cultural primitivism, claims Maja-Pearce, some writers persist in valorizing an indigenous heritage that is plainly unequal to late twentieth-century experience and to the psychic needs of the African in the modern world.

In fact, as Maja-Pearce wrote, a younger generation of West African fiction writers was already answering his call. The cultural matrix out of which these novelists write at the end of the twentieth century is altogether more complex, their experience more irredeemably alloyed, the modernity of their world more thoroughly hybridized, than those of their early 1970s' counterparts. In the works of the writers discussed in the last two chapters of this book—Ben Okri, Kojo Laing, Syl Cheney-Coker, 'Biyi Bandele-Thomas—this eclecticism and syncretism reach new heights. In this writing cybernetics and the supernatural, science fiction and animist mythology, postmodernism and the oral tradition mingle to form fascinating new combinations. The consolidation of traditionalist models of identity around notions of an authentic, precolonial African sensibility was one limited historical response to the political debacle of the first postindependence decade; it was an attempt to salvage African values from the swamp of political corruption and Westernized cultural confusion. For the new generation of novelists discussed in the second half of this book, however, it is no longer a viable endeavor. Over the past 20 years the migration and cross-fertilization of forms and ideas in African writing has produced ever more innovative and heterogeneous modes of fiction, and as the century draws to a close this continues to be the developing direction of the contemporary African novel.

Chapter Two

Lyric Fatalism and Mystic Utopianism: History as Myth and Ritual in Kofi Awoonor's *This Earth, My Brother...* and Wole Soyinka's *Season of Anomy*

One response to postcolonial political crisis by a minority of West African poet-novelists was to invest protagonists with mythic or ritual identities, often with ambiguous effect. On the one hand, the hero's worldly struggles and failures were placed consolingly in a more meaningful metaphysical and numinous context where they could appear to have some significance or distant consequence. At the same time there were ironic undertones in the merely allusive, secondary presence of mythology and in the token quality and limited relevance of ritual at the level of social reality; the combined effect of these was to question the practical effectuality of protagonal action and to accentuate the feeling of futility and despair. Thus Kofi Awoonor, in *This Earth, My Brother...* (1971), uses ritual process to subsume political betrayal and failed revolution into an indigenous religious metaphysic and eschatology; Wole Soyinka, with more irony and less fatalism, employs both myth and ritual in *Season of Anomy* (1973) to frame the horrors of civil war in a token seasonal cyclicalism that is constantly exploded by political realism. The ritual subtexts of these novels generate writing of great power and beauty, but they also have their problematic aspects, particularly in the case of Awoonor's novel.

In an interview discussion of *This Earth, My Brother...*, Awoonor has referred to the "theme of the priest, the carrier, the man who bears his burden of the terrible truth"[1] and likens his protagonist, the Western-educated lawyer Amamu, to "a priest, in the traditional African sense, taking upon himself all the burdens of his people."[2] The author appears here to conflate the priest who carries shrines at specific Ghanaian religious festivals[3] with the annual purification rite of the carrier who in a number of West African coastal settlements cleanses the community by carrying out to sea the burden of the dying year's sins and subsequent misfortunes in the form of a miniature wooden boat.[4] The function of this complex figure—who also features figuratively in Ayi Kwei Armah's *The Beautyful Ones Are Not Yet Born* (1968) and Gabriel Okara's *The Voice* (1964) and in much of Soyinka's writing—is to ritually introject the social consciousness into his own being and thus to suffer on society's behalf. In his literary manifestations, in both Awoonor's and Soyinka's work, the carrier's power to heal society's sicknesses depends, paradoxically, upon his decontaminatory removal and estrangement from society. The carrier's withdrawal thus gives special symbolic value to the role of the altruistic outsider and places communal salvation, doubtfully, with acts of solitary sacrificial heroism.[5] Implicit in this writing, it appears, is the mystic assumption that ritual, by virtue of its subtextual existence, has some sort of magical power and efficacy in the action of the novel. The latter, in the absence of any visible sign of communal regeneration, is deemed to have been accomplished invisibly by ritual.[6] The result is that the figurative is sometimes mistaken for the factual, and there is a confusion of metaphoric motif and narrative motivation, of ritual and reality.

Awoonor's experimental poetic novel, set in Nkrumah's Ghana of the early 1960s, is written in parallel, twin narratives that operate on two different levels of consciousness and reality. The realistic prose narrative bears Amamu through the despairing round of an average working day as a city lawyer, during which he encounters both the oppressed, in the form of beggars, criminals, and the unemployed, and their oppressors, the corrupt elite who are now running the country. This omniscient, third-person account establishes the social milieu in the panoramic fashion of objective realism. It also characterizes Amamu, externally, as a withdrawn, socially awkward figure, dreamy and distracted in manner, and given to outlandish scholarly monologues that cause him to be half-revered and half-derided by his fellow clubmen.

The prose chapters also include, in flashbacks to Amamu's past, vignettes of a typical colonial childhood and adolescence; this personal legacy is then accumulated and stored in what serves in the novel as both an individual and a collective consciousness, containing the debris of colonial history and awaiting a ritual unburdening. The prose narrative, however, is interspersed with poetic interludes that draw upon the worlds of myth, dream, and folklore, and are more closely connected with a specifically ritual consciousness. In contradistinction to the forward linear movement of the primary narrative, these dense lyrical passages carry Amamu back to the visionary rediscovery of his lost childhood cousin Dede, who, at the deeper level of his subconscious, is identified with a legendary precolonial innocence and a pre-European African mythology that has survived the depredations of colonialism. Preeminent among this body of myths in Amamu's fragmentary first-person narrative is that of Mammy Water, the mermaid or Woman of the Sea, who takes men into her element for periods of seven years and then sends them back, reborn, into society with supernatural healing and regenerative powers. As Gerald Moore has noticed, the Westernized linear time of the prose narrative merely measures the intervals between moments of vision; Awoonor, as in his poetry, incorporates linear advancement into a pattern of circular return, a pattern mirrored in the career of the homecoming, foreign-educated "been-to."[7]

This pattern is complicated, however, by other strands running across it. The cycle of return to the "second self" of the reborn childhood is tied to a parallel eschatological cycle, since the visionary liberation achieved by assuming, in Amamu's words, "the body" of Dede's death can be purchased only by his own passage, at the end of the book, through madness and bodily death. This death is part of a process through which Amamu is reborn into the spirit world from which he comes into the village of Deme at his birth in the first chapter. The two worlds are conceived spatially as areas of existence rather than phases of time. Subsequently, Amamu not only does service as the purgative carrier who releases the immediate past but also bridges the transitional gulfs between the worlds of the living, the ancestral dead, and the unborn and is the historical link between the corrupt modern state and a reservoir of lost myths and faiths. Thus Awoonor uses Amamu's intensely private and at times impenetrably introspective reverie to suggest an alternative African worldview in which death is not a meaningless event but is part of a process of continuity and renewal. He does not, however, show how this worldview is recoverable in the present, and the links in the novel between the visible historical and the unseen spirit worlds and, more particularly, between eschatological rebirth and the vision of social regeneration are often quite tenuous.

A more crucial superimposition in the novel is that of a ritual bearing away of a communal historical burden upon Amamu's return journey into his past and his attempt to annul his personal history. Dede's death from malnutrition in 1944 is made to mark the centenary of the colonial incursion into Ghana and is seen as the culmination of a century of theft, pillage, and neglect that brutally curtailed a precolonial African innocence: "And on that magnificent continent, the diamond diggers and washers, the gold-miners, the copper-miners, the farmers on the great European-organised plantations toil from sunrise to sundown so that their infants can die early of malnutrition.... So my cousin love, she who came from the sea at the hour the moon slashes the sea in two beneath the shadow of my almond died, long long ago I cannot remember. As infants we run through the naked land naked."[8] Independent Ghana struggles into a horrific birth after a long and violent colonial gestation: "Woman, behold thy son; son, behold thy mother. This revolting malevolence is thy mother. She begat thee from her womb after a pregnancy of a hundred and thirteen years. She begat thee after a long parturition, she begat you into her dust, and you woke up after the eighth day screaming on a dunghill" (*TEMB*, 28). The dunghill is contemporary Ghana, blighted at infancy because begotten by colonialism; the metaphor, which is graphically literalized in Amamu's final harrowing journey through putrescent city slums at the end of the book, carries the corruption beyond colonialism to its inheritors. Awoonor, like Armah in *The Beautyful Ones Are Not Yet Born,* is fond of long-distance retrospection from contemporary African dignitaries to slave-dealing ancestral prototypes, whereby precolonial and neocolonial evils are attached to colonial ones. Thus, Nkrumah's escape contingency is "an improvement on the same tunnel through which the slaves were shipped in ancient days," and he rules from "the same castle where the slave ship anchored, and received their cargoes through the tunnels to the Americas" (*TEMB*, 27, 30).

Furthermore, as in the dunghill world of the Armah novel, the vast entropized weight of material corruption legated by the colonial era takes the metaphoric form of the mounting mass of undisposed-of human excrement. In one satiric episode the night soil truck fresh from the dunghill rides in triumph at the head of the presidential motorcade, carrying symbolically before it the rottenness of the ruling regime. The uncollected refuse and unemptied latrines of the slum ghetto memorialize the neglected ills of a period still awaiting deliverance: "Two septic tanks, a fitting memorial to Nima, the city within a city, Nkrumah once said he would make it. These latrines are ever full. Those in a hurry take a shit right on the floor. Near the septic tanks are huge dunghills which in the language of the Accra City Council are called refuse dumps. No one ever removes refuse from Nima" (*TEMB*, 152).

This rot and decay may yet, however, develop the fertile regenerative capacities of manure and the sea may recover its mythic principle of creativity, and its power to refertilize a ruined earth. For Amamu casts himself metaphorically in the ritual purificatory role of the coastal carrier (there is ironic reference to the latrine carrier). The important difference is that his self-appointed task is to bear away not the accumulated pollution of the past year but the 113 years of colonial ills that were supposed to have ended with Nkrumah's declaration of independence in 1957. The expulsion of dying years inevitably invests the carrier motif with millenarian or utopian associations, colored as festival rites are by the New Year's traditional mood of revaluation, redefinition of roles, and long-term retrospection, which may be the prologue to permanent change. Thus the motif, as in Soyinka's work,[9] may imply some messianic political regeneration, the end of an epoch, or the changing of a world order.

Both the antiquity of Ghana's corruption and the foreboding of impending apocalypse are finely caught in the last part of the book where Amamu traces his forefathers' steps back to the village lagoon and the scene of his childhood dreams but first has to negotiate the squalor of the Nima slums in search of his houseboy Yaro, whose half-brother Ibrahim is in trouble with the law: "He [Yaro] suddenly looked old; he wore for the first time an indeterminable age, an oldness that was not time's, an agedness of hills and rivers. In that what was the true and more valid self of this peasant turned into a squatter on the dunghill of modern Africa was a final weariness that defied all description. . . . It had to do with a doom, a catastrophe, a total collapse of all things, his world, his all" (*TEMB,* 175–76). Amamu's ritual task, as he envisages it, is to roll back the years on the accumulated unpurged misery represented by the Nima dunghill: "The centuries and the years of pain of which he was the inheritor, and the woes for which he was singled out to be carrier and sacrifice, were being rolled away, were being faded in that emergence. Here at last, he realised with a certain boyish joy, was the hour of his salvation" (*TEMB,* 179).

This Earth, My Brother . . . is a hauntingly elegiac, richly textured achievement, a prose lyric of great poetic beauty. It remains, however, an overambitious work and leaves an impression of ungathered threads and unrealized purposes. The ritual themes of communal deliverance and rejuvenative annulment are weakly executed. In Awoonor's allegoric treatment of these ideas, the returning prodigal's recovery of a lost personal past is made to correspond with the acceptance of the traditional responsibility of annulling the community's time only by a leap of the narrator's wishful poetic imagination, resulting in a mere semblance of meaning.

The links between the novel's eschatology and social vision, between the posthumous progression of the protagonist's spirit and an implied social regeneration, are even more tenuously theoretical. Richard Priebe has tried to establish links between these two very different things by arguing that Amamu is a religious sacrifice who, because he represents "the greatest loss to the community, stands out as the most efficacious offering"; Amamu's death "adumbrates ultimate salvation for his land since he is better able as an ancestral force to effect the changes he had not the power to effect while living."[10] Plausible though this may sound in the light of African theology, it receives but doubtful support from the novel. Amamu's sociosacrificial value and the novel's eschatology are unprovable, imponderable properties of uncertain status insofar as they are both, finally, projections of the character's crazed consciousness, and the relationship between them is never properly worked out. Amamu's completion of a religious cycle through death, though it achieves a supernatural communion with the spirit of his lost childhood love, cannot be construed except in the most marginal terms as an act of communal deliverance that restores some collective loss. His personal "assumption" of Dede's death and a parallel substitution of himself as communal "carrier" are in fact given only the thinnest metaphoric connection.

Most importantly, perhaps, Amamu's vision of both his personal and historical pasts is romantically utopian, and he invests the carrier metaphor not with ideas of messianic change but with feelings of nostalgic regression and the desire for a return to innocence. "Let us return to the magic hour of our birth for which we mourn," he cries, identifying his dead childhood sweetheart with a retrievable sinless, precolonial world. This particular fixation has disastrous consequences for Amamu's sexual life, for all of his adult relations with women are dominated by the idyllic memory of "his first love," whom he tries futilely to reincarnate in each affair. Dede serves absurdly as the transcendent touchstone against which every casual liaison is measured and found wanting; she is the unattainable ideal that causes all present experience to savor of dissatisfaction and disappointment. Inevitably, in the course of these comparisons and in adult retrospect, the innocent, platonic boyhood romance comes to be imbued with obsessive sexual longings, and one of the components of Amamu's culminating madness on the beach appears to be an early middle-aged lawyer's impossible fantasy yearnings for a prepubescent girlchild:

> Then slowly he saw her, the woman of the sea, his cousin love of those years long long ago rising from the sea. She rose slowly, head first, adorned with sapphires, coral and all the ancient beads her mother left for her pubertal rites. . . . She rose now up upon the waves, her breasts bare, her nipples blacker than ever. . . . She walked on the sand, her arms outstretched; she strode towards him, a smile on her face; her breasts bobbing softly. From his island of joy, utter indescribable joy, he moved towards her. . . . She enveloped him in her warm embrace. (*TEMB,* 179)

In fact, all of the visionary aspects of Amamu's consciousness—his Edenic longings and spirit-life, his fantasies of Dede and of himself as carrier, the promise of national rebirth presaged by the child goddess's watery resurrection—can be seen, at the material level, as part of a single psychotic complex fueled by the same hopeless, self-destructive idealism. They are all instances of the lyric narrator's private, therapeutic myth-making, the self-obsessed inward drama that Amamu, and Awoonor too it seems, finds more interesting than the outward world of action. The author, however, leaves no doubts about the price of such self-absorption. Beginning at the end, Awoonor superimposes, in the opening unnumbered chapter, the boyhood fantasy-reminiscence upon the world of the nearby mental asylum to which Amamu is taken from the beach and where he commits suicide. The hero's final catatonic vision of Dede rising mermaidlike from the waves is, from the realistic perspective of the prose narrative, pure illusion, the fruit of his madness. His subsequent death at the scene of his childhood dreams is not invested in the renewal of society—which is in fact renounced, along with life itself—but is squandered, changing nothing. It is suicidal rather than sacrificial, more narcissistic than altruistic: It is not a public but a personal event, a private "salvation" in which ritual mystique has priority over social reality.

It is therefore to be seriously doubted whether Amamu's despair and death can be seen, either in social or in spiritual terms, as necessary stages of a regenerative process, a new flowering from decay that will transform the dunghill into a place of renewed creation. Indeed, in the novel's metaphoric network, the dunghill and the regenerative chrysalis, the nightsoil dump and the butterfly are antithetical rather than complementary images, with the result that even within the eschatological scheme ideas of decay and deliverance pull in different directions. The wry refrain "Fear death by shit trucks," with its ironic echoes of *The Waste Land* and *The Tempest,* mocks the idea of a miraculous sea change with a young army officer's unambiguous death under heaps of the body waste that is society's end product, the issue of the body's own death-circuit (*TEMB,* 113). Material and magical transformation, death as finality and as process, scatology and eschatology, all seem to be working in opposition. Awoonor's somber apocalyptic prose places more emphasis on an ancient heritage of unalleviated suffering and the sheer oppressive weight of past pollution than on regenerative deliverance in the present.

Amamu is, in any case, an unlikely, doubtful savior. His outsider status, which approximates the ceremonial estrangement of his ritual prototype, derives, at the level of realism, from his aloof, elitist social position. It is true that we see Amamu, after the fashion of the carrier and with the same paranoid compassion of Armah's unnamed hero in *The Beautyful Ones Are Not Yet Born,* assuming and appropriating the sufferings of others, notably the anguish of the drudge-barman at the club and the long-standing traffic policeman. Moreover, as a lawyer, he carries on his conscience the unprosecuted crimes and unexpiated guilt of his society. But we also see him profiting from the crime and corruption that provide his livelihood and "put a good deal of money in his purse" (*TEMB,* 23). Amamu's mood swings erratically from cynical fatalism about the inevitable failure of all revolutions to a high-minded moral indignation with corruption. Yet he appears to be little aware of the extent to which he himself, as a member of the privileged elite that rode to prosperity on the backs of the independence movement, is part of both revolutionary failure and corruption. "A lawyer is next to God. He is the one who gets you out of trouble; he is the one who puts you into trouble" (*TEMB,* 159). In this society Amamu's "magical powers" effectively constitute no more than corrupt influence over customs officers, policemen, and petty bureaucrats—a corrupt influence that, in his final mad vision, he sees himself as ritually purging—and they are too little and come too late to save Yaro, Ibrahim, or any of the Nima slum dwellers. Many of the latter are, after all, on the wrong side of the law that Amamu represents: "The law is an enemy to these captive people" (*TEMB,* 158). Amamu's moral gestures of identification with the poor and downtrodden and his desire for self-sacrifice to expiate his own complicity with the ruling elite's sellout to neocolonial values seem genuine enough. But they are inconsistent with his professional behavior and his real ignorance of, and distance from, the people who, in his self-conceived ritual role, he comes to deliver.

One of the weaknesses of the book's narrative technique is that it tends to obscure rather than heighten these inconsistencies. In the prose narrative Awoonor uses Amamu's vaguely socialist vision as the vehicle for a great deal of wry social criticism and satire of the corrupt establishment, so that the reader almost forgets that Amamu is himself part of that establishment. Meanwhile, in the lyric narrative, Awoonor is so committed to his hero's mystic inner vision and lavishes so much attention upon his poetic sensibility that for much of the time we forget that Amamu is a lawyer. As Gerald Moore has observed, Amamu is not convincingly situated in social terms, and the author clearly endows him with his own memories of conversations with artists and Bohemian intellectuals from many countries.[11] The confusion is exacerbated by Awoonor's lyric style, which tends to mawkishly indulge his protagonist's visionary ecstasies and self-pitying nostalgia, leaving too little critical distance between author and fictional character.

Awoonor's novel suffers—and Armah's *Fragments* is a comparable case in this respect—from its miscasting of the alienated intellectual as carrier and its romantic association of the ritual consciousness with the artistic sensibility. This confusion can be traced to the author's essays and interview statements: "Living outside Africa, removed from first-hand experience, imposes a certain burden of sorrow on my work. I cannot escape it, but I know too, that it sharpens my articulation in many ways. . . . All artists, all creative people are displaced persons by virtue of the burden of suffering they carry. This burden enables Amamu to stand aside and make a clear statement about his society" (Goldblatt, 42, 44). And in another interview in the same year:

> When I finally decided to use this theme of the priest, the carrier, the man who bears his burden of the terrible truth, I decided it was very easy for me to go into traditional society, to take a person from that society. . . . But rather I would choose a man who, by his upbringing and by his education, exists almost totally outside this world and its outlook. The lawyer, the sophisticated international man . . . is the one who is very much in need of this journey, in terms of the future and what the whole of Africa will become. He is the representative of the future . . . and we will all be like the lawyer in some basic general sense. (Lindfors, 62)

Awoonor exploits the carrier's limited estrangement to recast him in the role of expatriated and alienated artist whose absence from the African community sharpens his moral awareness and brings a fresh energy and objectivity to his role but whose saving mission stops short at contemplation of its sufferings and is not translated into action. Amamu merely assumes the moral and intellectual burden, the maddening weight of consciousness of the evil legacies left by Africa's past, but there is no evidence that his personal "journey" smoothes Africa's path into a future that daily becomes more and more like his own.

Awoonor's various oracular remarks on Amamu in his interviews and essays imply mystical identification between personal and social redemption. Amamu is "liminal yet central" and "strives towards the ultimate harmonic order."[12] In death he achieves "a personal, individual redemption," but his journey, which takes place on both "a very realistic level" and "at the mythical level," is "also a journey into himself, into the society—into the very entrails of his society in order to turn from it, as it were. It may be lonely and anguished, but it is achieved and fulfilled" (Lindfors, 60–61). But Awoonor's priestly conception of the carrier as special and set apart imposes severe limits on this fulfillment and its range of reference: "He runs himself into a state of trance and then, in the clear-eyed singular moment, the god of sense descends and communion takes place" (Goldblatt, 44). What appears to be envisaged here is supernatural communion between individual and deity or ancestral spirit, which Amamu achieves only in death and which refers only marginally to the ritualized social communion of carrier and community.

It would of course be a mistake to take Amamu's vision for that of the novel as a whole, particularly because the third-person narrator's sardonic ironies are occasionally at his expense. The community of his childhood that he mythicizes into a time of Edenic innocence and invests with hallowed associations is revealed by the impersonal narrator to be far from perfect. In reality it is spoiled by bribery, the drunken abrogation of social duties, and the desecration of customs even by traditional elders. Although the voice of the prose narrative urges the termination of the long decay of colonialism, unnaturally preserved in Nkrumah's moribund regime, this receives no direct impetus from Amamu's imaginative wombward journey to a precolonial innocence.

Neither is Ghana's contemporary historical crisis resignedly subsumed into the cyclic eschatology; rather, the novel's metaphysical fatalism is partly resisted by the note of horrified protest in the account of the Nima slums. Indeed, the graphic realism of this episode, whose power of disturbance eludes even Amamu's capacity for moral absorption and sublimation, infuses the novel with a more militant, socially oriented spirit. Nevertheless, the problem remains that, in the matter of Amamu's death, Awoonor appears to use ritual metaphor to present what is essentially a mystical and religious event as a material and social one. In the flawed execution of the ritual motif, societal regeneration is not successfully analogized to the posthumous progress of the spirit, no more than is the eschatological passage to the passage of terminal body wastes. The purification of the body politic in this world and of the soul in the next one, this earth and its shadow spirit world, remain obstinately polarized in their mutually exclusive orders of reality.

Wole Soyinka's *Season of Anomy* is more substantial and solidly structured than *This Earth, My Brother* . . . , but, like Awoonor's book, it is a poet's novel, richly textured and dense with metaphoric allusion, and is a comparable work in its attempt to make ritual and mythology meaningful at the level of social and political action. The two novels also share a preoccupation with the dilemmas and proper role of the intellectual or artist in periods of postcolonial emergency, in seasons of corruption (Awoonor) or catastrophe (Soyinka). *Season of Anomy* is a free adaptation of and transposition to fiction of the military crises and massacres of the summer of 1966, which led to the Biafran secession and the Nigerian civil war. The narrative follows the fortunes of Ofeyi, musician, songwriter, and promotions executive of the giant Cocoa Corporation in a country that is a look-alike for Nigeria. Ofeyi, to his disgust, has allowed his art to become cheapened in its mercenary and propagandist service of the corporation. He therefore begins, in his advertising campaigns, to undermine both the corporation and the ruthless military-industrial ruling cartel of which it is a part by disseminating the communalist political ideas of a village utopia called Aiyero (though thoroughly Africanized in Soyinka's version, this is in fact based upon a Christian community in the Yoruba creekland called Aiyetoro [Moore, 227]).

A scene early in the novel where his troupe's dancer Iriyese bursts, in self-parodying fashion, from a giant cocoa pod as part of a publicity stunt has threefold significance: It is at once a measure of the commercial corruption in which Ofeyi's art has become ensnared, a symbolic token of the struggle to break free from it, and an adumbration of Iriyese's final appearance in the novel as the dormant seed of a new revolutionary era. In addition to his own artistic subversions, Ofeyi borrows some of Aiyero's revolutionary cadres to spread its ideals through the cartel state in the hope that they will bear fruit beyond the commune's rural boundaries. The cartel's response is to arouse local tribal hatreds against all of the Aiyero men who are working in the region of Cross-

Rivers (thus these do service for the Ibos, from whose ranks many progressives and activists came and who were therefore indiscriminately targeted by the federal regime). In the wave of terror and massacre that is unleashed, most of Ofeyi's musical troupe is wiped out, and Iriyese is abducted. The ensuing quest for Iriyese takes Ofeyi on a nightmare trip through a relentlessly horrifying landscape of genocidal slaughter, a journey that is, however, underlain by the seasonal myth of Orpheus's search for Eurydice in the underworld. This mythical underpinning links together Ofeyi's personal pursuit of his stolen love, the nationwide revolutionary violence emanating from Aiyero, and nature's seasonal cycle of renewal observed by ritual, a continuum reflected in the chapter titles—"Seminal," "Buds," "Tentacles," "Harvest," "Spores."

Earth mythology is in fact omnipresent and perhaps overinsistent in the novel. The dissemination and violent protection of Aiyero's ideals are metaphorically grounded in the seasonal cycle and constantly linked with the ritual renewal and regeneration of the earth. At the beginning of the novel, during his visit to Aiyero, Ofeyi advises the head of the commune, Pa Ahime, that Aiyero's "grain must find new seminal grounds or it will atrophy and die."[13] The "young shoots" must be protected from the garden's "monstrous growths," most particularly the evil of the cartel, which spreads like "the poison tuber" through both the "bowels of earth" and the "tumoured belly of humanity" (*SOA*, 129, 195). As Ofeyi puts it, "The sowing of an idea these days can no longer take place without accepting the need to protect the young seedling, even by violent means" (*SOA*, 23). The cocoa seed's cycle of germination is, moreover, made to prefigure both a personal and a collective rite of passage—"the parallel progress of the new idea, the birth of the new man from the same germ as the cocoa seed" (*SOA*, 19). The ceremonial initiation of Ofeyi and Iriyese into the Aiyero community in the opening chapter, "Seminal," is incorporated into the rites of passage for the dead Custodian of the Grain, and from that point on their characters are conceived largely in ritual and mythological terms along a continuum of death and rebirth. In a succession of stylized tableaus, the dialogue of dancer and musician swings into the choric chant of mythic Feminine Principle and Spirit of the Harvest. The "bitch-goddess" of the metropolitan nightclubs is transformed, with an abrupt switch of register, into mystic Earth Mother, her sexuality endowed with powers of natural and political regeneration: "In wrapper and sash with the other women of Aiyero, her bared limbs and shoulders among young shoots, Iriyese weaving fronds for the protection of the young nursery, bringing wine to the sweating men in their struggle against the virgin forests. . . . Now she could even tell a blight on the young shoot apart from mere scorching by the sun. Her fingers spliced wounded saplings with the ease of a natural healer. Her presence, the women boasted, inspired the rains" (*SOA*, 20).

Meanwhile, at the pragmatic level, Ofeyi's Aiyero-inspired humanistic initiative and ritualized individual quest are counterpointed by the activities of the ruthless assassin and revolutionary Demakin, better known as "the Dentist" because of his "unassailable logic of extraction before infection" (*SOA*, 88). After much agonizing by Ofeyi over the rival options of Aiyero's utopian idealism and the Dentist's dedicated selective violence, it comes as something of a shock to learn that Demakin has secretly been an agent of Aiyero from the start and that these two are not in opposition but are working in concert. It is, in fact, Demakin who carries Ofeyi through the last three "circles" of his infernal voyage—the circles of cripples, lepers, and lunatics in the bowels of Temoko prison where Iriyese is incarcerated—and who accomplishes the dancer's rescue. In Soyinka's version Eurydice is not lost to Hades but emerges in a coma that not only represents the sleep of reason and sanity in the nation around her but also recalls her earlier stage-act in which she emerges, in triumphant fructification, from the sleeping seeds of the cocoa pod. Symbolically, her condition is described as an "egg," fertile with promise for the future, and in the novel's closing cliché, "in the forests life began to stir" (*SOA*, 320). Ofeyi's challenge to the cartel has been crushed, and the forces of Aiyero are in retreat, but their seeds have been sown and may, like Iriyese, stir into life.

Ofeyi's journey in the novel is across rather than through chaos and has in places a spectatorial, dreamlike quality. Indeed, he seems at times to lead the charmed life of the hero of a historical adventure novel who contrives to be magically and ubiquitously present at all the key events—the burning of barricaded church congregations, the setting up of political assassinations, the hunting down of fugitives—but who watches the violence and terror in comparative safety from a miraculously quiet corner. Compounding this sense of unreality, the recovery of the somewhat dubious revolutionary figurehead Iriyese is a ritual rather than a political event: At the material level, it is a symbolic salvaging operation, not an armed insurrection; a relief action, not a revolutionary one. Indeed, it is one of the peculiarities and inconsistencies of the novel that, with the reappearance of Demakin as an Aiyero agent, the political action begins to be dissipated into ritual and myth. After the cartel's massacre of their kinsmen, the survivors, in what is essentially a face-saving exercise, ritualize their trek back to Aiyero as a "cleansing act" that will "purify our present polluted humanity" and cure them "of the dangers of self-pity" (*SOA*, 218). Once virtue has thus been made of necessity, the political campaign is abandoned for the symbolic rescue of Iriyese. Even the Dentist is made, rather unconvincingly, to agree upon Iriyese's superior value as ideological weapon—as "torch and standard-bearer, super-mistress of universal insurgence"—thus giving the ritual "meaning of the event" priority over the event itself (*SOA*, 218–19).

In each of Demakin's appearances, his policy of selective assassination implicitly begs the question of whether societies benefit from any kind of sacrificial action other than that in which the ritual form is strategically directed at the actual source of infection, the very kernel of pollution (in this case, the cartel), as it is in Soyinka's version of *The Bacchae*.[14] The question, however, is left unanswered, and there follows a fantasy of abstract ideological concord that shelves but does not solve the moral debate, which lies at the heart of the book, between the humane scruples of the liberal individualist and the drastic surgical measures of the hard-headed assassin. Doubtless, rural utopians, revolutionary assassins, and liberals all have something to contribute to the struggle against tyranny, and the Dentist's violent eliminations and Ofeyi's visionary programs of reconstruction are conceivable as separate phases of a single process. Nevertheless, they are in themselves radically unlike and opposed in spirit. In Demakin's political praxis, the vision must come after the action, not inform or interfere with it; the violence stops at itself and leaves the business of renewal to others. In the hard terms of his realpolitik, the "sacred journey" of the Aiyero ideal back to its source in the commune has value only as a "good toughening exercise," and the rescue operation is an obscure diversion that draws attention away from active opposition to the cartel.

The ritual motif of the quest for Iriyese and the Orphic seasonal archetype underlying it tend, however, to align the novel's sympathies with Ofeyi's lone sacrificial quietism and against Demakin's committed activism. As in Awoonor's novel, this has the effect of upholding and valorizing the artist's or intellectual's merely mental assumption and moral absorption of the burden of suffering—"the terrible truth," which in this case is the futile genocidal sacrifice of ethnic groups by military despots at fake altars of national unity. More seriously, there is a tendency to subsume the cartel's massacres into the rhythm of natural cycles, camouflaging pogrom as purification. Watching the corpses float past the Shage Dam, Ofeyi battles with the consoling fiction that the slaughtered men of Aiyero are not only scapegoats for the nation's guilt and carriers of its conscience but also regenerative sacrificial offerings in a mass vegetation rite; he is struck with the realization that seasonal and political revolution—and nature's and man's deaths—are the same. Earlier in the novel we see Ofeyi brooding on history's "violent untimely cycle of waste" and taking refuge in the prospect of "a parallel transformation to that of rotted earth-flesh reborn into life-giving oil" (*SOA*, 90–91). Confronted by this latest round of human carnage, he indulges a similar hope that the destruction of life will "tear up earth and throw it back in stronger, fructifying forms" (*SOA*, 174). Here are his dreamy meditations at the dam:

> There was the marvel, although the bodies were swelled and the faces decomposed there hung about the scene a feeling of great repose. Perhaps the shroud of miasma dulled all sense of horror, or the abnormal stillness of giant machinery made it all a dream, a waxwork display of shapes, inflated rubber forms on rafts in motionless water, perhaps it all seemed part of the churned up earth, part of the clay and humus matrix from which steel hands would later mould new living forms.
> I am lying to myself again he said, seeking barren consolation. . . . It was becoming a habit, running lines in his head to stop the negative flow of implications from stark reality. (*SOA*, 173)

Importantly, the novel's mythic seasonal frame is questioned, and the protagonist's position undermined by the closing ironies. The sudden, sharply self-critical element has an unmistakably personal urgency—which is not surprising, since Ofeyi's temptations, to which he is alert in his more astute moments, reflect his author's own desperately embattled faith in sacrificial death and rebirth.

In a 1975 interview Soyinka said that he mistrusted the transposition of terminologies in Western literature that first turned the defeated challenger or failed revolutionary into a tragic hero and then proceeded to compress the alternatives into the unitary concept of the sacrificial revolutionary. He remarked that "inherent in all struggle on behalf of society is always the element of self-sacrifice" (Gates, 37). In the quoted passage from the novel, Soyinka has his hero turn this idea on its head and push it to extremity. Ofeyi's instinctive tendency is to see elements of constructively beneficial action or even revolutionary struggle as, conversely, present and inherent in all sacrifice, which is therefore never construed as mere waste; he then is apt to dissolve anger into self-deluding fatalism or indolent justification. This is very close to home. In his prison diary, *The Man Died,* Soyinka wrestles with the insidious temptation to cast himself in the consolatory role of the fated sacrificial victim, warning himself that the "poetic snare of tragic loftiness" uselessly diverts constructive energies into martyred egoism. He reminds himself that his death will not be morally or socially beneficial but futile because it will not challenge but only advance the interests of a genocidal military regime.[15]

The fatalistic currents in Soyinka's thought can be traced to the transitional metaphysics of his seminal 1968 essay, "The Fourth Stage," reprinted as the Appendix to *Myth, Literature and the African World.* According to his reading of Yoruba cosmology in this essay, the conduit of vital transitional energy necessary to recharge the universe and keep it in motion is provided by an unceasing, alternating cycle of disruption and reparation, a complementary dialectic of infraction and restoration, disturbance and conciliation. Cyclic patterns, of course, often have fatalistic resonances, and Soyinka's picture of cosmic disintegration and restitution is morally neutral and, at times, disturbingly complacent: "Offences even against nature may be part of the exaction by deeper nature from humanity of acts which alone can open up the deeper springs of man and bring about a constant rejuvenation of the human spirit. Nature in turn benefits by such broken taboos, just as the cosmos does by demands made upon its will by man's cosmic affronts."[16] Evil and its complementary reparation are alike necessary for the fruitful upheaval and rejuvenation that they generate: They are both part of the nature of things, so no moral obloquy attaches to them. In a similarly indifferent vein, Soyinka describes his version of Euripides' *Bacchae* as a "prodigious, barbaric banquet" in which "the more than hinted-at cannibalism corresponds to the periodic needs of humans to swill, gorge and copulate on a scale as huge as Nature's on her monstrous cycle of regeneration."[17] In *Season of Anomy* this "monstrous cycle" includes the bestial deformation of humanity in savage acts of mutilation and murder, presented not in the distanced, stylized form of ritual drama but in realistic close-up to the last gruesome, sickening detail. Ofeyi, who repeatedly dreams himself transformed into a rabid dog, witnesses atrocities—human hunts, disembowelments, infant massacres—which in their shock power surpass anything in Soyinka's writing. The book excels in moments of startling, horrifying wit, as in the "spattering [of] schoolroom walls with brains hot from learning" or a child corpse plummeting down a ravine "like a plump wild duck" (*SOA*, 110, 194). And yet there is still more than a token attempt by the mythopoet in Soyinka to absorb human suffering and death, as in the lyric poems of *Idanre,* into the neutral contexts of nonhuman nature and cosmic cycles, where their individual pain and horror no longer impinge. For all its graphic and horrifying realism, *Season* finally seeks a suspiciously facile refuge in the seasonal fatalism of myth, and, after the rendings of pain and terror, harmony and wholeness are restored with a puzzling ease. Meanwhile, on the ritual front Ofeyi becomes a kind of reverse carrier who, instead of conveying the infections from an otherwise healthy community, bears the healthy seeds from the nerve center of an infected system. But the real effect of this ordeal on the blasted, wasted society appears to be no more redemptive or purificatory (unless too much is pinned on the conversion of the prison gatekeeper, Suberu) than that of Amamu in Awoonor's novel.

Season of Anomy, although stylistically and mythologically complex, is a politically simplistic novel, not least in its rather crude, cartoonlike polarization of wicked imbecilic potentates and impotent visionaries. Political history is conceived conveniently in terms of cartelized, powerful individual personalities, untouched by the ethnic currents they manipulate and who are removable en bloc by policies of selective assassination, as are their victims by concerted rescue actions. In his characterization of the principal figures, Soyinka presents not rounded individuals but composite personalities who, through the archaic morality tradition of externalized alter egos, embody different aspects of the awareness or temperament of the author. Thus the Indian woman Tailla and the Dentist are merely functional characters who have no existence except as Ofeyi's "good and bad angels," the rival custodians of his fate who tempt him with the alternatives of mystical contemplative withdrawal and revolutionary activism. "Can't you see I am meant to save you?" he is implored by Tailla, the "mystery virgin of a transit lounge." "If we were destined to meet, so was my meeting with the Dentist," replies Ofeyi, remembering an earlier fateful airport encounter.

Another casualty of the novel's mode of characterization, and suffering from the same expressionistic thinness, is Iriyese, an impossible combination of "gin and tonic siren" and Earth goddess who has little real substance outside Ofeyi's male imagination ("Vision is eternally of man's own creating") and who, like the expatriated Aiyero youths, remains miraculously untouched by the corrupting influences of the modern state. Repeatedly, the habits of metaphysical rationalization and mythologizing that Ofeyi tries in vain to shrug off have the effect of obscuring rather than sharpening understanding. For example, he frames the misshapen Cross-Rivers man Aliyu in a "metaphysic condition called evil," seeing him as determined by apolitical factors such as climate, geography, disease, and innate "natural" forces, and as a mere instrument in one of history's cyclic seasons of anomy. But Aliyu turns out to be a good Cross-Rivers native who has outgrown infection by the regime's racist poison as he has outgrown his smallpox; his subsequent courageous, altruistic deeds indicate that the tribal mob-evil engineered and orchestrated by the cartel is a political, not a metaphysical, phenomenon calling for a practical, not a ritual, remedy.

The main movement in *Season* is an inward retreat from public catastrophe into an uncertain private mythology of captive regenerative powers awaiting ritual deliverance and release from the underworld. *Season*'s "floating style" of reportage, though it catches eerily the unreality of horror and atrocity, also blurs their objectivity into Ofeyi's introspective consciousness; his spectator-verbiage of "recognizing," "confronting," and "understanding" evil is not a great advance in real terms on the dreamy idealism of Amamu in *This Earth, My Brother*.... It remains to inquire what the uses are of Ofeyi's effort, through his search, to "immerse [himself] in the meaning of the event" and to acquire "a new understanding of history" (*SOA*, 218) if they do nothing concretely to stem the tide of contemporary cataclysm. One is also inclined to ask what a "consciousness" of the need for armed resistance to tyranny practically amounts to if it does not lead its owner to join the struggle. Ofeyi espouses violence only in the curiously externalized form of acknowledging the necessary role of the assassin, and this is the sum of his mental harvest and ideological ripening; he does not practice violence himself, so we are left uninformed about any real changes in his inner nature resulting from this decision and, therefore, of the degree to which he is actually implicated.

Gerald Moore has argued that *Season* is about "Ofeyi's attempt to transform the larger society (Nigeria? Africa?) in the image of Aiyero" by building up the nation, Maoist-style, from an agglomeration of small communal units (Moore, 226–29). Soyinka's acerbic response to Moore's criticism was that Aiyero was not intended as a model for the "cellular mobilization of the country" but as an agent of "transformation."[18] He gives little indication in the novel, however, of the direction this transformation is to take, and, arguably, Aiyero is more a strategic defensive model for survival against the onslaughts of political tyranny than a force for active transformation. Certainly *Season* offers no blueprints for popular revolution but is concerned, rather, to pinpoint the tormented individual conscience of the liberal-humane artist. It is not Soyinka's wish to persuade us that years of isolated contemplation have made Aiyero's experimental ideologies ready for export into the larger society or that they have the capacity to transform a militarized monopoly-capitalist despotism into a nation of decentralized communes. Rather, Ofeyi's failure to extend Aiyero's values beyond its rural boundaries implies a critique of its parochial utopianism.

Neither is Ofeyi's "lone-hero" individualism necessarily incompatible, as Moore claims, with the village-state communalism of Aiyero, which still needs special, talented individuals to promote its interests, or proof of his author's obstinate faith in messianic "world-changers" (Moore, 230). What is suspect in *Season of Anomy* is the process by which such individuals arrive at public collective commitments, the form these commitments take, and what they actually amount to in concrete terms. The novel suggests, albeit not very persuasively, that the paths that lead deep into the recesses of the private consciousness finally—by some mysterious process analogous with Ahime's restorative cavernous pool, where Ofeyi has his first mystic communings with revolutionary ideology—bring the lone visionary hero out into the public domain and into sociopolitical reality. The problem is partly that, in his adoption of the Orphic motif, Soyinka has saddled himself with an excessively individualistic Western myth of the artist-hero, a myth that, because of the essentially private nature of the artist's quest and his ultimate powerlessness to change anything, does not easily blend with the revolutionary political myth of Aiyero.

Chapter Three
Orature Revisioned: Yambo Ouologuem's *Bound to Violence* and Ayi Kwei Armah's *Two Thousand Seasons*

While Soyinka and Awoonor enclosed 1960s' postindependence corruption and the horrors of civil war within the token framework of ritual, other novelists writing at the end of the decade turned away from the present and attempted, with the aid of a simulated orature, to remythologize the colonial and precolonial pasts. This was essentially a new development. Apart from the folk narratives of Amos Tutuola and Gabriel Okara's experimental novel *The Voice* (1964), which rendered Ijaw idioms directly into English, there had been no thoroughgoing attempts to transmute oral literary forms into written ones in African fiction of the 1960s. The survival of the styles and narrative techniques of the oral storyteller into the modern African novel had, in any case, always been an unpredictable and haphazard affair. The exuberant hyperbole of the traditional *griot,* or oral historian, was in fact as pervasively in evidence in novels with contemporary urban settings (such as Soyinka's *The Interpreters* [1965] and Armah's earlier *The Beautyful Ones Are Not Yet Born* [1968]) as were his other stock-in-trade in historical novels that dealt with traditional cultures in an earlier period; examples of the latter are Achebe's *Things Fall Apart* (1958) and *Arrow of God* (1964), where the idiomatic oral wisdom that carries the novels' main themes is encapsulated marginally in the proverbs, fables, and folktales that punctuate the narrative. As it transpired, the most adventurous experimentation with oral narrative forms was not to be found in the historical novel proper, set in a specific and limited period, but in two visionary, half-mythical reconstructions of whole eras of African history published early in the next decade: the Malian writer Yambo Ouologuem's *Le Devoir de violence* (1968), published in its English translation as *Bound to Violence* in 1971, and the Ghanaian Ayi Kwei Armah's *Two Thousand Seasons* (1973).

This chapter examines the relative gains and losses of these two exercises in simulated orality—the one largely negative and deflatory, the other corrective and constructive—and assesses their polemical implications for the literary status of oral tradition.

In *Bound to Violence* Yambo Ouologuem constructs an idiosyncratic pseudohistory of the barbaric cruelty and oppression of Sudanic Africa, represented in the novel by the fictional kingdom of Nakem. As Thomas Hale's researches have demonstrated, Ouologuem's tale is not a wholly invented history that has nothing to do with reality. But, as Hale reveals, the novelist's anagrammatizations are erratic: Whereas Nakem is an anagram of the medieval empire of Kanem, now modern Chad, and the Ngodos of Ouologuem's own Dogon people, more distant allusions extend the cruelties of the Sahel to the Zulu of South and the Masai of East Africa.[1] Ouologuem openly identifies his sources: These are the written chronicles, the *Tarik al-Fetach* and the *Tarik al-Sudan*, and the oral epic of the Songhai emperor Askia Mohammed,[2] the historical original of the fictional Saif Isaac el-Heit. He then proceeds, however, to garble them with deliberate misattributions and misdatings and makes a point of compressing the horrors and atrocities of many generations and hundreds of pages in the chronicles into a 23-page first chapter, concentrating exclusively on murder, violence, and sexual perversion, and blurring the distinction between one reign and another.

As numerous commentators have observed, the novel's multivocal narrator unapologetically mixes up both the matter and the styles of his sources.[3] Some parts of the narrative attributed to oral epic are indistinguishable from episodes in the written chronicles, and the griot Koutouli's gruesome catalogue of the Saifs' imperial slaughters in the opening chapter owes more to the graphic realism of the chroniclers than to the more formal and elevated epic style of the griots. Ouologuem's historiographic metafiction may not be a total iconoclastic satire or a statement of nihilistic relativism. Its radical fabulative strategies inquire into the ways in which history is constructed—through judicial records, oral epics, folklore, chronicles, and contemporary fictional discourse—and demonstrate in the process that neither the oral tradition nor its written counterpart may be very accurate or reliable in their recounting of the past.[4] What sounds most ominously in the opening pages of *Bound to Violence,* however, is a note of critical dissent from a problematic and contestable oral tradition.

Ouologuem delivers a sardonic pastiche of oral narrative that mockingly reproduces the traditional griot's pietistic formulae, rhetorical invocations, and stock hyperbole, and begins at the breakneck pace of a storyteller who is narrating something for the umpteenth time:

> Our eyes drink the brightness of the sun and, overcome, marvel at their tears. Mashallah! wa bismallah! . . . To recount the bloody adventure of the nigger trash—shame to the worthless paupers!—there would be no need to go back beyond the present century.
>
> What is more interesting, when the elders, notables, and griots, peering wide-eyed into the bitter deserts, speak of that Empire, is the desperate flight, before God's implacable "blessing," of its population, baptized in torture . . . torn by internecine rivalries and warring with one another for the imperial power with a violence equalled only by the dread it called forth.[5]

In this narrative two voices are heard. There is a parodic pandering to denigratory European stereotypes of Africa, too blatant to be anything but ironic, and at the same time a demystification of the accepted indigenous notion of Askia Mohammed/Saif Isaac el-Heit as the millennial pinnacle of Sahelian civilization. But more important, perhaps, is Ouologuem's concern to implicate the oral tradition in both the vagaries of recorded history and the original historical mystification:

> At this point tradition loses itself in legend, for there are few written accounts and the versions of the elders diverge from those of the griots, which differ in turn from those of the chroniclers. . . . When the Immortal One makes the sun—diamond of the house of his Power—set, then, along with the tales of the oral tradition, the elders intone the famous epic (the value of which some contest because they deny Saif's Jewish descent, insisting that he was a plain ordinary nigger) written by Mahmud Meknud Trare, a descendant of griot ancestors and himself a griot of the present-day African republic of Nakem-Ziuko, which is all that remains of the ancient Nakem Empire. (*BTV,* 6)

This oral tradition, for so long the prized repository of African values in opposition to Western literate cultures, is unmasked at the outset of Ouologuem's tale as the apologist and legitimizer of tyrannical social structures and political systems, no less collaborative with the feudal status quo than were the scribes and chroniclers. The author's footnote on the first page of the novel directs the reader toward the traditional definition of the griot as "a troubadour, member of a hereditary caste whose function it is to celebrate the great events of history and to uphold the God-given traditions" (*BTV,* 3).

Ouologuem's reinvention of Sahelian history is not, however, a celebration of the divinely sanctioned epic exploits of the hereditary caste of feudal overlords from which the griots come. Far from being a saga of dynastic glories and conquests, it is a savagely ironic indictment of that caste's vicious despotism and its exploitation of its suffering peoples. Ouologuem borrows from the oral tradition only to challenge the values that it upholds and to subvert the ideological underpinnings—for example, Islamic ideologies of domination—that are encoded into it. Far from imparting a solemn dignity to the modern griot's discourse, the incongruous juxtaposition of oral rhetorical devices with the Saifs' sadistic cruelty, duplicity, and repression brings a devastating irony to bear upon both the events narrated and the mode of narrative: "In reality the nobility, warriors in the days of the first Saifs (Glory to the Almighty God), had become intriguers for power: Amen. At the death of the accursed Saif (Blessed be the Eternal One!), conscious of their own need of stability (So be it!), they had flung the people into a bath of pseudo-spirituality, while enslaving them materially (And praised)" (*BTV,* 23). The parenthetical exclamations, elliptical slogans, and prayer tags borrowed from oral narrative are brought into disrepute and their seriousness undermined by the author's scurrilous attachment of them to unworthy and lurid subjects—perversion, rape, slave raids, and massacre. Subsequently, the praise songs bestow only ironic eulogies upon the public personalities they ostensibly proclaim. Ouologuem's mock-heroics are a double-edged sword that, at the same time as it lays bare the faulty heroism of the subject, also belittles the narrative form that heroizes it and implies doubts about its moral and historical reliability.

Thus it comes as no surprise when it is revealed that the myths and legends of many of the tales in the oral culture are no more rooted in indigenous folklore than the phony antique masks collected by "Shrobenius" (the ethnologist Leo Frobenius) and the bogus "mixture of pure, symbolic and religious art" concocted for him by the witch doctor Sankolo. Like the art and religion, the tales too are mere fabrications designed by Saif-el-Heit himself to dupe gullible and suspiciously motivated European ethnologists into taking a falsely heroic, "Afrolotrous" view of traditional culture. Here, in Saif's spurious negrology, are the roots of negritude's romanticized version of a glorious pre-European, spiritually holistic, African past that would serve later generations of African dictators as an opiate to divert attention from the abuses and sufferings of the present:

> Madoubo ... spoke indefatigably of symbols, as did his father, who spouted myths for a whole week.... Shrobenius's head teemed with ideas. Reeling off spirituality by the yard, the men paced the courtyard with anxious, knit brows.... Saif made up stories and the interpreter translated, Madoubo repeated in French, refining on the subtleties to the delight of Schrobenius, that human crayfish afflicted with a groping mania for resuscitating an African universe—cultural autonomy, he called it—which had lost all living reality.... African life, he held, was pure art, intense religious symbolism, and a civilization once grandiose. (*BTV*, 86–87)

As the farrago served up to Fro/Shrobenius by Saif selects only those elements of the African past that glorify it, Ouologuem's version of history, by hypothesizing an alternative oral tradition that has the Saifs themselves as its subjects, selects only those elements of the past that debase it.

In the author's self-conscious countercreation of Sudanic history as a chronicle of primitive cruelty and enslaved misery, an acrobatic fancy juggles with one outrageous invention after another, with the result that the response to Saif's cynical inventions itself becomes suffused by a Saif-like arbitrariness and deadly whimsicality. Both versions are imaginative projections that put biased constructions on the past to suit the political and polemical needs of their authors. The mirror-image correspondence they acquire means that the story we are reading raises reflexive, self-implicating doubts about its own authenticity (the last part of the novel, "Dawn," in fact describes a film scenario about the history of Nakem, which is the story we have just been reading). Many of Ouologuem's mischievous counterfictions are deliberately and grossly unhistorical, as with his ruling caste's restriction of a French education to the serf class. Alternatively, as with his portrayal of the colonists' cunning manipulation by the colonized, they are exaggerated half-truths (only a handful of Sudanic nobles profited from their ability to negotiate with the French). In the case of the proposed Semitic origin of the Saifs, moreover, Ouologuem's counterfictions are of doubtful authenticity. Although there is abundant evidence of the Jewish presence in the medieval Sahel and of the Jewish role in trans-Saharan trade between the Songhai empire and North Africa (Hale, 148–50), the Jews have a somewhat legendary status in the *Tarik* chronicles. It is likely, as Christopher Miller suggests, that Ouologuem's Saifs merely "exploit the prestige of this birthright to lord it over the *negraille*."[6] The implication is that, given the immensity of the African historical vacuum assumed by the author and the impossibility of historical objectivity, this particular grotesque griotatary guess at Sarahan history is probably as accurate as the Frobenian version or that celebrated in works such as the Malian epic *Sundjata*. For Ouologuem, remembered legends preserved in oral form by the communal memory are no more reliable than recorded histories of selected "facts" kept by the colonizing powers.

In the manner of other projected histories that make use of oral memory to relate the odyssey of a whole people—for example, André Schwartz-Bart's *Le Dernier des justes,* the formal prototype of Ouologuem's book—*Bound to Violence* handles the notion of some kind of racial ancestry and destiny running across the centuries and periodically resurfacing in the lives of selected individuals. In Ouologuem's novel, however, the ongoing continuum is nothing so positive as the indigenous spirit of communalism celebrated in many oral folk cultures or the inherited burden of redemptive suffering that is the theme of Schwartz-Bart's book. It is simply the unchanging and apparently unchangeable feudal order of Nakem that has miraculously survived into the twentieth century: the barbaric tyranny of the hereditary Saifs, on the one hand, and, on the other, the perpetual servitude for which the doomed "Negraille" or "niggertrash" develop a fatalistic "imbecile vocation."

The choice of oral forms is integral to the author's vision of the past insofar as these forms, like Nakem's history, are irredeemably bastardized: Thus, Koranic parentheses are interspersed with and finally outnumber the Bantu ones. Implicit in Ouologuem's flamboyant iconoclasm is a denial of the idea that there was ever a time when native values and forms were wholly separable from those of the Islamic Saifs. The indigenous colonialisms of the early Negro-African overlords preceded foreign imperialism, and their exploitative practices anticipated the atrocities of the Arab invaders with whom they were happy to collaborate. In spirit, the appalling Saifs have ruled from time immemorial and are our contemporaries and successors. It is no accident that ruling African elites of the postindependence period have professed roots going back to medieval empires and that some contemporary African leaders—Senghor of Senegal, Modibo Keita of Mali—have identified with or even claimed descent from feudal despots. Significantly, the contemporary killers in Ouologuem's novel are schooled in the same sadistic tactics and techniques—knives, snakes, razor blades—as those used by the ancestors whom they reincarnate. Thus the hope expressed toward the end of the novel that "the golden age when all the swine will die is just around the corner" is derided as "a false window offering a vista of happiness" (*BTV,* 174). The conclusion declares that "Saif, mourned three million times, is forever reborn to history beneath the hot ashes of more than thirty African republics" (*BTV,* 181–82).

Ouologuem's novel appears therefore to hold out little hope for either past or future. He dismisses with contemptuous zeal the idea of a pristine, precolonial value structure, indigenously and authentically African, presided over by enlightened pure-blooded elites, prior to the Arab and European incursions. This is regarded as but another European ethnological myth about Africa, as deluded in its way as the more pernicious myths of "nigger-hating" imperialists. Even the indigenous Songhai chronicles written in Arabic are mischievously misattributed to Arab historians, implicitly denying the existence of any native art and literature. Thus critics have observed that Ouologuem, although disallowing Arab claims to indigenous antiquity in Saharan Africa, takes no interest in destroyed or corrupted indigenous values outside the undifferentiated feudal context of overlord and slave and, in Wole Soyinka's words, "still leaves the basic curiosity about black historical reality unsatisfied" (*MLAW,* 106). For some, albeit limited, measure of satisfaction on that score, we must turn to a comparable African historical novel of the same period: Armah's *Two Thousand Seasons*.

Armah's book, written after a six-year stay in Tanzania, marks its author's search for a more genuinely African form and focus than those offered by his three previous novels about alienated Westernized Africans, *The Beautyful Ones Are Not Yet Born* (1968), *Fragments* (1970), and *Why Are We So Blest?* (1972). After the psychological intricacies and historical particularities of these earlier novels, the fourth book, with its panoramic sweep across time, its Manichean reduction of humanity to primal racial forces, and the relentless polemical harangue of its collective narrator, comes as a powerful and often alarming corrective. *Two Thousand Seasons* uses as a microcosm for the historical experience of the whole African people the troubled migrations of the Akan nation (here called "the people of Anoa"). The book traces the Akan from their supposed Sudanic origins, through slavery, exile, Arab and European imperialism, guerrilla resistance, and decolonization, to their settlement in modern Ghana and their future task of reconstruction. As such, it is only in part recorded history, and the narrative draws not upon specific local tribal memories but upon the hypothetical race-consciousness of a fictitious Pan-African brotherhood of undifferentiated ethnicity, whose names are taken from all parts of the continent. In this book Armah bursts the bounds of historical realism and moves into the terrain of myth, legend, and racial memory. The group experience is now paramount, so characterization is minimal and is concerned with the representation of collective states and feelings and, most particularly, of collective heroism rather than the delineation of individual personalities and deeds. The reader is addressed by a pluralized narrative voice, an anonymous and timeless "We" that represents the whole social body throughout its wanderings across history.

Two Thousand Seasons does not purport to be a novel in any sense of the word, and to approach Armah's daring experimentation with indigenous narrative techniques with critical assumptions governing discussion of European fiction is to mistake both the formal design and spirit of his book. Rather, he has created a strange and arresting new literary form out of the tradition of the oral historian who, unlike Ouologuem's mock-griotatary narrator, speaks with the voice of the whole community and whose legends, folktales, and proverbs are stored in the communal memory. Few novels create deliberately unmemorable characters who are merely functions of a collective will or who ramble episodically over vast spans of time in pursuit of racial destinies. Even fewer novels start from the premise that certain racial groups have engrossed most of the human vices and are helpless before the evil of their own natures, whereas others have acquired a monopoly on the virtues. Although Armah's narrative makes no simple distinction between foreign vice and indigenous virtue, the precolonial disruptions of the community from within are chiefly of interest for their anticipation of colonial values. The African "askaris" who are targeted for abuse are entirely the creation of the Arab "predators" and European "destroyers"—both described as "whites"—whose destructive work they carry out. Armah attempts no critical investigation of his "white" invaders and their African quislings but characterizes them through stock epithets and invective after the partisan fashion of the Ewe *halo* (a traditional song of vitriolic insult and abuse) rather than the more balanced tone of Western satire. These features are more commonly the stock-in-trade of oral epic and undoubtedly have their written European equivalents in Saxon and Norse chronicles, which similarly trace the migrations of whole peoples and celebrate the founding of nations and empires.

It has been observed that graphic cultures favor complex, "round" characters whereas oral narratives make more use of the generic type-character.[7] Armah's deliberate use of orature's heavy, flat characterization without psychological interest or detailed motivation is a crucial part of his negotiatory polemic. His adopted mode of characterization in *Two Thousand Seasons* makes no claim to realism and has no pretensions to psychological plausibility. The slave-king Koranche is an unashamedly pasteboard villain, and the invading whites are unilaterally and pathologically evil: "The white abomination: violence in its pure state, hatred unmixed" (*TTS*, 87). The women Anoa and Idawa, in their superlative beauty, have mainly representational value as negritudinous abstractions in the collective consciousness, while the prophetesses Noliwe and Ningome are ethereal voices without physical presence. Through the depiction of mass mentalities and stereotyped folkloric heroes, the complexities of naturalistic narrative are sidestepped in an effort to provide modern Africa with a strong, curative mythology as an antidote to the sicknesses spread by colonial myths, notably the corrosive inferiority complexes they have induced.

Armah's self-conscious griotlike discourse strives to correct the method of narrating African history as well as the history itself. There are therefore some significant departures from story-telling traditions. For Armah the destiny of a whole people is too important to be entrusted either to individual heroism or to mythic higher powers. From his avowedly anti-elitist standpoint, the collective narrator shuns the griot's customary glorification of the matchless deeds of past heroes that is derisively parodied by Ouologuem and, as Isidore Okpewho has observed, rejects the supernatural along with the superhuman.[8] The book's narrative discourse is not only communalist but also essentially secular and humanist in its worldview. Armah systematically subverts and debunks not only the elitist myths of African legend and epic tradition with their supernaturally ordained kings but also the mythic vision of a historical millennium issuing from the prophetess Anoa's mystic pronouncements. Thus the rebellion and escape of Anoa's people from the slave ship in the last quarter of the book are not presented as utopian fulfillments of the oracle's promised emancipation but as makeshift victories in an ongoing, unfinished saga. They are further represented as stages of progress in a history that is left liminally open ended and incomplete. Subsequently, communal and egalitarian ideals are perceived only as potentially realizable in the contemporary world, not as actually being achieved.

Nonetheless, it is important that these ideals are reflected in the narrative's aesthetic strategies. Accordingly, and contrary to traditional practice, the individual creative personality of the narrator in Armah's epic is denied any domineering proprietorship over the events narrated (Okpewho, 8–9). The narrative strategy emphasizes instead the griot's self-effacing assumption of a common identity with both the specific audience that his tale is designed to educate and the characters of the tale itself. Thus *Two Thousand Seasons* is not only about the reciprocity that it loudly proclaims: Its technique enacts reciprocity between the storyteller, the tale, and the listeners.

Armah's plural narrative voice formally announces its agnostic viewpoint in the opening chapter: "We have not found that lying trick to our taste, the trick of making up sure knowledge of things possible to think of, things possible to wonder about but impossible to know in any such ultimate way. We are not stunted in spirit, we are not Europeans.... What we do not know we do not claim to know."[9] In Armah's first two novels his skepticism about the difference between the present and an ultimately irretrievable past contributed greatly to their ironic and pessimistic vision. In *Two Thousand Seasons,* however, he capitalizes upon the uncertainty of the past and turns it to positive ends. The narrator does not, like Ouologuem, cynically negate all retrieved "authenticities"; on the contrary, he proceeds to the imaginative hypothesis of an indigenous, precolonial African mode of life that he calls "the Way." The line between the supposedly rational ideology of "the Way" and its rivals—those sentimental mystifications and nostalgic hankerings for unreal pasts—is at times ironically thin, but the narrator strains to differentiate them, presenting the latter always as betrayals of the Way's essential aims.

Armah's didactic purpose is to cure an errant Africa of its diseased distrust in its own indigenous forms and values, not to reproduce the exact historical origins and developments of those forms and values. It is accompanied by an awareness that the communal memory drawn upon by the remembrances of oral narrative is no more unreliable than recorded history, especially when the written record is a European one colored by colonial prejudices, and that a starkly monochromatic portrait of white devilry and black victimization is at least compatible with Africa's narrow experience of the white man as enslaver and colonizer, as material and spiritual destroyer. The dogma of the Way works from the premise that one constructed ethnocentric history, serving one set of ideological needs, is as good as or better than another one that serves different and alien needs. *Two Thousand Seasons,* as Soyinka has observed, stands in the same relation to the work of black ethnologists and historians such as Cheikh Anta Diop and Chancellor Williams as Rider Haggard and Conrad do to the Eurocentric ethnology of Western scholarship (*MLAW,* 107–8). The prologue's rhetoric of fragmentation and dismemberment issues a reminder that it is the fragmented part of Africa's history—the colonial period that cut the continent off from its past—that until recently has alone constituted "African history" in

Western study. Of course, the past is not a total void into which any fiction may be projected. There is a bedrock of verifiable fact to provide yardsticks for authenticity. Even Armah's highly postulative, theoretical history, although less concerned with the past than with promise for the future, retains a strong attachment to historical time-bound reality: Witness the Arab invasions, the slave trade, the many historical personages. The griot's didactic purposes may, however, license historical inaccuracies such as the notions, in *Two Thousand Seasons,* that kings, classes, private property, and even adult genesis fables were all foreign importations and that African hunting skills were merely defensive. The poet-historian of the African oral tradition is, if only by way of compensation, as entitled to vagaries of chronology and causation as the Western historian is.

Armah's innovative, pseudo-oral narrative is, of course, a simulated exercise, a literary affectation rendered in English, not in Akan or Kiswahili, and the traditional communal intimacy between local artist and audience is here a mere fiction of the plural voice. *Two Thousand Seasons* is the kind of "novel" that would have been written if a griot had had access to literary form. It is, self-consciously, an epic written in the age of the novel, expressing the epic's integrated vision in a period of atomization. In it Armah artificially resolves the problems of the contemporary African artist by setting his tale in an indeterminate past when the artist was not yet alienated from his society but still immersed in a collective ethos and then using the griot's voice for the vicarious advocacy of communal commitment and popular revolution in a time of fragmentation and elitist privilege, when such conditions no longer prevail. Since the book's message is aimed not at a traditional audience, however, but at those anglicized Africans who have ventured furthest from what Armah hypothesizes as Africa's true self, there is no necessary inconsistency between its form and its initial African publication. Neither does it matter much that the narrative, in its ideological urgency, draws not upon local tribal memories of a specific community but on the hypothetical race memory of a fictitious Pan-African brotherhood whose names are taken from all parts of the continent. The migrations of the People of the Way suggest the legendary origins of the monarchical Akan of Ghana in the medieval Sudanic kingdom of the same name, whereas their acephalous communalism seems to have more to do with the Igbo of eastern Nigeria, and the concept of Reciprocity would appear, in light of the book's Tanzanian genesis, to owe something to the ethics of Tanzanian tribal cultures utilized by Nyerere's *Ujamaa*.

Armah's experimentation with oral form in *Two Thousand Seasons* is much more adventurous and risk-taking than in the historical novel proper, where it is usually restricted to the culture of a specific period and place. Armah is not content merely to reproduce selected oral features in a traditional novelistic context, as in Achebe's novels of traditional society; neither is he simply out to capture the spirit and energy of the griot, as in Ouologuem's extravaganza, but makes the more ambitious attempt to find precise written equivalents for oral stylistic devices. In his effort to approximate the auditory resonances of orature, Armah deliberately destabilizes and ruptures literary English as his code of cultural inscription. It is possible to regard the resulting passage, or slippage, between African oral and anglophone written modes as a source of fruitful tensions; indeed, one might consider it as the tactical springboard for the negotiation of a new creative freedom, a liminal third space, between the polarities of rival linguistic codes. The resulting transnational, stylistic mishmash can be seen as the expression of a tolerant pluralism that reflects the continent's multiculturality and resists simplistic notions of cultural and linguistic hegemony. In theory, the communal, composite identity of the narrative "we" contains boundless possibilities for the development of protean, polyphonic voices and for democratic dialogue between them. In practice, however, Armah's narrative voice proves to be an oppressively monolithic and authoritarian one. Moreover, even if one turns a blind eye to the simplifying effects of the book's monotonous racial chauvinism and monoculturalizing Pan-Africanism, it is hard to ignore the fact that the aesthetic profusion is really, at the formal level, confusion and that the balance between language codes is, in practice, maintained only with great difficulty.

No matter how resourceful and inventive the author's labor, the fact remains that the oral tale is designed to be spoken, not read, to be declaimed, not decoded, with the result that its greatest strengths seldom survive transposition to written form. Armah's imitative version, oral in conception but literary in expression, strains after an illusion of orality through what A. N. Mensah has described as a "high mimetic," special ceremonial style.[10] In actuality, however, the book employs an erratic variety of registers and devices, mixing dense poetic description with the strategic pauses and digressions of oral delivery, and ranging from the oracular and invocatory to the popular and idiomatically American: The harem women effect "the discombobulation of the askaris," and two mad fugitives from the Arab "predators" have to be restrained "from trying more homicide" (*TTS*, 31, 47).

Within the oral-ceremonial idiom itself, Armah strives to reproduce an illusion of vatic utterance through a formidable battery of rhetorical questions, lamentations, frenetic alliteration—"This is no hurried hustle hot with sweaty anticipation" (*TTS*, 158)—and portentous-sounding adjectivally sprung inversions: "Painful was the groping after lost reciprocity. Fertile had been the rule of women" (*TTS*, 26). The attempt frequently overreaches itself, however, and produces a lugubrious, almost self-parodying rhetoric that is at home in neither the oral nor the literary form. Traditionally, the "backward scanning" techniques of oral narrative edit out errors and eliminate discrepancies by glossing over them or, as a very last resort, by self-correction.[11] Once something has been said, it exists ineradicably, so the option of omission is not open to the oral narrator, who is apt to convey emphasis quantitatively rather than qualitatively: by the frequency rather than the manner of expression. Oral expression favors repetition, which is compounded by the contingencies of oral delivery that force the performer, who picks up the thread of his story after a break of weeks or months, to recapitulate and relive his narrative to refresh his audience's memory. The resulting failure in economy, translated into written form, leads inevitably to rhetorical redundancies. For example:

> The disease of death, the white road, is also unconnected sight, the fractured vision that sees only the immediate present, that follows only present gain and separates the present from the future, shutting each passing day in its own hustling greed.
> The disease of death, the white road, is also unconnected hearing, the shattered hearing that listens only to today's brazen cacophony, takes direction from that alone and stays deaf to the soft voices of those yet unborn.
> The disease of death, the white road, is also unconnected thinking, the broken reason that thinks only of the immediate paths to the moment's release, that takes no care to connect the present with past events, the present with future necessity. (*TTS*, 8)

The point labored here—that a fractured vision cannot see the connectedness of two thousand seasons of fragmented racial memories and hopes—is principally a point about time, not perception and community, and is actually not given threefold expression but is monotonously restated in the same form without any regard for the chosen vehicles. The narrator does not, after the fashion of the traditional griot, attempt to draw and elaborate upon the peculiar attributes of sight, hearing, and thought, which might just as well have been taste, touch, and smell. The treatment of the ideology of the Way is similarly marked by a vagueness of definition and a disregard for concrete particulars that are in fact alien to the oral tradition. The obsessive repetition of the Way's sacred trinity of neologisms—"Reciprocity," "Connectedness," and "Creation"—is accompanied by so little explication of what they practically involve as a lived social pattern that they eventually become lifeless verbal tags. The prose has a tendency to collapse into a lusterless jargon—"our way, the way," "the destruction of destruction," "the unconnected consciousness"—which is perhaps at its most stark in the formulation of the Law according to the Way, the 10 commandments as handed down to the visionary leader Isanusi in the form of an incantatory scriptural chant: "Our way is reciprocity. The way is wholeness. Our way knows no oppression. The way destroys oppression. Our way is hospitable to guests. The way repels destroyers. Our way produces before it consumes. The way produces far more than it consumes. Our way creates. The way destroys only destruction" (*TTS*, 39). Mensah remarks of this litany to the Way that "the most salient feature is repetition—repetition with variation, balance, antithesis" (Mensah, 7). In fact, this passage, like the previously quoted one, appears to lack all of these and to be sheer repetition, without elaboration or qualification. Only in the prologue, where thwarted racial destiny, frustrated generosity, and failed reciprocity are powerfully realized in the imagery of springwaters flowing into the desert, do Armah's poetic powers appear to be at full stretch and to do any real justice to his oral models. Paradoxically, the dazzling inventiveness and exuberant hyperbole of the griot are more in evidence in Armah's supposedly Western-oriented first novel, *The Beautyful Ones Are Not Yet Born*, than in *Two Thousand Seasons,* where the literary compromise with oral form, far from being enriched by it, results in a comparatively restricted and impoverished verbal code.[12]

Two Thousand Seasons remains, however, an important turning point in Armah's career. The author's penitential submergence in a communal vision of the isolated artists and visionaries of his early novels is clearly an attempt to give his art a more democratic basis and a more overt grounding in traditional African values. The rejection of despair and the rousing call for a halt to the further fragmentation of African society by the doubtful blessings of Western culture are positive gestures in a new direction. In Frantz Fanon's tripartite scheme for the African writer, *Two Thousand Seasons* clearly belongs to the "fighting phase," in which a polemical, future-oriented literature strives to revolutionize its African readership (*WOE,* 179).

Armah's book is essentially a therapeutic exorcism on both the private and public levels. On the level of private penance, the alienated individuals of the early novels are implicitly reproved and outgrown in the harsh treatment of Dovi—"The selfish desire of the cut-off spirit was so strong in him" (*TTS,* 183)—and in the selfless sacrifice of Abena: "There is no self to save apart from all of us. What would I have done with my life, alone, like a beast of prey?" (*TTS,* 111). At the public level the therapy is twofold. First, the systematic direction of hatred toward both Arab and European "whites" exorcises the sensations of helplessness induced by colonialism and clears the air of negative feeling so that the work of construction may begin. It is a catharsis that prepares the mind for the creation of radical alternatives to the societies left by the imperialists. Second, the "destruction" that the whites inflict and that, to the narrator's delirious glee, they eventually draw upon themselves, provides the relief for the oppositional, mainly negative, definition of the Way: "Leave the destroyers' spokesmen to cast contemptuous despair abroad. That is not our vocation. That will not be our utterance. . . . We are not a people to nurture kings and courtiers. . . . We are not a trading people" (*TTS,* xvii, 95, 98).

Forgotten and not yet rediscovered, the Way is an unknown, hypothetical quantity. Any sociopolitical models encoded in it are therefore of necessity bound to be theoretical and imprecise, like the model of oral discourse that serves as its vehicle. The indigenous communal ethic to which Isanusi and his disciples act as spiritual guardians leads a hovering existence somewhere between the restricted village communalism of precolonial Africa and the mass socialism of the postcolonial nation-state. It does not materialize, however, into either of these or into any other historical form, and so, problematically, it never becomes the accepted way of life of the community, where it is repeatedly undermined by the selfish materialism and imbecilic greed of powerful individuals. In terms of immediate practical, political action, the Way appears to amount to little more than resistance of oppression and the destruction of destroyers; it seems at times to be a mere convenience category for lost virtues.

Armah had already anticipated the problem of definition in his early essay on African socialism: "Negative, anti-colonial feeling is relatively easy to come by. At any rate it does not demand any genius. The development of positive programmes and ideologies is a much more difficult proposition."[13] In practice, this means that the rather drab communalism that the writer hypothesizes as the indigenous African way of life emerges as something that is more non-European and anti-European than specifically and recognizably African. In fact, certain features such as the total rejection of family and kin urged upon Dovi and Araba Jesiwa in the name of a higher ideal and the overriding of territorial instincts by abstract ideological loyalties would appear to be highly un-African.

Meanwhile, at the level of the larger historical vision, contemporary Africa's futile cycles of recurring colonialisms and neocolonialisms, which feature so prominently in Armah's early novels, become, on the larger canvas of *Two Thousand Seasons,* temporary aberrations in a wider "cycle of regeneration" that is destined to carry the continent back to indigenous roots. This circle of regeneration is momentarily "burst with the invading line of destruction" (*TTS,* 154), but the "white road" of linear destruction proves finally to be merely part of an immense curve on the circular trajectory of the developing way. The completion of the cycle and the return to unitary beginnings is achieved, however, only by correctively reinventing history. Isanusi's successful slave rebellion reveals the Way's potential for victory, albeit a temporary one in this instance: It is history as it might and should have been and as it might be yet if the conditions of the Way are adhered to. Armah's principal aim is the remythologizing of history or what Soyinka has called "the visionary reconstruction of the past for the purposes of a social direction" (*MLAW,* 106). As Kofi Anyidoho has observed, there is never very much distance in the narrative between historical and present experience and never enough time in the present to absorb the lessons of the past. Thus, Isanusi's recounting of the disastrous history of Anoa's people contains "immediate, urgent knowledge" that his disciples, in imminent danger of enslavement at the hands of their own leaders, fail to heed at their peril.[14] The words *vision* and *seer* alternate in the narrative with the words *remembrance* and *rememberer,* stressing the link between knowledge and foreknowledge and the importance of a usable version of the past that will provide guidance and goals as well as cautionary warnings for the future.

The utopian socialism of Isanusi's fifth grove is, self-consciously, a reality-negating mythopoetic construct of no more historical validity than the individualist warrior traditions of African epic debunked by the book's communal narrator. It is not meant, however, to be ranked along with such traditions as another precolonial Golden Age mythology. The ideal of an egalitarian, nonethnic African fraternity flies with a polemical deliberateness in the face of the continent's real tribal, social, and national divisions. The concept of the Way is thus an imaginative tool for the work of the future, an ideal projection that is yet to be realized and that must be believed in to be created, not an already or previously existing form to be retained or restored. The book's ethical manifestos belong to a higher, speculative order of reality and provide a frame of reference from which the prevailing destruction in the existing reality can be condemned and surmounted. Armah, as griotlike activist, joins in the struggle between creation and destruction in his tale and paradoxically valorizes his new models for progress by inventing an ancestry for them, thus urging the creation of what does not yet exist by insisting that it has always existed. These two orders of reality—the actual and the postulative—are evident in the book's naming of characters. The rogues' gallery boasts names and accompanying deeds that refer, directly or satirically, to historical personages—Kamuzu to Hastings Kamuzu Banda of modern Malawi, Koranche to the Portuguese-controlled puppet Kwamina Ansa, "the Golden" to Mansa Musa I of ancient Mali—whereas those who serve in the struggle for African freedom—Dedan Kimathi, Irele, Soyinka—are merely items in a list of names. Projected Pan-African virtues are thus vaguely opposed to specific historical villainy. Against the latter's stark reality, the Way remains elusively and evasively theoretical.

In the years following its publication, *Two Thousand Seasons* was widely hailed by African critics as an epochal work that evolved a major new style for African fiction even though its forced conclusion, determinedly envisaging victorious struggle and ultimate reunification (however distant), appeared to leave little further to be said. In fact Armah himself, in his next book, *The Healers* (1978), advanced only a little way beyond his position in *Two Thousand Seasons;* another 17 years passed before the appearance of his sixth novel, *Osiris Rising* (1995). Other African writers, meanwhile, did not rally to the call: Although novelists of the next generation have occasionally picked up on the mythology of the African Way,[15] the book has had no imitators. Armah's hypothesis—for purposes of future reconstruction—of a pristine, authentically African Way and Ouologuem's use of a similar imitation-griotatary mode to debunk the same idea were exciting formal and intellectual innovations. Yet, though not exactly dead ends, they now have the appearance of experimental false leads. Certainly they have not proved to be enduring models for African fiction, which over the last 20 years has headed off in quite different directions. In retrospect Armah's Pan-African polemics, like Awoonor's nostalgic poetic lyricism and Soyinka's myth-based cellular utopianism, look increasingly like dated and backward-looking products of a certain historical era. After the mid-1970s there was a slowing of the momentum to extricate "authentically African" values and styles from the increasingly complex cultural matrix of African fiction. The movement of this fiction into the 1980s was to be an outward, expansive movement, away from cultural homogeneity and toward greater diversification and hybridization. As the following chapters will show, the writers of this period were less ready to discover future potential in visions of the traditional past; more particularly, following Ouologuem's rather than Armah's example, they were less willing to award absolute and unequivocal value to the oral tradition.

Chapter Four
Orality and Dictatorship: Ngugi wa Thiong'o's *Matigari* and Nuruddin Farah's *Sweet and Sour Milk*

In a 1986 interview the Ghanaian author Kojo Laing spoke of the gap between oral and written history as being the potential source of an original thrust in creative and inventive ideas.[1] It is in this area of slippage between literature and orature that much of the innovative writing of the next decade, the 1980s, is situated. In this chapter I examine novels by two very different writers, the Kenyan Ngugi wa Thiong'o and the Somali Nuruddin Farah, both of whom conspicuously feature elements of oral discourse in their work, albeit to diametrically opposed ends. In the parable of *Matigari* (1986), Ngugi self-consciously reconstitutes oral narrative for revolutionary purposes, creatively investing its indeterminacy with a timeless, mythic dimension. Meanwhile in the earlier *Sweet and Sour Milk* (1979), published at the turn of the decade, Farah places the oral tradition in a more local and more specific and, subsequently, a more problematic context and with altogether more negative and sinister political implications.

The titular hero of Ngugi's novel, Matigari Ma Njiruungi (in Gikuyu, "the patriots who survived the bullets") is a stark and unsubtle embodiment of the spirit of militant insurgency left over from his unnamed nation's armed struggle for independence. After expelling the colonial settler and his African stooge, John Boy, Matigari emerges from the forest and, assuming that injustice has ended with the fighting, buries his gun, puts on "the belt of peace," and makes a belated reentrance into civilian life to seek his family and home. He finds himself, however, in a dystopian society where orphans live in the wrecks of cars and feed off garbage dumps and police unleash dogs on defenseless women. This "upside down world" is ruled by the corrupt dictatorship of a neocolonial elite that passes itself off, in the parroted ideology of its imperial masters, as "democracy and the rule of law" but that is really the comprador puppet of multinational corporations. In his futile search for "truth and justice" in this land, the hero discovers that the truth of contemporary history is a story of inherent injustice, which the dictatorship uses law to dispense.

The regime of "His Excellency Ole Excellence" has even rewritten history to exonerate those who collaborated with the colonial powers in the war of national liberation and to vilify the ones who bore arms; this brings the fictional narrative very close to the actual history of postindependence Kenya, in which the inheritors of colonial power included some of Mau Mau's staunchest opponents. In the absurd Orwellian doublespeak of the sinister Minister for Truth and Justice, "it is those who obeyed the colonial law . . . who made the colonialists give us independence on a platter. . . . Major Howard Williams and John Boy went to fight against terrorists during the war for independence."[2] The sons of Williams and Boy have now usurped the national "house" that Matigari built and comes to reclaim.

In his subsequent nationwide quest for truth and justice in the company of an orphan, a prostitute, and a striking worker, Matigari effects a number of apparently miraculous escapes from prisons, mental hospitals, and burning houses, which invest him with legendary trappings and render uncertain his ontological status in the narrative. In addition to his Christlike ability to appear and disappear at will and to go without food, drink, and rest, the character begins to incorporate elements of specific messianic prototypes from contemporary history. Among these are the exiled Mau Mau general Stanley Mathenge, whose threatened imminent return haunted Kenya's successive postindependence governments. Also included is the millenarian religious and political leader Elijah Masinde, around whom there evolved an oral mythology of miraculous works, including escapes from locked cells, rapid travel over immense distances, sudden unaccountable appearances, and a talent for turning bullets into water (Masinde died in the year of the book's publication).[3]

His supernatural powers notwithstanding, Matigari is unable to convert people to the cause of truth and justice—a representative student, teacher, and priest each sell out to or comply with the order of oppression—and he even begins to feel that he is "the only one preoccupied with what was happening," that he is one man "all alone in the entire country" (*M,* 85). Finally he accepts that the enemy cannot be defeated and justice achieved with words alone but only with words backed up by the force of arms, though his incitements to armed rebellion prove to be no more successful than his efforts at peaceful persuasion. In the novel's ambiguous climax Matigari sets fire to his own house and is pursued to a river where, true to his millenarian prototype, he charms the police bullets that cut down his companions and disappears into his own natural, protean liquid element, leaving the orphan Muriuku to exhume his rifle and continue the struggle.

The original Gikuyu version of *Matigari* was published in Nairobi in October 1986, and about 3,000 of the 4,000 printed copies made it as far as the bookstores before government authorities stepped in to ban the book. Though initial sales were brisk and some prepublication copies had already been smuggled from the printers to roadside stalls, there were still plenty of unsold copies on the shelves for the police to confiscate when they raided the bookstores in February 1987. The sales figures were misleading, however, because it had been customary since Ngugi began writing in his native Gikuyu for his novels to be read aloud at social gatherings and eating places and to be narrated on public conveyances, so that, as the author put it in a 1989 interview, "every copy would have a multiple readership,"[4] giving the book a broad circulation in a relatively short space of time. Thus it was that people who had never set eyes on the novel had heard of a character called Matigari who was roaming the country posing subversive questions about truth and justice and that they began to talk about him as if he were a living person; thus it was also that the Kenyan police, acting with a farcical incompetence matched by their behavior in the book, issued orders for Matigari's arrest. Upon discovering that the prime public enemy was a fictitious character in a novel, they seized the book instead. This extraordinary train of events was ample testimony not only to the power of Ngugi's writings, in their oral renderings, to leap censorship barriers and electrify mass audiences but also to the intrinsic capability of oral modes of transmission to erode the boundaries between the real and the imaginary, fact and rumor, and, in the process, to give to fiction the power and currency of actuality. By denying access and thus attracting publicity to the book, the Kenyan government then turned the text into an event and ironically empowered its oral authority, energizing its hero's circulation as a publicly owned property and conceding to him the mysterious, charismatic status that he has in the novel. Whether or not Ngugi foresaw the seizure and enhanced oralization of his book, he had already, in anticipation, built these possibilities reflexively into its form. Even before the vagaries of the novel's oral transmission blurred the lines between fact and fiction, Ngugi had already done this within the text itself, for in the surviving English translation of the book Matigari is a self-consciously mythic creation of the popular imagination, a folkloric hero who has already passed into contemporary oral legend.

Matigari was originally written to be read aloud, and a number of its oral features are evident even in the 1989 English translation, notably the recapitulative devices, the rhetorical questions, the strategic pauses for interjections, and the storytelling styles adopted by the hero's companions. Moreover, as Ngugi's introductory note to the translation indicates, the narrative is modeled on the popular oral quest motif of the hero's search, whether in the next town or country or (as in Tutuola's dream-narratives) in the next world, for a cure for an illness or disease—in this case, a moral disease that afflicts a whole society.

But the orality of *Matigari* is not merely a formal matter limited to style and technique. Ngugi said, in another 1989 interview, that he was interested in the way that myths are made and grow, in the process by which historical figures are imaginatively transformed into legends.[5] The character of the titular hero is, accordingly, a fluid, protean one who, very much in the oral mold, hovers between history and fable, the natural and the supernatural, and material and mythic realities. Matigari, Ngugi has insisted, should not be seen as a highly individualized character inhabiting a specific historical period but rather as a collective and timeless construct whom the choric oral narrator is able, in his mental wanderings, to transport magically over enormous distances in limited time scales and even across time itself (Jaggi, 243, 247). Thus the hero taps, archetypally, the national and racial consciousnesses in his response to the latest round of colonial usurpers: "I was there at the time of the Portuguese, and at the time of the Arabs, and at the time of the British" (*M,* 45). As in orature, the narrative moves freely not only in time and space but also from one plane to another, from literalism to fable, from historical to magical realism. In the split-level dialogue favored by the fable form Matigari, like the titular heroine of Yeats's play *Cathleen ni Houlihan,* refers to the occupied "house" (the nation) and "yesterday" (the past) in parabolic and generic terms that operate on a level over and above that of his literal-minded interlocutors. Of course, the protagonist's personal circumstances—the recalcitrant Mau Mau fighter belatedly returning from the forest in the heyday of neocolonial corruption—are highly implausible at the level of historical realism, as the prostitute Guthera's pragmatic response makes clear: "This man has indeed spent a long time in the forest, she thought to herself. He should first go home and sleep off the fatigue of many years" (*M*, 40). The symbolic point of Matigari's prolonged absence is twofold. First, it is important that his moral vision is kept pure and free from contamination by the distortions of postcolonial political indoctrination. Second, he is able to embody more immediately the folkloric mythology of the "Matigaris," the warriors who remained in the forest or in exile to keep the fires of freedom burning and who, in popular legend, will one day regather and return to complete the unfinished war of independence left over from a militant past: The etymology of *matigari* refers in fact to the leftovers of food and drink (Gikandi, 161).

The discourse of Ngugi's narrative is not only driven by collective myths and popular legends, however: It also seeks to enact and transform them into political reality. Like Armah in *Two Thousand Seasons,* Ngugi takes a revolutionary and idealistic view of the oral tradition that invests myth with power and in which language, though it needs to be strengthened by armed force, is itself regarded as an empowering and emboldening agent. Songs, slogans, and war chants are seen to mediate between the thoughts and deeds of their performers, infusing a new militancy into their actions. The novel's Gikuyu title, "Matigari Ma Njiruungi" (literally, "the leftovers of the bullet"), refers not to a character, as in the English version, but to an event, if only an unfinished event left over for another generation to complete, and thus signifies not a name but the eventual translation of words into deeds (Gikandi, 165). Therefore Matigari, although anchored at the level of historical realism to Kenya's contemporary postcolonial repression, is conceived at the visionary level as a messianic agent of transformation, and his astonishing capacities for self-transformation are part of the book's polemical strategy. Matigari is, of necessity, an unstable and destabilizing force, a polymorphous phenomenon who exists in rival versions and changes his shape to adapt himself to his people's varying needs. Hence he is by turns singular and plural, male and female, young and old, fat and thin, a dwarf and a giant; his very countenance alters with circumstances, aging when it beholds cruelty and deceit and growing youthful again when it encounters kindness and integrity. Ngugi capitalizes on and turns to positive effect the unsettling indeterminacy of the oral text, floating somewhere between rumored speculation and verifiable fact: "Was Matigari a man or was he a woman? A child or an adult? Or was he only an idea, an image, in people's minds? . . . Is he real or just a figment of people's imagination? Is he a person, or is it a spirit?" (*M,* 158, 170).

Since all of this makes Ngugi's novel sound like a much more complex and sophisticated piece of writing than it actually is, some qualification is necessary. Whatever their empowering and enabling effects, oral influences are also at least partly responsible for what—to the orthodox pieties of Western criticism—are the book's most glaring weaknesses. On the negative side of the balance, the flat, minimalist characterization favored by orature results, as in Armah's book, in a bland parade of exemplary unimpeachable heroes and shameless villains who seldom rise above the level of cartoon figures. Matigari is the flawless patriotic martyr, Kiriro the upright worker hero, Muriuku the rightful disinherited heir to the land, and Guthera the golden-hearted prostitute and paragon of degraded, deserving virtue who now plies her trade only in the service of the revolution. Next, as in Armah's simulated oral epic, there are the usual inevitable redundancies that accrue from the translation of oral into written modes. Orature, because of its reconstructive, recapitulative style of narration, is full of twice-told tales. Thus the history of Matigari's defeat of Settler Williams and John Boy in the war of independence and the episode of his miraculous escape from prison are recounted, ad nauseam, to each new character he meets on his odyssey (and, by implication, to each new listener who joins the storyteller's audience). Only occasionally does the repeat version supply any new information: For example, Matigari's narration of Guthera's history to the priest adds the important fact that his deliverance from the locked cell was accomplished by her gift of herself to the prison guard, not by supernatural aid. The proverbs, slogans, catchphrases, and refrains beloved of orature—"Truth never dies," "Too much fear breeds misery in the land," "A farmer does not stop sowing just because one crop has failed"—also feature with a monotonous frequency and with a solemn intensity that unfortunately offsets the stark hilarity of the satire on police incompetence, media confusion, and the official government ideology of "Parrotology."

On the other hand, oral tradition cannot be held responsible for all the faults of *Matigari,* which often occur when the author departs from the essentially communal spirit of orature in pursuit of his own partisan political purposes. Thus the sloganeering rhetoric is heavily reinforced by Marxist ideology—"Those-who-reap-where-they-never-sowed," "Give the wealth back to the owners," "Claim the products of our labour"— and the authoritative voice of the griot is used for crudely propagandist purposes: "No government, not even the most repressive, has ever managed to silence the voices of the masses" (*M,* 72, 75, 78, 127). *Matigari* marks the extreme point of the shift in Ngugi's later writing from purist to functionalist literature, realism to polemic, and to the doctrine of art for the sake of political reconstruction. It is, of course, arguable that the correct criteria for the judgment of such works is not so much aesthetic excellence, after the canons of Western taste, as the persuasiveness of their arguments and their practical efficacy, but in practice these things are hard to measure. Ngugi's work is widely known in his country, but its effectiveness—in the sense of being translatable into useful action— is an unproven and perhaps unprovable quantity. Whatever the ultimate persuasiveness of dogma and diatribe in other forms of writing, they are sadly unconvincing in the rhetoric of Ngugi's novel.

Certainly it is in the book's polemic that Ngugi's use of orature is most questionable. In the oral tale on which *Matigari* is ostensibly modeled there is, in addition to the narrative voice, the assumed or implied presence of an audience of listeners and the possibility of their participatory response through applause, interjection, or counterstatement, after the negotiatory, polemical pattern of the debate. In practice, however, the oral paradigm of statement and response is of only limited and selective formal relevance to *Matigari,* in which the peremptory, hectoring harangue of the narrative voice is anything but negotiatory and is really, in its way, as authoritarian and dictatorial as the regime it targets. There is no dialogue here, no reciprocity between teller and listener, and there are no competing judgments; only, under the cover of an assumed common identity with his audience, the narrator's repeated assertion of an ideological position. The relentless foregrounding of the author's political message leaves no space for criticism or irony; as Dianne Schwerdt astutely observes, the characters in the novel do not struggle or argue their way toward enlightenment but are simply acted upon by the charismatic protagonist and submit passively to his will.[6] It is likewise demanded that the reader/listener acquiesce to Matigari's crude and intolerant polarization of people into patriots and traitors, "those who love the truth and those who sell the truth" (*M,* 90, 92), and accept his doctrinally "correct" view that, since peaceful persuasion has failed, there is nothing left but to fight. The expected agreement of an already converted audience is one of the givens of the novel, and the reader is left with a sense of not being able to have it any other way. There is subsequently no serious attempt to grapple with the complex, problematic forces and issues that make up the multifaceted, plural reality of Kenya and every other postindependence African society.

Ngugi's relation to the oral mode that he purports to valorize is, finally, as problematic as that of the authors discussed in the previous chapter. For example, he initially makes selective strategic use of the vagaries of orature and its unstable order of meaning. He utilizes its ability to improvise alternative versions of events and thus erode the line between fact and fiction in order to write back to the doublespeak of a regime that habitually presents lies as truth, tyranny as law, and oppression as justice. In the service of this cause he puts to polemical use oral modes of transmission that rely heavily on report, rumor, and hearsay, and in which human speculation and credulity therefore play an important role. Thus the strategy is carefully qualified from within the narrative, for Ngugi, at the same time, is quick to expose false rumor and human gullibility, particularly with regard to the desire for miracles, both in his tale's fictional populace and by extension in his audience of listeners. Matigari does not claim messianic status but has it thrust upon him by a credulous public. And yet, having critically exposed this superstitious credulity, Ngugi then appeals and panders to it; indeed, he proceeds unapologetically to exploit the popular fantasy of a miraculous redeemer and sacrificial savior-hero to enlist public loyalty and subservience to the special authority of Matigari. This is a largely "magical" authority insofar as the hero's leadership and right to speak for the oppressed are never questioned or rationally inquired into. It is also, as Abdulrazak Gurnah has argued, a patronizingly paternal form of hegemony that inclines to present patriotism in a masculine and patriarchal guise.[7] Although Ngugi has argued that Matigari is a collective portrait in which "both the woman and the boy are really different aspects of Matigari, and Matigari is different aspects of the woman and the boy" (Wilkinson, 133), this composite self tends to subsume the female character into, rather than combine it with, the tutelary male one, and Matigari envisages woman as an essentially domestic creature: "Women are the ones who uphold the flame of continuity and change in the homestead" (*M*, 27).

One final reservation that is difficult for the Western critic to resist concerns Ngugi's ideology. In the novel the regime peppers its pronouncements with hostile references to Eastern-bloc socialism and interdicts on the teaching of Marxism, both apparently revered by the author. Of course, Ngugi's orthodox Marxist-Leninism now looks dated and somewhat primitive in the post-Soviet world. However, even when *Matigari* was first published, his old-fashioned utopian Marxism had for some time sounded romantically naïve in light of the Soviet Union's neoimperialist interference in Africa and elsewhere during the Cold War era. In his habitual identification of colonialism with capitalism, Ngugi turns a blind eye to these interventions. This then begs the question of whether his Marxist socialism, though more socialist than the bogus kind fabricated by the current Kenyan regime, is in truth any more African or is merely an alternative form of parrotology, uncritically mouthing the axioms of another foreign ideology. For a more searching and sinister account of Soviet-African political relations in the postindependence period and a more complex view of the oral tradition, we now turn to a much more subtle and sophisticated writer than Ngugi.

The Somali writer Nuruddin Farah, unlike Ngugi and the writers discussed in the previous chapter, grew up in a genuinely oral world that communicated in a virtually unwritten language, his imagination nourished by the legendary oral poets of his Ogaden childhood (Somali acquired no orthographic script until 1972). His novels, in his own description, chart the passage of a "society coming out of the oral tradition into a written form,"[8] though he has insisted that "you cannot divorce the oral and the literary from one another,"[9] and in his fiction the two modes have an interpenetrative existence. From the illiterate Ebla in his first novel, *From a Crooked Rib* (1970), to the educated Askar in the later *Maps* (1986), Farah's characters live idiomatically as oral beings on the pages to which they are transcribed, their questing intelligence and intuition fed by remembered anecdotes, parables, and folk wisdom imbibed with the oral cultures of their childhood. These continuities notwithstanding, Farah's fiction has been slower than that of Ngugi and Armah to recognize the positive strengths and reconstructive potential of oral cultural values and modes of expression, and, unlike them, he has not conceived these values and forms in an unequivocally polemical way: for example, as unsullied alternatives and possible modes of counterdiscourse to the evils of postcolonial politics.

In his trilogy of novels, *Variations on the Theme of an African Dictatorship* (1979–1983), Farah seeks neither to rehabilitate traditional forms, like Ngugi and the later Armah, nor to discredit and repudiate them, like Ouologuem, but rather to show how indigenous traditions—both oral and domestic—have themselves been implicated in the new political tribulations and terrors of the independent state. On the domestic front, the totalitarian tribal oligarchy imposed on postrevolution Somalia by General Siyad Barre's Soviet-supported regime is revealed to be but the old patriarchal (and matriarchal) despotism writ large. Thus, in the first novel of the sequence, *Sweet and Sour Milk,* the police informer and "grand patriarch" Keynaan connives at the death and defamation of his dissident son, the government minister Soyaan, to stamp out subversion at both state and familial levels; in the next novel, *Sardines* (1981), the tyrannical Idil, when evicted by her son Samater (also a government minister), is able to invoke the wrath of the state to bring about his political degradation.

With regard to the oral tradition, Farah had already provided, through the medium of Ebla in *From a Crooked Rib*, a glimpse of an oral culture in a pristine healthy state prior to its perversion by the General. Meanwhile, at the other end of the spectrum he presents in the barely literate, vivid figure of Dulman in *Sardines* a revolutionary image of an ancient, oral Somalia, a guest in a century of high technology that it now turns to its own account by fighting despotism with its own weapons. "Our tradition is oral," says Dulman. "One can communicate with the hearts of Somalis only through their hearing faculties."[10] Moreover, Deeriye, the hero of the third novel of the trilogy (*Close Sesame*, 1983), is a living reminder of a radical Somali oral tradition that fostered the talents of the warrior-poet the Sayyid and the Sultan Wiil Waal, who fought colonial and clan enemies with the power of the spoken word as well as with conventional weapons.

Farah, however, has also described the Somalis more skeptically as a people "moving straight from the oral tradition in the African sense to the oral tradition in the technological sense (television and radio) without going through that middle stage of the written word" (Langille, 7). This process acquires sinister implications and the oral tradition darker dimensions in *Sweet and Sour Milk*. Here the oral culture is effectively allied with the reactionary forces of tribal authoritarianism and obscurantism, thus polarizing oral despotism and written revolution, unalphabeted tyranny and textual subversion. It is Koschin, the narrator of the earlier novel *A Naked Needle* (1976), who sounds the first warning note about the dangers of excessive reliance on the oral code's modes of communication. "There is no government-fixed price, neither do you get a receipt," Koschin remarks ominously. "All is done orally, we are an oral society, and one has to trust."[11] In the somber trilogy of novels that follows, the Somali populace is shortchanged by a military dictatorship that lives in terror of the written word and whose repressive surveillance techniques thrive on oral exchanges and are steeped in the existing oral traditions of a still largely illiterate society. The General knows as well as Dulman that Somali hearts are won through their ears; the subversive cassettes that she smuggles abroad, recorded direct from the poet's mouth and worked into unscripted pieces for performance, are the oral tradition's answer to the debased oral techniques that help to keep him in power. Throughout the Dulman episode, Farah gives a nod of acknowledgment to the outspoken oral poets who also fell victim to the Barre regime,[12] but it is his sole concession to the oral mode's radical possibilities in a trilogy that generally opposes a progressive sophisticated literacy to a primitive reactionary orality.

In the Somalia of *Sweet and Sour Milk* and *Sardines* the status quo is a repressive, text-exclusive oral culture. There are embargoes on books and written information, and banning orders force writers like Medina, the protagonist of the second novel, to adapt her work for domestic oral consumption only (by her young daughter Ubax). Texts such as the "Clowns" essay by the posthumous hero of *Sweet and Sour Milk* (which apparently had a real underground circulation in a Somali translation) are ruthlessly hunted down, with dire results for those found in possession. More insidiously, the mechanics of power in this world are still oral based. According to the system of "Dionysius's Ear," the oral network uncovered in a secret memorandum, a barely literate General recruits his security corps of spies and informers from illiterates working entirely in the oral medium and reporting verbally everything they hear. Under the "ear-service" of tyranny, little or nothing is written down: There are no death certificates or epitaphs on graves, no lists of detainees or arrest warrants (phoned instructions suffice), and no written reports and particulars. "No writing pad, no pen," the protagonist of *Sweet and Sour Milk* notes of the heavy-booted official who hauls him briefly into detention. "He had not come to take Loyaan's particulars.... No minutes would show how long he had been kept here.... [H]e might be here for six months, a name untraceable, a person unregistered, a man inexistent."[13] "In this country, rumour rules," the woman Margaritta tells him, and it is rumor rather than information that is published: "The politics of mystification rendered rumours credible. Nothing was ever confirmed.... No information was released until a rumour had been published, and nothing was made official until the General's informants had reported back the mood, the feeling of the general public" (*SSM*, 196).

In *Sardines* Medina argues that gossip, libelous rumor, and speculation are fostered to sustain the atmosphere of suspicion and uncertainty, of being "kept guessing," required by the dictator. In apparent confirmation of this, a Somali poet referred to in the novel notes that the ear, the organ of both the oral culture and the General's police system, is shaped like a question mark. Medina has scarcely made her decisive departure from home and husband when a generous supply of oral versions of the event are already in circulation and on their way back to her, presenting her with four possible reasons for her action: Idil's threat to have Ubax circumcised, the compromising of her antigovernment position by Samater's ministerial appointment, Samater's rumored infidelity with the maid, and the creation of a need for herself through absence. The result is that the agent herself is no longer sure of her motives, and neither she nor her author ever confirm that any one of these alternatives is to be preferred above the others. Whatever private certainty exists is thus dissolved into public indeterminacy, and the oral convention, in its reconstruction of multiple possibilities, poses not merely an invasion of privacy and a moral usurpation but an ontological threat: What is uncertain is not only who but what and *if* people are.

In *Sweet and Sour Milk* the reader is plunged into a deranged, nightmare world of Orwellian unpersons, dawn disappearances, and rearranged history controlled by a psychotic dictator. In the prologue to the novel Soyaan Keynaan, economic adviser to the President, dies, apparently poisoned at a dinner with a government minister. By falsifying his last words and the facts of his life, the regime then immediately proceeds to turn the dead man into a revolutionary hero, an undertaking that his father, ex-policeman and now informer to the dictatorship, willingly collaborates with. Soyaan's twin brother, Loyaan, a country dentist with no experience of the labyrinthine passages of political life, embarks upon a reconstruction of the events of Soyaan's last weeks. From coded messages in his brother's diary, a seditious memorandum hidden in his clothes, and evidence scrambled together from various people—Soyaan's mistress Margaritta, a fellow conspirator Ibrahim, and a suspicious doctor Ahmed-Wellie—it becomes apparent that the dead man had been a leading figure in subversive, anti-Soviet activities and was probably murdered with the aid of a Russian doctor as part of a government plot. In the atmosphere of fear and suspicion sown by the dictator, however, Loyaan is unable to trust the testimony of any of Soyaan's confederates and confidantes: Margaritta is also an ex-mistress of the Minister of Police, and Ahmed-Wellie appears to be a government spy. After a futile interrogative assault on the minister who was present at Soyaan's last meal and a brief spell of detention, Loyaan's lone quest for the truth peters out inconclusively with the government's decision to pack him off to Belgrade as a "diplomat" in the Soviet embassy. The exact motive for and manner of Soyaan's death and the reliability of a revolutionary underground "Group of Ten" formed around him remain uncertain. As Loyaan awaits his departure, the novel ends with an ominous, ambiguous knock on the door.

One of the key problematic issues of this frightening novel is the fate of the written text in a political system geared to oral discourse. The written sign would appear, in theory, to pose to an oral-based power system the greatest challenge: The sign marks limits, defines, and identifies, and certifies reality by keeping an evidential record of people and events that insists that things happened. In the oral malaise of Farah's Somalia the underground Group of Ten who challenge obscurantist power pin their faith to the few signs that exist because there is nothing else with which to fix the flux, or even prove the existence, of human experience. Loyaan entertains the naïve hope that a written public statement will refute the lies fabricated about his brother by his father; Ibrahim trusts optimistically that "the written word, more powerful than the gun, will frighten them" (*SSM*, 139); and Soyaan, who kept his official memos short because of the semi-illiteracy of the ruling oligarchy, seems from the scraps of his writings that survive to have shared this perhaps deluded faith in the subversive potential of the written word, not realizing that the real sources of power lay elsewhere. In fact, the fate in store for literate protest against unalphabeted dictatorship is sounded proleptically during the retrospective beach scene between Soyaan and Margaritta at the beginning of the book: "The solidity of his body in the water's transparency flowed into ripples of fantasy. . . . She wrote his name on the sand. The sea washed away her writing. They silently watched the water recede. He wished he could read her message in the water receding" (*SSM*, 12–13). Here, in the novel's prologue—in the dissolving of solid, stable realities into fantasy, the washing away of words—the pattern for the book is set. What are the implications for written texts, including Farah's own, in a mode of reality built on oral discourse? What happens to language when nothing is happening, in the sense of being written, in it? With a technical ingenuity and a degree of reflexiveness far surpassing those of Ngugi's novel in sophistication, Farah's text sets out to answer these questions.

One possible reaction to this floating, indeterminate oral reality is for the text to retreat deeper into its "writtenness" and for its peculiarly literary texture to grow denser. Partly in imitation of, partly in resistance to the polymorphous political order of the dictator, it becomes a darkly hermetic, opaque hieroglyph layered with mysteries, its meanings driven underground into secret codes. Soyaan scribbles cryptic poems on the backs of photographs and devises a private "alphabet of mysteries":

"I/M" (Ibrahim/Medina?) and "M to the power of 2" (Margaritta and her child Marco, Mogadiscio and Moscow?). Margaritta scratches enigmatic signs in the sand, and Ibrahim speaks on the telephone in mysterious monosyllables, designed to thwart the General's Dionysian cave of listening devices. Given the paranoid context of persecuted print where written texts are both threatening and threatened, Farah's narrative develops into a correspondingly obscure and evasive text in the face of the reader's interrogation of it for possible clues. Indeed, it seems at times as if the implied reader were conceived as a kind of hermeneutic thought-police conspiring with the political plot and as if the text's defensive behavior were reenacting Loyaan's suspicions of "friends" to whom he is afraid to tell everything he knows. In the process, the uncertainty of the questing protagonist is magnified in the reader's responses. Much of the text is taken up by questions, but they are, in Loyaan's phrase, "Whys and no wherefores . . . endless questions, unprovidable answers" (*SSM*, 51, 62). Thus the novel does not so much *tell* but *is* its story. The book itself retreats finally into Soyaan's secret codes, re-creating the atmosphere of confusion and mistrust spread by the General. The awaited clarifying closure of the political thriller and detective novel encouraged by its form is finally dissolved in a polygraphy of possible meanings (the detective novel's authoritarian messiah-figure who traditionally ties up all the loose ends is here, in fact, the obscurantist mystifier who creates them).

Alternatively, the public oral code begins to infiltrate the written text that, if only at a figurative level, takes on certain selected characteristics of the oral modes of discourse privileged by the regime. Most relevant to Farah's novel in this respect are the oral narrative's reinventive capacities and talent for the improvisation of alternative versions in the retelling of tales. Also pertinent are its susceptibility to variation, omission, and shifts of emphasis and its vagaries of characterization. Finally, most dangerous in the present political context is the interpretative openness that follows inevitably from a form of discourse that is audience oriented rather than performer centered. "Let everybody interpret things as they wished," Loyaan laments, in despair at the systematic misinterpretation of the facts of his brother's life by their policeman-father and the police state that he serves (*SSM*, 138). In this novel human lives are like plots—coming and going ephemerally in an epic narrative, reimaginable and reinterpretable. *Sweet and Sour Milk* is, in fact, full of multilayered, miniature oral "texts" that require an audience's complementary interpretation, notably the symbolic vignettes of weather and skyscape that open the chapters and the recurring epigraphic refrain of rival poisons fed to an infant who is denied his mother's milk. The latter may be variously construed as the "sour" and "sweet" sides of the Somali temperament, represented by Loyaan and Soyaan or by Keynaan and his wives. They may alternatively be perceived as the mixed bag of colonial education that offsets Keynaan's flat, preheliocentric conception of the universe with a fully rounded global view but also teaches that Africa had no precolonial history. Finally, one may conceive of them as the successive poisons of colonial and the General's regimes.

Of this order of experience is the Keynaans' family butcher's riddling "text" of the tribal goat, tortured for its own enlightenment before being ritually slaughtered: "I am training her so that she can grasp the meaning of death before I slaughter it. Your father has, with the money he paid for her head, taught her what it means to be separated from where she was born and her tribal masters. She grasped that being dragged here. Now I've cut the tribal ear. A little later, I shall gladly administer death to her" (*SSM,* 209). Exactly how the butcher intends his fable to be read is far from clear. Is the goat the murdered Soyaan, either as a sacrificial martyr to a spurious revolution or as a scapegoat, focusing the wrath of the regime on the rising tide of anti-Soviet activities and issuing a warning to the other members of the Group of Ten? Or does the butcher's parable present a broader image of modern Somalia, decaying and moribund under a tribal dictator, and of its Westernized intellectuals, uprooted from their birthplaces but still psychologically scarred by their tribal heritage and facing a choice of exile or torture and execution? Perhaps the point is that the regime's political imbecility resists intelligibility in any terms other than those of sadistic powermania. If so, then the parable of the goat stands reflexively as a sinister paradigm of Somali reality under an obscurantist dictator: a reality that, because it is infinitely interpretable, is fundamentally uninterpretable.

In *Sardines* the oralist Idil, the matriarchal representative of the General on the domestic front, is fully at home in this many-versioned reality that she can easily remold into the shape of her own obsessive vision: "Idil's ball of thread rolled away. . . . She began to thread-draw in her mind a past with patterns different from the one she had the intention of re-narrating. . . . Idil counted the number of holes she had to jump in order to form a pattern" (*S,* 78). In the tangled webs of both the General's and Idil's oral texts, the interpretative spaces around the words— the "holes" or lacunae, the "antimatter" generated by the text—are as important as the words themselves in the forming of patterns. The oral mode is, in a quasi-postmodern way, an oblique or off-centered mode of discourse, and there is in the novel a prevailing motif of uncenteredness that indexes its political themes and its protagonist's existential crises and dilemmas to oral conventions.

In the polemical exchanges of ideas between Margaritta and Loyaan in chapters 8 and 10, Somalia, serving as a microcosm of modern Africa, is itself envisaged as a featureless void inhabited by inauthentic foreign and indigenous presences but without any inner core of identity. Its preliterate, precolonial history is conceived as an endlessly reinvented oral narrative improvised over a factual vacuum, a text on which each successive regime plays its own variations before an obliging mass audience. Meanwhile, its more recent, postcolonial history is reconstituted at the personal whim of dictators, usually in terms of flat, cartoonlike fictions. At the funeral celebrations that remake him into a myth, Soyaan, we are told, was "the centre of this festivity," but the real Soyaan "wasn't there" (*SSM*, 231). Because there is no route by which his writings might pass into the oral discourse privileged by the regime, Soyaan's fate will be to be remembered not by their complex truths but by the oral slogans that refashion him into a revolutionary hero. The lives of Soyaan and his confederates are, in fact, satellites of other forces, rotating in an interpretative void and existing in a multiplicity of versions.

The manufacturer of this many-versioned malaise and the ringmaster of its peculiar epistemological circus is, of course, the General. In theory, Somalia's Islamic militarism is centered on key political and religious signs in a written code: the Revolutionary Council's constitution and the Koran. In practice, however, the General has substituted his own personality for the constitution ("I *am* the constitution"), and he has bowdlerized the Koran into a collection of slogans and hackneyed praise songs ("There is no General like our General") parroted by his military stooges, a debasement that leaves the original text corrupted beyond restitution: For Loyaan at his brother's funeral, the Koran stands "open and unreadable." The effect, Soyaan notes, has been to decenter Somalia's political reality by placing phrases like "radical governments" and "revolutionary socialism" in parentheses and quotation marks that hold them at a remove from the real thing.

A similar indeterminacy informs characterization. Under the stage-management of the General, "Mulki," the sister of Ibrahim who is allegedly arrested and tortured for typing Soyaan's secret memorandum, is also enclosed in quotation marks and is entirely "oral" in conception, a character for whom there is neither documentary evidence in photographic or written records within the contexts of realism nor any other form of narrative confirmation. We are given only others' representations of Mulki's doings and never meet the woman herself. She suffers—indeed, she exists—on hearsay alone, and on doubtful hearsay at that: of the police informer Keynaan, the suspected government spy Ahmed-Wellie, and the tribally antagonistic receptionist at the government office where Loyaan goes in futile pursuit of Soyaan's death certificate (possibly a spy recruited from the tribal group most hostile to the General to divert suspicion). The ministerial files disclaim all knowledge of Mulki's existence, and it is not even completely clear that the unnamed typist and Ibrahim's sister are one and the same person: The name is supplied by Loyaan himself, who has previously never heard either of Ibrahim or his sister, and its source is one of the text's many lacunae. Although Ahmed-Wellie insists that a blindfolded torture-victim he was taken to tend was not "Mulki," Loyaan does not believe his claim to know her, and the suspicious doctor is later called away to deal with "a mad case of euthanasia administered to a woman." Is this Mulki? In the "badly written farce" staged for Loyaan by the Minister to the Presidency in the interrogation scene, "Mulki" is represented by an incompetent actress, wheeled onto the set at ministerial cue to protest that she has been neither detained nor maltreated; she further promises to be there at the airport to wave him off to the foreign diplomatic post that the embarrassed regime has hastily created for him. If Mulki really does exist, clearly this is not she, but, depending upon oral testimony alone, we have no way of knowing whether there really is such a person.

Moreover, Mulki's torture, like Soyaan's fatal injection by Russian doctors ("pale, ghostly beings which jabbed with needles"), is presented in the form of frenzied dream and delirium in the protagonal consciousness, blurring the true and the imaginary, what does and does not exist. As a result, we can no more distinguish the "real" from the merely "represented" Mulki than we can the "real" Soyaan from the revolutionary artifact into which he is posthumously transformed. In what sense, for example, can Soyaan be said to have existed except as a mythical property of the government, like the parks, streets, and buildings named after him? Loyaan is repeatedly mistaken for his twin and eventually comes to doubt his own reality. He imagines that he hears his dead brother's voice speaking inside his head, tempering his impetuosity with its discretion, and begins to wonder if he is perhaps not really an autonomous being at all but part of a composite imaginative construct, a Siamese soul called Loyaan-Soyaan, with interchangeable parts. Both Mulki and Soyaan are "unwritten" entities: They, and perhaps even Loyaan himself, begin as figures in Farah's written text but end as figments of the General's oral scenario. Farah has said in his essay "Why I Write" that "Somalia was a badly written play" and "Siyad Barre was its author. . . . [H]e was also the play's main actor, its centre and theme; as an actor-producer, he played all the available roles."[14] The more precise analogy that suggests itself in *Sweet and Sour Milk* is of the General as a species of debased oral performer. He appears as a malevolent, diabolically inventive kind of oral historian, producing endless surprises and variations on the theme of silencing dissidents, fabricating imagined alternatives for the lives of his trampled victims, and, with the help of men like Keynaan, breathing a false life into lies that travesty their real ones. Farah appears to have conceived Somali political reality in terms of a grotesque parody of orature, with the General as an astute and wily performer, serving up for his nation's oral epics, sung by his "griots in green," new "heroes and legendary figures about whom one tells stories to children and future generations" (*SSM*, 183). In Farah's dark parody, however, there is none of the usual reciprocity between teller and listener, and this effect is deliberate, not something that the author tries to disguise as in Ngugi's novel. Instead of the griot's self-effacing assumption of a common identity with his audience and his instilling of a common sense of reality, the aim is, through sheer imposition of the dictatorial will, to render the audience's hold on these things unsure. The listener, Loyaan learns, must make himself alertly receptive to each new variation—he must "plot, plan, wriggle and struggle the best he could, and let nothing surprise him" (*SSM*, 208)—for the General's ideal audience consists not of active, contributing participants but of passive assenters. This audience comprises brainwashed buffoons mouthing official dogma ("Soyaan, the Hero of the Revolution"); political stooges like Keynaan, men with no core of identity who will stoop to any baseness to ingratiate themselves with power; and beggars who are so attuned to the General's protean oral reality that they have become compliantly impressionable and manipulable: "Here was an audience willing to hear anything," notes Loyaan (*SSM*, 229).

The novel's vaporous political reality is reflected in its highly poetic meteorological descriptions. Cloud formations, the night's phantasmagoric skyscapes, and the sun, which "poured its blazing vapouriness upon everything," constantly assume different shapes—camels, trees, garments, pillars, skulls—to the imagination playing its variations upon them. But when night falls "in a veil of darkness," Loyaan discovers at one of the novel's crucial reflexive moments that the artwork is really shoddy, the scenery badly painted, and that, like the political order of which it is a metaphor, there is really nothing behind it: "Empty at my touch like a soap-bubble, everything reducible to nought, nothing. Inexistent at my remembering, like a dream" (*SSM*, 143). "You always lose hold of your own reality," the dying Soyaan is informed by his mother, and those who try to track down the reality of the dead man's life—Loyaan, the reader—find their own hold upon the world weakened. Somali reality under the dictator constitutes not so much a slippery and confusing multiplicity of signs as a signless void, providing no forms in which coherent meanings can be expressed:

> The night unrolled like a cotton thread, unfolding inch by inch; the night wove words of thready thoughts; the night stitched for him a blanket of comfort and warmth. . . . Every movement he heard had a meaning, and if it didn't he gave it one. The security men were following him and making sure he stayed indoors, in one version. . . . Then, right before Loyaan's and the world's eyes, all suddenly began to disintegrate like a worn-out piece of cloth a thick set of fingers has pulled asunder. (*SSM*, 205–6, 210–11)

The sun's sudden dismantling of the "fabric of schemata," the text written upon the night by Loyaan's imagination, is indirectly an image of Farah's own text deconstructively unstitching itself. What looks like an unfolding of meaning turns out to be an unraveling of the entire fabric in which meaning should reside. The novel's ontological barriers are themselves breached, and the proliferation of "versions" precludes the literary representation of reality as the discovery of indivisible truths. Subsequently Loyaan, as a character within the novel's realistic frame, comes increasingly to rely on instinct and touch for his sense of reality: on the stark immediacy of his brother's corpse, his almost visceral hatred of his father, and the tender pragmatism of the flesh that (though his feeling for Margaritta is more erotic than sexual) becomes the final touchstone for his existence.

As Loyaan is unable to unravel the butcher's tortuous text of the goat, so the novel's narrative plot of his quest for the truth of his brother's death is unable to unravel the political-criminal plot to murder and mythologize Soyaan. Obscured by a malaise of misinformation, this plot never materializes. It is, finally, unwritten and unwritable and peters out unresolved in a series of loose ends or dissolves in a welter of conflicting oral testimony. We are told in the final chapter that only Ladan, who has hidden Soyaan's writings in a place known to herself alone, will be able to resume control of Loyaan's narrative quest and restitch the true text of Soyaan's life: "Ladan is that Solomonic thread which connects all, which stitches the holes its needle has made. Follow the hints of that thread, follow it with patience" (*SSM*, 225). Yet Ladan is, puzzlingly, one of the few characters who fail to appear or even get mentioned in the next two volumes of the trilogy. Significantly, the precise whereabouts of Soyaan's scripts and, by extension, of the written word in oral Somalia are left uncertain. "The sky is too high to reach and hide them in," Loyaan tells his sister, "the earth too earthly and too exposed and the boxes are not sufficiently secretive" (*SSM*, 224).

At the end of *Sweet and Sour Milk*, Keynaan's second wife, Beydan, dies giving birth to a child called Soyaan, who may or may not recover the truth about his dead namesake: "Twenty years later, for all one knew, a Soyaan who survived Beydan's death in childbirth might walk a street named after a brother Soyaan knighted by a false revolution, made a hero in order to hide in the virtuosity of the generosity of politics" (*SSM*, 218). Exactly what is delivered, achieved, or brought to fruition at the end of Farah's book, what value it has, and what promise it holds for posterity are left unclear. It may be the new offspring's gesture of hope for the future, the truth about Soyaan, or the promised revival of the written word that will give it expression. Or it may be the book itself, which contains these hopes and so still poses a threat to totalitarian power.

In retrospect, Farah's caution in forecasting the future of Somalia in *Sweet and Sour Milk* appears to have been justified by events. In the following decade the General's clan hegemony narrowed to a family dynasty, the one-party state to one-man rule, and the cohesive political institutions and infrastructure of the nation were undermined and eventually dismantled by the dictator's ruthless manipulation of clan animosities. Consequently, when the Barre regime finally fell in May 1991, it left behind a political vacuum that was filled by feuding warlords with private armies, plunging the country into a nightmare of anarchy, famine, and abortive international relief actions from which it would take years to recover.

Chapter Five
The African in White South African Fiction: Landscape and Mythology in J. M. Coetzee's *Life and Times of Michael K*

Until the last decade of the twentieth century, democracy was unknown by the African population in the southern tip of the continent. In this, Africa's last bastion of white colonial rule, a minority of 5,000,000 whites wielded political power and owned most of the land and wealth. Only with the slow dismantling of institutionalized apartheid, which led to the end of white minority rule and the election of the nation's first black president in 1994, did an excluded majority of 28,000,000 people of African, Asian, and mixed ancestry finally receive legal rights, voting privileges, and freedoms of movement and speech that had long been denied them. The writer who, during the previous two decades, had perhaps done the most among white South African writers to target the embattled national myths and the authoritarian, patriarchal modes of discourse that had helped to keep the white Afrikaner regime in power for so long was J. M. Coetzee. It was in Coetzee's writing that reflexiveness and self-referentiality, fitfully present in Farah's fiction, assumed the dimensions of a controlled polemical strategy. Coetzee's writing, and that of his white contemporaries (Gordimer, Brink), has been rapidly overtaken by political events and is to some extent already history and of dated documentary value. Nonetheless, it marks an important staging area in the nation's end-of-the-century political upheaval and transformation and remains a milestone and landmark in South African fiction.

Coetzee's novels are sophisticatedly self-conscious and at times insidiously self-implicating, self-subverting fictions. His fourth novel, *Life and Times of Michael K* (1983), in which the white narrator takes it upon himself, inauthentically, to assume voices and compose stories for the silenced black Other, and his fifth novel, *Foe* (1986), in which he emphatically denies himself this right, are in some respects the culminating points of Coetzee's fiction. But the author's reflexive and metafictional tendencies have in fact been abundantly in evidence throughout his work, his return to realism in *Age of Iron* (1990) notwithstanding. In *Dusklands* (1974) he traces the infantilizing paternalism of apartheid to the eighteenth-century Afrikaner expeditionary narrative—to its dualistic and ultimately solipsistic separation of imperial self and colonial Other—and proceeds, in an act of imaginative decolonization, to deconstruct the settler-narrative "realism" (and its latter-day equivalents) that has long served as a literary tool of imperial oppression. In *In the Heart of the Country* (1977), Coetzee explores cross-racial sexual phobias and devises an antipastoral that harkens back to the South African *plaasroman* or farm novel, specifically to its iconography of woman as mother-martyr and sustainer of racial purity, and to its fantasy of paternal landowner, supportive wife and mother, and grateful Africans all bound together by a mystique of earth. *Waiting for the Barbarians* (1980) examines paranoid colonial fictions of "barbarians," the fantasy images of primitivism with which empires define and promote their own self-images as forces for civilization. It also poses the dilemma of the writer who cannot remain silent but who is impotently aware that, in depicting torture realistically in fiction and arousing a voyeuristic fascination with the forbidden, he may be guilty of complicity with the oppressor.

Each of Coetzee's fictions gives expression, to some extent, to abstract ideas about earth and the land that have been enduring preoccupations in white South African literature, usually in the form of expropriative territorial mythologies or mystiques that automatically exclude the non-Afrikaner. The Afrikaner writer, notes Breyten Breytenbach, has a tendency to mythologize landscape through "passionate and mystical descriptions of flatland and hillock," whereas for his black African counterpart the land is simply there and is taken much for granted.[1] In *Life and Times of Michael K* the perspective adopted is, for the first time in Coetzee's work, a nonwhite one. The book's ruling metaphysic, however, is still of earth and the land, though with the key difference that the conditions for and terms of the mythology constructed around its black protagonist, instead of taking refuge from historical reality, are themselves set by South Africa's historical situation as Coetzee sees it.

The novel depicts the strange nomadic peregrination of Michael, a municipal gardens laborer, from the Cape to the Karoo with the sick body, and then the ashes, of his mother: a pilgrimage that is blocked at every border by army and military police and that leads to his triple internment—for vagrancy and on suspicion of running a staging-post for guerrillas—in prison, camp, and hospital. There is a war going on in the background of his journey, but this war, whether civil or revolutionary, remains vague. It is fought, says Noel the camp commandant, "so that minorities will have a say in their destinies,"[2] which appears to refer to the ruling white minority keeping their say rather than to any of the excluded majorities obtaining theirs. Throughout his wanderings and internments Michael "barely knows there is a war on" (*MK*, 179) because he is busy existing on his own terms, unresponsive and minimally touched by historical events that, in his marginal existence, acquire the unreality of dream. The medical officer into whose care he drifts in the rehabilitation camp, and whose narrative takes up the second part of the book, refers to him as "a human soul above and beneath classification . . . untouched by history . . . the last of his kind, a creature left over from an earlier age" (*MK*, 207).

In the long first part of *Michael K* there is a curious passage in which the white South African writer is discovered trying to imagine what the South African black himself imagines to be the Afrikaner heritage, a legacy presented here in terms of landscape and silence:

> He filled his beret with more of the feed, thinking: At last I am living off the land. Sometimes the only sound he could hear was that of his trouser-legs whipping together. From horizon to horizon the landscape was empty. He climbed a hill and lay on his back listening to the silence. . . . I could live here forever, he thought, or till I die. Nothing would happen, every day would be the same as the day before, there would be nothing to say. . . . He could understand that people should have retreated here and fenced themselves in with miles and miles of silence; he could understand that they should have wanted to bequeath the privilege of so much silence to their children and grandchildren in perpetuity (though by what right he was not sure). (*MK*, 63–64)

Momentarily, Michael achieves the Afrikaner's pastoral ideal of "living off the land" and sympathizes with his pursuit of silence. The irony, quick to sound, is that this rural bequest of silence has long been verbalized into noisy propagandist myths to uphold a dubiously authorized system of political oppression ("by what right he was not sure") of which Michael is himself a dispossessed victim. The difference in Michael's case is that he has none of the Afrikaner's need to affirm through verbal posturings his puny presence in this landscape. For him, the topography lends itself to no myths, offers no mystical bond or blood-intimacy, and altogether lacks humanizing dimensions, being not merely silent but empty—a place where nothing happens.

Coetzee's Cape gardener, faced with the harsh, inhospitable earthscapes of the Karoo, finds himself perfectly at home with their refusal of human meanings, their preverbal nothingness. Coetzee shows him virtually turning into the landscape and assuming its character, exchanging the vegetal soil and rotted leaves of the Cape's parks for the bare mineral scrubland: "I am becoming smaller and harder and drier every day" (*MK*, 93). But the ecstasies afforded at the extremity of this "arid landscape that tilted and threatened to tip him over its edge" (*MK*, 78) are ecstasies of vacancy and negation, in which faint echoes of Wordsworth's anthropomorphic scenery are quickly dispersed into the brooding nullity:

> Even on the stillest of days no sound reached him save the scurrying of insects across the ground, and the buzz of the flies that had not forgotten him, and the pulse of blood in his ears.... There was nothing to look forward to but the sight, every morning, of the shadow of the rim of the mountain chasing faster and faster toward him till all of a sudden he was bathed in sunlight. He would sit or lie in a stupor at the mouth of the cave, too tired to move or perhaps too lackadaisical.... [H]e sometimes locked his fingers behind his head, closed his eyes, and emptied his mind, wanting nothing, looking forward to nothing. (*MK*, 91, 93, 94)

Language exists at a tangent both to this minimalist, almost comatose, landscape and to its occupant: K's pursuit of silence, paradoxically rendered into rhetoric by his white Afrikaner author, is in fact a nonverbal one. Almost inarticulate as a result of his harelip, he lives in terror of a life spent with people and in language (he is "not clever with words" and cannot handle "quotients" and town names like Prince Albert). At one point he envisages himself as an earth-hole into which words disappear: "Always, when he tried to explain himself to himself, there remained a gap, a hole, a darkness before which his understanding baulked, into which it was useless to pour words. The words were eaten up, the gap remained" (*MK*, 150–51). When he takes shelter in an abandoned white homestead, he is forced to reengage with the language order of white authority in the form of a deserter from the war who tries to turn K into his "body servant." But he soon feels "the old hopeless stupidity invading him" and has only silent truth to oppose the Afrikaner's verbal falsehoods. The deserter, Visagie, vacuously parrots Herrenvolk platitudes like "People must help each other," referring to the Afrikaner's due from his fellow whites and compliant blacks. Michael, meanwhile, "did not seem to have a belief regarding help." Visagie prattles of a "separate peace": "There is no war here on the farm. You and I can live here quietly till they make peace everywhere. . . . You must help me. Otherwise there is no future for either of us" (*MK,* 88–89). The fallacy is obvious: the division between the "You" and "I" of this sentence, the black and white, is presumably what the war is being fought over. The hard fact is that, on the existing terms, there is now no future in the same country for both. But the counterassertion comes from within the text of Visagie's contradictions, not from Michael, who seems to be almost outside the language order of contemporary history and whose only response is to get away from the man and forget him.

The camp medical officer of the second part of the book sees Michael not as part of the substantial modern world that he himself inhabits but as "scuffled together" from "a handful of dust" into "the shape of a rudimentary man." To this philosophical white observer Michael is not a creature of human history. He is, rather, "a genuine little man of earth . . . with fingers ready hooked back ready bent for a life of burrowing, a creature that spends its waking life stooped over the soil, that when at last its time comes digs its own grave and slips quietly in and draws the heavy earth over its head like a blanket and cracks a last smile and turns over and descends into sleep, home at last, while unnoticed as ever somewhere far away the grinding of the wheels of history continues" (*MK,* 220). As with all myths, however, it is out of history that Michael K comes and, specifically, out of South Africa's contemporaneous political situation, from which Coetzee extrapolates, and projects onto a civil war footing, the real options for the country's blacks. These comprise a life lived in camps—educational, rehabilitative, or penal—or life as a survivalist, out in the open with only the earth for protection. For "people with nowhere to go," as the camp inmate at Jakkalsdrif characterizes them, there is only a choice of underground existences, represented by the airless, windowless understairs cupboard that Michael's mother, Anna K, lives in at her white employer's flat and the earth-cave that it anticipates: " 'I feel like a toad under a stone living here,' she whispered" (*MK,* 12). The alternatives boil down to likely death inside the camps and certain death outside them, and the sympathetic white-liberal medical officer at the rehabilitation camp does not oppose this status quo but is himself a party to its enforcement. Seeking, finally, to do to K exactly what other officials have done to him his whole life long, he concludes that K would have been better off either shut away in a high-walled institution or "quietly suffocated" at birth and thrown out with the garbage.

Anna K's fate is envisaged in similar terms. "When she died they threw her in the fire," K tells the doctor. "Here is your mother, take her away, she is no good to us" (*MK*, 186). When K refuses to eat or speak in the hospital, the medical man's moral integrity is tested to the limit by the strange creature who looks at him "from beyond the grave" and invites him to cross the fine line between wanting to be rid of his charge and wanting to destroy it. As the camp militant Robert puts it: "If we just grew thin and turned into paper and then into ash and floated away, they wouldn't give a stuff for us. They just don't want to get upset. They want to go to sleep feeling good" (*MK*, 121). Put in its crudest form, the unspoken wish of the white authorities in the novel is for the blacks to vanish from the face of the earth and preferably into it. K's frightening image of blacks being forced to dig their own mass graves anticipates the doctor's later fantasy of K as earth man pulling down the lid after himself:

> If these people really wanted to be rid of us, he thought . . . if they really wanted to forget us forever, they would have to give us picks and spades and command us to dig; then, when we had exhausted ourselves digging, and had dug a great hole in the middle of the camp, they would have to order us to climb in and lay ourselves down; and when we were lying there, all of us, they would have to break down the huts and tents as well as every last thing we had owned upon us, and cover us with earth, and flatten the earth. *Then*, perhaps, they might begin to forget about us. (*MK*, 129–30)

The passage presents the prison camp, potentially an extermination camp, as a microcosm of the South African state: It points K and all the invisible men the way to a life lived—politically, physically, metaphysically—underground. Disenfranchised from a human existence on the earth's surface, they are directed back toward the earth itself: "A man who wants to live cannot live in a house with lights in the windows. He must live in a hole and hide by day. A man must live so that he leaves no trace of his living" (*MK*, 135).

Yet, over and above the conditions set by South Africa's historical situation, Coetzee erects around Michael K a special chthonic mythology with its own ahistorical order, into which the "wheels of history" have been rerouted. K goes literally underground, burrowing without trace, like the animals, insects, and grubs that he eats and likens himself to, or is plowed back into the earth like a fallen seed, to be resurrected from three dungeonlike incarcerations. Earth has become his element and is a constant touchstone and referent for his existence. He thus feels "like an ant that does not know where its hole is" when removed from it to the camp (*MK*, 154). He grubs, plants, and hides in it, he carries his mother's ashes to the part of it whence she came, and he will take back as food only what he has put into it: his seedling-children, growing into a family of sister-melons and brother-pumpkins, the fruit of his other mother, to whom he is connected by an invisible "cord of tenderness." In the course of this earth-odyssey the protagonist's figurative parentage begins to eclipse his actual progenitors. "My father was Huis Norenius," K remembers of his childhood. "My father was the list of rules on the door of the dormitory" (*MK*, 143). When Anna K falls sick, her son rejects everything represented by the father in South African culture, encompassing the military establishment, special institutions and penal system, and the war fought to defend and preserve them ("War is the *father* of all," runs the novel's Heraclitean epigraph). He decides at that moment that "he had been brought into the world to look after his mother" (*MK*, 9). It is part of his quest in the novel, however, to discover who his true mother is.

From the beginning of the book, K's two mothers are closely associated. On the first page his harelip forces his natural mother to feed him with a teaspoon, and on the last page he is "fed" water in an identical manner by the earth, whose hills are elsewhere represented as "two plump breasts." He transports his mother across the Cape in a converted wheelbarrow, used in his work as a gardener for the transportation of earth; he crawls under it for sleep and protection as he will later crawl under the earth's surface. At the end of the novel, when he is bound again for earth, he sets off to recover the same abandoned barrow (K moves circularly, in fact, like the seasonal movements of the earth). What is most revealing, however, is that, after first burying his mother's ashes in a hole in the ground, he then has misgivings and decides instead to plant them like seeds in individual spaces, distributing "the fine grey flakes over the earth, afterwards turning the earth over spadeful by spadeful. This was the beginning of his life as a cultivator" (*MK*, 80–81).

Thus out of the burial of his natural, biological mother is conceived the tending of his greater, cosmic one, and K can reply ambiguously to the doctor's inquiries about her whereabouts: "She makes the plants grow" (*MK*, 178). The maternal power presiding over K's life passes both literally and symbolically into the soil and, by a Whitmanesque metaphysical chemistry, is "drawn up into leaves of grass . . . after her season in the earth" (*MK*, 171). Michael's progress is thus a kind of reverse-initiation rite, returning from city to unspoiled earth, from being to elements, and from adulthood to mothered child. Indeed, in his imagination, he travels all the way back to his origins, tracking his descent "from a line of children without end" and conjuring up the images of an original, amorphous Earth-Mother and a prehistoric earth moving in geological time:

> He tried to imagine a figure standing alone at the head of the line, a woman in a shapeless grey dress who came from no mother; but when he had to think of the silence in which she lived, the silence of time before the beginning, his mind baulked. . . . He also dreamed of his mother. He was walking with her in the mountains. . . . The green lines of river-courses stood out against the fawn of the earth; there were no roads or houses anywhere; the air was still. . . . He was learning to love idleness . . . as a yielding up of himself to time, to a time flowing slowly like oil from horizon to horizon over the face of the world. . . . [H]e was living beyond the reach of calendar and clock in a blessedly neglected corner, half awake, half asleep. Like a parasite dozing in the gut, he thought; like a lizard under a stone. (*MK*, 158, 160–61, 163)

The figure constructed here by the white narrative voice has a recognizable literary ancestry, including the mad King Lear's "Poor Tom" ("Thou art the thing itself—naked unaccommodated man") and those rocklike, elemental Wordsworthian presences, the Old Man Traveling, the Leech-Gatherer, and the Old Cumberland Beggar. Reminiscent of the latter figures, K is, in the mind of the white doctor, "like a stone, a pebble . . . having lain around quietly minding its own business since the dawn of time . . . a hard little stone, barely aware of its surroundings, enveloped in itself and its interior life" (*MK*, 185).

Onto this prototype, however, Coetzee then grafts a more up-to-date myth, one more in line with the ecological orthodoxies of the 1980s. "What grows is for all of us," says K. "We are all the children of the earth" (*MK*, 190). Yet this earth barely keeps him alive and seems rather to adumbrate his grave, for his desire to grow food is inversely proportional to his hunger to consume it, his need to eat growing ever slighter as he tends his seeds and waits for them to bear fruit: "When food comes out of this earth, he told himself, I will recover my appetite, for it will have savour" (*MK*, 139). He plants to keep the earth, not himself, alive—by giving it seed to grow, work to do—and it is done, if for anyone, not for the present but for posterity. His papers give him the designation *opgaarder,* a storage man, and what he stores up on his allotment, it seems, is hope for the earth's future. In his sleep K grows food for this dreamed-of future: "I don't need food in my sleep," he tells his interrogators (*MK,* 180). But this food is then brutally dug up before it can take root by a skeptical, war-ravaged present, represented by the cynical despair of the medical man who mocks K's "fantasy of making the desert bloom with pumpkin flowers" (*MK,* 217). K has "no desire to father" and has "nothing to pass on": He offers to the faithless present not his own surviving seed but the message of survival itself and of the earth's spirit of survival, which is crushed by the camps and jails imposed upon it by human history. His eye trained upon a visionary tomorrow, K denies himself to the point of unimaginable privation today, his every move governed by stern ecological necessity. Wary of prodigality, he frugally adjusts his energy intake to the earth's capacities, thinking "only of growing enough for the seed not to die out" and pumping from the borehole only as much water as his garden needs for "the earth to be restored" (*MK,* 82, 154). Principally for concealment from the view of roaming warplanes but also desiring only what is best for the earth, he builds his lairs and hovels out of biodegradable material blending with and returning to the earth and concludes at the end of the book, "I am more like an earthworm": K passes harmlessly, like a worm "through the bowels of the state undigested" and "like a stone through the intestines of the war" (*MK,* 185, 221, 248). As Nadine Gordimer has suggested, he appears to represent the need "to keep the earth alive, and only one salvation, the survival that comes from her. . . . Hope is a seed. That's all. That's everything. It's better to live on your knees, planting something."[3]

Coetzee seems in this novel to be founding, albeit in a partly ironic way, a new myth of the land: the myth of earth minus man or at least Western Technological Man (i.e., white), as distinct from Vegetarian, Macrobiotic Man (here, black), who eats only what the earth supplies and does not damage her in its cultivation. Living always at extremity, drifting in and out of consciousness, Michael K appears at times to be more wraith than man—more a spirit of ecological endurance, a Gaian ideograph. It is pertinent, therefore, to ask where his relevance lies, whether in the contemporaneous political situation of South Africa of the 1980s or in the ecological one of the African continent at large. The African earth is here opposed not to industrial overdevelopment but to colonialism and war specific to the South African context. It is not poisoned by industrial waste but destroyed by colonial agriculture (the Visagie farm is a wasteful "adventure") and by rival armies (the rebel soldiers allow their donkeys to trample K's crops while the government forces mine his allotment). It is not industrial plants but jails and camps like Jakkalsdrif that cause "earth [to be] stamped so tight" and "baked so hard... that nothing would ever grow there again" (*MK*, 148). Sowing is the earth's alternative to history as war: "The pineapples don't know there is a war on," K tells his mother and he is careful to keep himself, both physically and symbolically, apart from and unknown to the soldiers who plunder and mine his allotment because the business of growing is opposed to war in all its forms. "There must be men to stay behind [from the war] and keep gardening alive, or at least the idea of gardening," he argues, "because once that cord was broken, the earth would grow hard and forget her children" (*MK*, 150).

Nevertheless, there are inevitably planetary reverberations in this constant insistence upon earth's exhaustibility, upon resources that are not infinitely renewable, and upon the human "cord of tenderness" that can be cut "only so many times before it would not grow again." The range of reference and implication is naturally extended beyond African ecosystems to the more troubled ones of the developed world. If the book's mother/Mother Earth association is taken to its logical conclusion, then the recurring image of Anna K's cremation and K's nightmares of a "mother with flaming hair," "the very embodiment of great Mother Death" (*MK*, 194, 205), translate into the consumed, burned-up earth at a general ecological apocalypse that has nothing specifically to do with South Africa.

It is, arguably, possible to "Africanize" the novel's earth myth by discovering in K's withdrawal from society not utopian pastoral longings but a sort of mystical radicalism, whereby he remakes history on his own marginal terms through notions of mutual survival and a strength-giving interdependency with the earth.[4] Alternatively, the earth myth can be given a localized political construction by allegorizing the references to "the bread of freedom" and underground seeds growing in the dark into black land claims and deferred political resurgence.[5] Coetzee, however, fails to locate K's earth consciousness, either at the spiritual or political level, in any indigenous African worldview. The mythological drift of the novel—problematically, for a white writer using a black spokesman—is that the land is to be returned not to the blacks but to itself. These two things could conceivably be the same, although there is no indication in the book that they will be, since earth care and ecological awareness are not made synonymous with or concomitants of Africanity or blackness. In fact, the ahistorical, mystical-ecological dimensions of the myth tend to eclipse the political ones. It is clearly not Coetzee's purpose in the novel to debate how much or how little Africa's human populations are to blame for ecological damage, relative to those of the industrialized world. Rather, what he appears to have constructed, if only half-seriously, in the figure of Michael K is a kind of surrogate hero for the white, ecological decade of the 1980s. In this white-authored text a white liberal spokesman—the camp medical officer—interprets a black character to promulgate what is essentially a "white" myth (insofar as it expresses the anxieties and preoccupations of Western industrialized cultures, whether Euro-American or white South African).

The medical officer's first instinct, in the role of colonial physician and psychologist, is to demythologize and demystify K: He is simply "a person of feeble mind" and a case of "chronic malnutrition," no natural earth spirit but a "city mouse" who "did not know how to live off the land and began to grow very hungry indeed"(*MK,* 179, 187, 200). But it is not long before he supplies the object of his strange fascination with its chthonic mythology ("a genuine little man of earth"). The saving factor in the doctor's narrative is that this mythmaking is but part of his own (and, implicitly, his author's) baffled envy and frustrated attempt at understanding. To this man, who is in fact no more a doctor than "Michaels" is Michael K (he is really a pharmacist), K is a space that he craves to fill with meaning, "a privileged site where meaning erupted into the world" (*MK,* 227), and thus an index to his own inadequacies.

> Michaels means something, and the meaning he has is not private to me. If it were, if the origin of this meaning were no more than a lack in myself, a lack, say, of something to believe in . . . if it were a mere craving for meaning that sent me to Michaels and his story, if Michaels himself were no more than what he seems to be (what you seem to be), a skin-and-bones man with a crumpled lip, . . . then I would have every justification for retiring to the toilets behind the jockeys' changing-rooms and locking myself into the last cubicle and putting a bullet through my head. (*MK,* 226)

It is the white official who, out of his chronic need for meaning, transforms K into a new myth. Subsequently, it is part of the book's self-subverting aesthetic that at its close this white quest for meaning is put by K into its proper political context and is seen, in his scathing last word, to amount to no more than a mixture of philanthropic sentiment and guilt preying upon black suffering, consuming it as entertainment:

> They want me to open my heart and tell them the story of a life lived in cages. . . . And if I had learned story-telling at Huis Norenius instead of potato-peeling and sums . . . I might have known how to please them. I would have told the story of a life passed in prisons. . . . When my story was finished, people would have shaken their heads and been sorry and angry and plied me with food and drink; women would have taken me into their beds and mothered me in the dark. Whereas the truth is that I have been a gardener, first for the Council, later for myself, and gardeners spend their time with their noses to the ground. (*MK*, 247)

The "story of a life lived in cages" is perhaps what Coetzee's novel ostensibly sets out to be. Coetzee and his doctor, however, are not Michael K, and Michael K, by virtue of his deprivation as a South African black of the early 1980s, is no storyteller, so the story cannot be written, only distantly imagined by the white writer in the novel's convoluted and reflexive form. Michael K—the "real" Michael K—simply works in the garden: The rest is the doctor's/novelist's myth. The author gesturally remythologizes his hero in the short last section. Here K recovers some of the precious seeds stolen by Cape down-and-outs, is shamed by a prostitute's wasteful spilling of his own seed onto drifted sand, and finally sets out, albeit with a fantasy companion, for his pumpkin patch with half a packet of seeds in his pocket. But by this stage the epistemologically bleak conclusion has become inescapable. The earth man makes his own kind of history, exclusive of war and colonialism, but the reader is warned that he *is* his own meaning and that this is not ponderable in the philosophical terms of the oppressor. Thus it is not safe (*pace* Gordimer, 6) to discern in K's closing comment, "there is time for everything," a note of irresponsible, fatalistic complacency convenient for the continuing hegemony of the white colonial worldview. Rather, the implication is that those who of necessity live moment by moment transcend the white historical time of waiting, the wasteful, suspended time of war inhabited by the white doctor and commandant, and experience a mode of time unimaginable to them. For the black nurse Felicity, "time is as full as it has ever been"; for K, who seems to experience one moment as intensely as another, there really is time enough for everything insofar as time is ever geared to the fruitful eventfulness of nature in ways inconceivable to the white characters, as to the white author and reader. Coetzee frames the narrative not to distance or dissociate himself from his doctor-pharmacist's interpretation but self-implicatingly to declare all such readings of the racial or colonial Other (including, retroactively, his own narrative presentation of K) as invalid because unavailable to the white interpreter.

A principal source of critical discontent with the novel has been Coetzee's failure to provide his protagonist with a surname that would particularize him as a South African black. (The "Michael Visagie" of the prison report is, of course, a police error, tagging the vagrant with the family name of the homestead where he is picked up. The cryptic encoding "CM"—Colored Male—on the same report would be recognizable only by those familiar with the South African penal system.) Neither the author nor his white representative respond to K in the obvious racial terms but choose instead to surround him with earth myths and with Kafkaesque trappings from the European literary tradition. For example, he is moved restlessly on by authority derived from "the Castle" and made to feel unspecified guilt over an unnamed crime that could be any one of vagrancy, spying, feeding guerrillas, or having no identification papers or residence permit. Of course, K's circumstances and experiences leave the reader in no doubt about his nonwhite racial status. At issue here are the different reasons that the white narrator and his author have, apart from the obvious one of not wanting to repeat the dehumanizing labeling of apartheid, for avoiding classification. On the one hand, Coetzee has allowed his doctor to pursue his earth mythology, whether he himself believes it or not. In this scheme K appears to represent something so elemental and irreducible that it is beyond formulation in any of the existing historical codes: He is "above and beneath classification," outside of language and history, as inarticulate as the seeds and humus of the earth cycle into which he is locked. On the other hand, the author is anxious not to equate or confuse K's historical condition with this attributed mythological status; he is aware of the latter's tendency to obscure K's material position as an African black, locked *out* of history by white colonialism. In both cases K is by definition outside the range of understanding encompassed by the articulate, historically conscious, white interpreter. However, whereas the medical officer has a mystical-philosophical alibi for his nonclassification of K, Coetzee has a more straightforward and obvious one that is more readily understandable in terms of the book's political hermeneutics.

On the first page of the novel the reader's attention is drawn not to K's color but to the harelip that allows him only a minimal articulateness. Coetzee's critics have been quick to point out that his typical, privileged white protagonists are all lucid and intelligent (if mad), whereas his first nonwhite hero is barely articulate (Gordimer, 5–6).[6] In fact, K is made inarticulate precisely because he *is* black; because in the colonial South African context, where speech is politically dangerous for four-fifths of the population, functional inarticulateness is a ready-made mark of racial identification. The racial division in the book is also, crucially, a language division, and language has problematic value in the given aesthetic milieu. The medical officer, for whom life is lived and history made in language, pleads in vain with K to break his silence: "Listen to me, listen how easily I fill this room with words.... Give yourself some substance, man, otherwise you are going to slide through life absolutely unnoticed.... *Talk,* make your voice heard, tell your story!... [N]o one is going to remember you but I, unless you yield and at last open your mouth" (*MK,* 192, 208). But K, he has already admitted, is not "wholly of our world," the world of language. What becomes increasingly transparent in these later passages is the "faking," from the enemy camp, of a nonwhite perspective by a white author who cannot presume to speak for the black but whose self-conscious fictions the black, because he is voiceless in his own country, is deemed to depend upon for his artistic existence.

This was a dilemma that was to become acutely relevant to Coetzee's personal situation during the 1985 state of emergency, when he was increasingly regarded by the international community as a literary spokesman for a land immersed in silence.[7] Thus the reader of *Michael K* is made ever more aware that at one and the same time the landscape's alleged imperviousness to myth is being demonstrated and the black protagonist turned into an alternative earth deity and unlikely ecological savior by an Afrikaner author who is himself steeped in his people's ancestral mythology and traditional religious view of the land. Note, for example, the references to "God's earth" and "miracles" in Michael's narrative and in his wondering "if he were living in what was known as bliss" (*MK,* 93).

Coetzee has said that during the composition of *Michael K* he began to feel dissatisfaction with the limitations of traditional form,[8] and if the novel is, finally, an unsatisfying work, it is perhaps partly because the self-implicating reflexiveness that would enable the author to make clear his degree of commitment to his white liberal's position is not available to conventional realism. In his next novel, where K's place is taken by Friday in a revision of the Robinson Crusoe fable, the dilemma Coetzee found himself in in the second half of *Michael K* is resolved by keeping the black character mute for the whole novel. Only in the surreal last scene of *Foe* (1986) is the black slave's mouth prized open; from it issues "a slow stream, without breath, without interruption.... [I]t runs northward and southward to the ends of the earth."[9] As Michael K's harelip is correctable and articulation restorable, so Friday's dumbness, a culturally enforced rather than a physical condition, is remediable. But we do not hear what Friday says because Coetzee does not and cannot know what he *would* say, and if he were made to speak he would, in any case, speak only in the colonial language of Cruso and of Coetzee himself.[10] Since the author cannot speak for the oppressed without becoming a party to their oppression, he explicitly questions his right to speak through his own characters, and in this way *Foe* aspires to revise the discourses that it is itself written by. In his revisionist version of Defoe's tale, Coetzee dramatizes the oppressive structures that render blacks voiceless and specifically demonstrates the complicity of the colonial settler narrative with exploitative political processes. The "foe" is the imperial fiction employed by the white author to shut the racial and cultural otherness of colonized peoples into closed European myth systems and codes of interpretation.

In *Michael K,* however, the black protagonist's thoughts, in the fashion of realistic fiction, are laid open to us as if of their own accord, although in fact by the white author who then has to resort to internal stratagems within the novel's realistic frame, such as making the white doctor unable to pry open K's mouth and make him say anything that he can understand. The reflexive metafiction of *Foe* is the logical next stage after this impasse, totally abandoning the token psychological realism of *Michael K* and, with it, the attempt to write from a nonwhite perspective. In *Foe* the devices of postmodern fiction render the novel capable of subverting its own ethnocentricity—a freedom that is denied conventional historical realism—and allow the author candidly to abdicate from the fictionalizing process. *Michael K* marks the end of a phase in Coetzee's writing and in South African fiction: Realism has also gone temporarily to ground, the imperial text to earth.

Chapter Six
A Wounded Nation: Shimmer Chinodya's *Harvest of Thorns* and Zimbabwe's Legacies of Liberation

During the war of liberation that in 1980 transformed colonial Rhodesia into independent Zimbabwe, the nation's oral culture provided many songs, slogans, and revolutionary war lyrics that celebrated guerrilla heroism and sanctified armed struggle and by these means helped to mobilize the rural populations.[1] There was, however, no simple and stable relationship between national liberation and written literature, and the war and postwar years produced a very varied crop of fiction.

Much Zimbabwean fiction of the 1970s was apolitical and indifferent to the liberation struggle that, as in Charles Mungoshi's novels, figures as a largely peripheral presence. Meanwhile, although depicting the social deprivation and disempowerment of the 1960s' generation that subsequently fought in the war, exiled writers such as Dambudzo Marechera eschewed both the war and the style of social realism that became the favored mode of war fiction. At the other extreme, there were inevitably, in the wake of postindependence euphoria, a few works of crude patriotic propaganda—such as Edmund Chipamaunga's *Fighter for Freedom* (1983)—featuring flawless idealized partisans and supportive peasants. At a much more sophisticated level, some novels written during the early stages of the war—before the most bitter fighting— present somewhat romantic portraits of nationalist unity and of harmonious affiliations between guerrillas and peasants, together with mystic supernatural connections between the First and Second *Chimurengas* (national uprisings). The most notable of these are Wilson Katiyo's *Son of the Soil* (1976) and Stanlake Samkange's *Year of the Uprising* (1978).

In Samkange's novel, as in Chenjerai Hove's *Bones* (published eight years after the war, in 1988), the ancestral voices of the martyrs of the 1896 rebellion speak oracularly through *svikiros,* or spirit-mediums, to the guerrillas of the 1970s and incite the people to take up arms, thus awakening the nation's conscience and guiding its historical destiny. At the same time, there were more skeptical and realistic contemporary depictions of the war that contested the myths of svikiro and guerrilla infallibility and explored the more complex and sometimes conflicting relations between freedom fighters and rural villagers. In Mungoshi's *Waiting for the Rain* (1975) and Stanley Nyamfukudza's *The Non-Believer's Journey* (1980), popular heroism is the exception rather than the rule, and the war is used to settle private scores and tribal grievances and for purposes of corrupt self-advancement. Mungoshi's Old Man, moreover, concedes only a negative connection between the two Chimurengas, concluding that the new war of liberation is as doomed to defeat as the first one; thus there is no acceptable way out of the political malaise and paralysis of the period following Ian Smith's Unilateral Declaration of Independence (UDI) from Britain in 1965.

The fiction published after the war, colored by postindependence political disillusionment, engaged in a more explicitly demythologizing dialogue with nationalist discourse and expressed an even more critical and cynically disenchanted view of national liberation. In Charles Samupindi's *Pawns* (1992) the freedom fighters are so torn by ideological frictions within the liberation movement that they are unable to maintain a united front. In Alexander Kanengoni's *When the Rainbird Cries* (1987) and Isheunesu Mazorodze's *Silent Journey from the East* (1987), they enlist for purely personal, self-serving, and often criminal, reasons. Kanengoni's guerrilla group comprises fugitive rapists, fraudulent mediums, and sadists who abuse and terrorize the support villages, one of which is wiped out by the colonial army as a result of their cruelties and carelessness. In Hove's later novel *Shadows* (1992), the peasantry are caught defenseless in the crossfire between rival colonial and revolutionary militias, each as bad as the other, and are rendered powerless by a war ostensibly fought to empower them.

Shimmer Chinodya's *Harvest of Thorns* (1989) is a seminal work in this body of fiction, which generally takes after its stark realist mode in preference to Hove's more poetic and mystical vision. Chinodya's guerrillas-on-the-run are solid, hard-edged historical figures, their sensations of fear, hunger, panic, and guilt vividly and viscerally conveyed; they are far removed from Hove's lost soldier-son who in *Bones* makes only a brief appearance at the end and whose pervasive presence in the novel is more mythic than real. At the same time, Chinodya's book is not quite like any of its contemporaries. First, *Harvest of Thorns* does not focus exclusively on the war but deals also with its immediate prehistory and its aftermath. Thus the liberation struggle is not placed against a purely contemporary social canvas, as in most of the aforementioned novels, but neither is it seen in relation to a timeless mythic view of the ancestral Shona consciousness, as in Hove's book; rather, it is incorporated into a collective history of the nation during a particular period of development. Second, Chinodya's guerrillas are not men but immature youths, barely out of boyhood but burdened with experience and wisdom beyond their years. Hence their squabbles and bickerings arise not from ideological conflicts (there is no questioning of the group's indoctrination programs) but from personal rivalries and temperamental differences and from all the usual pressures of adolescence magnified by the crisis situation of the guerrilla. Among these, for example, is the need to find physical and emotional relief while maintaining an impossible code of sexual ethics that outlaws personal relations with civilians and invites rape charges. These boy soldiers are motivated neither by patriotic zeal nor by fugitive criminality; instead they drift passively into the war, ignorant and confused, swayed by pressures and conflicts in their home and school lives that they cannot resolve. Finally, their relationship with the local rural population is not solely one of harmony or of conflict but is a shifting, problematic contact, an erratic makeshift solidarity with a people whose culture and beliefs they share only to a very limited degree.

Chinodya sandwiches the long account of his protagonist's war experiences between two short narratives of his homecoming that effectively serve as prologue and epilogue to the book. The picture of independent, postwar Zimbabwe that emerges in these sections is neither celebratory nor cynical but is a bleakly sober portrait of a period of great bitterness and disenchantment. Benjamin Tichafa, formerly Pasi NemaSellout in his combat identity ("Down with Traitors"), returns from the war, the sole surviving member of his guerrilla group, to discover that "a guerrilla is only a hero while the war is raging."[2] He comes home to unemployment, his education interrupted and set back by his war service, and to estrangement, general incomprehension, and even a degree of stigmatization. Family, neighbors, ex-teachers, and friends are embarrassed by their revolutionary hero, whom they regard as an alien curiosity, "as if he were a creature from another planet" (*HOT,* 12); they show little gratitude toward or understanding of those who won independence for them. Benjamin's conversations with his father consist of unconnected fragments of one-line dialogue, the stichomythic staccato suggesting the impossibility of communication, characteristic of much postwar writing, between those who fought and those who stayed home. When the father asks how Benjamin's in-laws died in the war,

Benjamin responds: "What would it help if you knew? What would it help if you knew anything?" (*HOT*, 235). His mother is unable to understand her son's bitterness, and when she accuses him of having blood on his hands, Benjamin, accustomed to pigeonholing his fellow Zimbabweans as patriots and sellouts, retorts angrily, "We'd have killed traitors like you in the war" (*HOT*, 22). The authorities provide no trauma therapy or counseling to help him and his fellow ex-combatants to cope with their war ordeals and subsequent disorientation.

What rankles Benjamin most, however, is that the war appears to have changed little:

> The worst thing is to come back and find nothing has changed. I look at my father and mother and brother and sister, at the house in which I was born, at the township in which I grew up—people prefer to call it a suburb now—and I see the same old house, the same old street and the same old faces struggling to survive. We won the war, yes, but it's foolish to start talking about victory. All this talk about free schools and free medical treatment and minimum wages is just a start. The real battle will take a long, long time; it may never even begin. (*HOT*, 243)

In the squalid, dilapidated township the bus service still functions erratically, water and food are rationed, and the intermittent television antennas indicate the unevenness of progress. Benjamin's hapless father clings to obsolete and inappropriate patriarchal traditions and double moral standards that take no account of a changing world. He puts on a hypocritical facade of moral indignation with the son who brings a pregnant wife back from the war and a daughter who elopes with her lover while he himself has an illegitimate child by his mistress. The surrounding society, like Benjamin's family, is in a state of disintegration and collapse. Nepotistic influence is used to disadvantage ex-servicemen, and the army is besieged by fraudulent financial claims from civilians posing as ex-combatants. In this state of anomy and confusion, white racism maintains a frustrating, tenacious hold on economic and commercial life. The white foreman at the building site where Benjamin scrounges work sacks him when he hears that Benjamin is a former combatant; a white checkout operator at the supermarket insultingly asks if he has enough money to pay for his purchases. "They didn't learn a thing from the war," asserts his young wife, whose whole family was wiped out by the Rhodesian Selous Scouts (*HOT*, 8). Benjamin is subsequently amazed "that certain areas could completely heal, while some festered on like stubborn wounds and others, like the suburbs on the hill, chose to remain untouched by war" (*HOT*, 7). Worse still, there are those, like the new black mayor in the old colonial hill station, who have actually profited from the war. On his way out of the demobilization building Benjamin symbolically collides with a suited businessman, a member of the new black bourgeoisie that took no part in the war but has ridden to prosperity on the backs of the militants; Benjamin receives a jab from the man's briefcase and a scowl of disapproval.

The titular phrase "harvest of thorns" is used only once in the book, by the guerrilla leader Baas Die at a village indoctrination session, or *pungwe*, where it refers to the meager harvests reaped from their own neglected farms by native laborers tethered to the colonial land system. But in the course of the novel it comes to have a wider application, taking in the "wounded nation" left by the war[3] and the whole confused, bitter legacy of the liberation struggle that was fought to end the colonial order. This legacy is summed up in the plight of Benjamin's lost generation: "I never had the chance to experience what other young men experienced. The church robbed me of my childhood and the war took away proper school, friends, holidays and all that" (*HOT*, 244). Deprived of his adolescence and of every one of his human supports—family, war comrades, a girlfriend killed in an air raid—Benjamin finally accepts that the work of sowing has to be done all over again. The novel ends with the planting of a new seed, symbolized by his newborn son, and with a desperate, defiant gesture of hope for the future, albeit one that expresses no faith in the new social order: "He's only twenty and he has no job or house of his own yet but he tells himself he'll do all he can to raise the little bundle of humanity in the cot. He'll do all he can, even though all he has is a pair of chapped hands. He tells himself he'll do it" (*HOT*, 248).

If the contextual narratives to the war look forward to its consequences, however, they also look backward to its prehistory, for the prolegomenary chapter of Benjamin's homecoming is followed by a long sweeping flashback to the 1950s and 1960s, to the courtship of his parents and his own formative childhood years. Clopas and Shamiso Tichafa, a semiliterate, white-aspiring government menial and a humble country girl, suffer all the hardships and indignities of 1950s' township life. These include curfews and permits; supervised relationships in regimented, segregated accommodation; overcrowded, unsanitary living conditions; rigid census control and predawn police raids carrying out spot checks on population movement. Added to these are the humiliations inflicted by white racist officials who, when applied to for marriage certificates, crassly vulgarize the African marriage's complex rituals of deference and esteem to the level of a crude commercial exchange. As the 1950s become the 1960s, the Tichafas find themselves living through a period of cultural confusion, mounting political repression, and, increasingly, crisis and emergency. The denial of black political rights is exacerbated by the arrival of Westernized tastes in fashion and music that erode the authority of the indigenous culture and that, by purveying a new ethos of freedom and opportunity, awaken expectations that cannot be satisfied at the local level. In the post-UDI wilderness years, feelings of political helplessness and frustration gather intensity. The hordes of youths drifting to the towns grow listless, disillusioned, and finally militant; houses are stoned and burned, men sleep with wooden clubs under their beds; and families furtively tune in to guerrilla broadcasts on muted shortwave radio stations.

None of this, however, has much effect on the lives of the Tichafa family: "Clopas was promoted from tea-boy to the chief messenger and allocated a bicycle with a silver 'On Her Majesty's Service' badge on the carrier for use on government business. . . . The Federation of Rhodesia and Nyasaland broke up; Ian Smith signed the Unilateral Declaration of Independence and Mr. Clopas Wandai J. Tichafa was appointed the new deacon at The Church of the Holy Spirit" (*HOT,* 69). Chinodya registers Rhodesia's seething political upheaval in this oblique, offhand way partly because it is fleetingly glimpsed through the eyes of the child Benjamin, "who saw the traumas of our country from the doors of township houses, peeking through the restraining skirts of our mothers" (*HOT,* 69). His main purpose, however, is to show how marginal the nation's turmoil is to the life of a family preoccupied with petty careerism and evangelical Christianity. When political groups come to their door, recruiting for popular movements based on land claims, the Tichafas take refuge in religious fatalism—"If it is God's will to change a government, then He will change it Himself, in His own time" (*HOT,* 75)—and reply that they are children of God, not of the soil.

Significantly, when violence erupts in the townships, the noises of police sirens, exploding tear gas canisters, and beaten rioters are almost drowned out by the fanatical amens and alleluias of the revivalist congregation. The sounds of battle, however, grow progressively louder in the ears of the child Benjamin, who is subsequently dubbed a "sellout" and persecuted by his schoolmates—not inappropriately, since the children of the Church of the Holy Spirit are trained in an ethos of informing and betrayal. In the ensuing psychological crisis of Benjamin's teenage years, the rival promptings of social guilt and religious hysteria, familial embarrassment, and a killjoy, sin-ridden Christianity become dangerously confused. Persuading himself that the rebels' slogan "child of the soil" has a Biblical ring, he tries at once to do the bidding of both his political and his biological parents and, in this confused mental state, participates in the arson of a government beer hall. Eventually his political guilt gets the better of his religious feelings, and he is arrested for carrying a banner proclaiming "The Boys in the Bush are Our Brothers" in a demonstration against black conscription. Released on bail, he slips quietly away from school, takes a train to a village at the country's northern extremity, and, after a terrifying encounter with the colonial army at a mountain border post, strays across the frontier into a revolutionary guerrilla cell.

Benjamin, Chinodya has explained, is "trying to grow up and then he suddenly finds himself a fighter."[4] The use of the passive voice here is revealing, for it implies that the life of the freedom-fighter is something that happens to him, not the outcome of his own volition. As Flora Veit-Wild has cogently argued, Benjamin "appears as a passive victim moved by forces outside himself," and his decision to become a guerrilla "results more from a series of outer circumstances than from deep-rooted inner conviction" (Veit-Wild, 325). The victim, as he later describes himself, of "an exaggerated Christianity," he is moved by forces he does not fully understand and that at the time he can apprehend only dimly, through the immature vision of someone still "trying to grow up." Benjamin, unlike the guerrillas of other Zimbabwean war fiction, runs neither toward nor away from something. Not knowing where he is going, he simply runs in a state of aimless confusion and joins the partisans without really knowing why. Chinodya has painted a portrait of the combatant not as patriotic hero or as cynical antihero but as innocent.

To convey Benjamin's psychological confusion and insecure identity and to create the impression of an unformed, still developing consciousness impinged upon by conflicting forces, Chinodya devises a fractured, shifting narrative mode that moves between rival appellations for its hero ("Benjamin," "Pasi"), first- and third-person forms, interior monologue, and external impressionism. The result is a vivid evocation of the dislocating, disparate nature of Benjamin's and his generation's experience and of the pain (as he tells his brother-in-law) of "trying to piece together the broken fragments" of a life (*HOT,* 243). Thus the narrative of *Harvest of Thorns* is really many modes in one, a kaleidoscope of shifting styles and forms. The intensely personalized account of Benjamin's anguished homecoming in the opening section gives way, in part 2, to a panoramic, omniscient narrative of the 1950s of his childhood, which is really a collective history of the nation. Then, as the novel moves on to the 1960s, this epic historical style is in turn replaced by a more individualistic first-person-plural narration that identifies Benjamin with and makes him representative of his generation and formative decade. In the long, third part of the book, which deals with his hero's war experiences, Chinodya returns briefly to the panoramic style for a survey of the civilian population enmeshed in the liberation struggle; he also draws upon the vagaries of orature to present conflicting versions of a legendary battle and the killing of a traitor.

For the greater part of this pivotal section, however, the author abandons the comprehensive, explanatory mode and, after the fashion of most authentic war fiction, opts to render war in perhaps the only way that it can be rendered: as fragmented, highly subjective experience and through the closely mirrored notation of the individual consciousness in states of extremity. Thus Benjamin's panic, horror, and chaotic guilt traumas are registered through a series of frantic interior, italicized monologues—really improvised mental letters to his mother—that capture the very quick of feeling and sensation at the moment of crisis. The horrific climax of Benjamin's war experiences is the brutal murder of a village "sellout," the woman Mai Tawanda, at which point Chinodya switches to an impersonal, anonymous, second-person narration. This mode has been used earlier in the narrative of the campaign to evoke the unheroic monotony of war and the tedium of doctrinal propaganda—"You sat there and listened, your fist raised over your head, stabbing the air, chanting slogans" (*HOT,* 115). Now, however, it is used to mark the sacrifice of individual integrity to group identity and to the inhuman demands of a programmed killing machine. Significantly, the other members of Benjamin's guerrilla cell, although they are named, are essentially little more than their names: They are not closely characterized as individuals and so remain basically indistinguishable and anonymous, being merely the separate functions of a group self. In the identity of Pasi NemaSellout, Benjamin—as part of this collective "you"—is able to kill another human being. He beats to death a defenseless woman while his individual self, in a state of hypnotized, zombified horror, looks on helplessly, as if the deed were being done by another person. Although its traumatic effect on the perpetrators subsequently divides the group, the murder is the culminating expression of the group's collective identity. After this deed Chinodya returns to the objective third person to register, as if describing another character, Benjamin's newly initiated identity and concomitant loss of self: "Pasi NemaSellout marched in a daze. His body pitched itself forward with a force and will of its own" (*HOT,* 217).

The novel's shifting, broken narrative structure purposes more, however, than its hero's changes and crises of identity and the disparateness of his generation's experience. At a broader level, the multitude of fragmented voices also creates a sense of the thoroughly hybridized, multifaceted, and pluralist nature of life in modern Zimbabwe and resists any single authoritative, monolithic view of postcolonial society. Furthermore, Chinodya's densely variegated portrait makes impossible any unified, definitive statement about the place of the war in the nation's history and rules out any simple relationship between the present liberation struggle and the ancestral past. In these respects his atomized historical vision is at an immense remove from the all-encompassing mythic unity of a novelist like Hove. In Hove's *Bones* an almost pristine peasant consciousness is still able, with the aid of spirit mediums and the intercession of a guerrilla's mother recently killed by the colonial police, to establish solidarity with the contemporary freedom fighters; hence it achieves a direct bonding with the martyred spirits of the 1896 uprising that takes no account of the complex historical changes that have occurred in the 80 years between the two Chimurengas. "Arise all the bones of the land," exhort Hove's ancestral spirit voices. "Arise all the bones of the dying cattle. Arise all the bones of the locusts. Wield the power of the many bones scattered across the land and fight so that the land of the ancestors is not defiled by strange feet and strange hands."[5] No ancestral bones speak in Chinodya's book, where the past exists not in the race memory but principally in living remembrance. In one of the bush villages Benjamin's comrades present themselves to an octogenarian grandmother in semimythical fashion, as "the children of Chaminuka and Nehanda," the legendary leaders of the First Chimurenga. The only link with this last-century event, however, turns out to be a solidly historical, not a mystic telepathic, one: It exists in the old woman's infant memories of being hidden by her mother in a cave when the fathers had gone off to fight a war with the white man (*HOT,* 133–35).

Chinodya's handling of the myths of national liberation differs from Hove's in three important respects. First, in Hove's mythic, ahistorical vision, the Chimurenga mythology appears as an immaculate, petrified body of wisdom retrieved intact and the maternal ancestor and martyr Mbuyo Nehanda as an absolute symbol of resistance presiding over the destiny of the nation. In Chinodya's demythologizing perspective, however, this legendary heritage is not a timeless absolute and forms no stable, seamless continuum with the present. On the contrary, it is an evolving body of knowledge that is constantly being added to, modified, and adapted to meet changing needs; it is itself a stage in the process of historical change, a function of what is being changed and made part of the present. For example, at the village pungwe, the "little story" of the nation's history of dispossession and disinheritance narrated by the guerrilla leader Baas Die is basically a reworking of the Chimurenga myth in the oral mode, updated with additions from distant and recent history to serve pragmatic present purposes.

A second important difference is that, in the case of Die's fable, it is the guerrilla leader himself who takes over the role of the spirit medium, the svikiro, to interpret the national folk memory to the people, while the svikiro herself, in both Die's story and the surrounding society, no longer has absolute authority. In the pungwe parable the fictional svikiro constantly revises the advice she dispenses to the indigenous population to deal with the mounting colonial threat; unfortunately, this advice—wary conciliation, sabotage, open revolt—always lags behind the action, coming too late to be of any practical use. Hence her wisdom tends to be of the hindsight kind, more cure than prevention, explanatory rationale rather than foresight. Thus, in the very process of adapting ancestral myths for contemporary use, the traditional transmitters of those myths are diminished in importance. During their campaign Die's guerrillas do in fact seek out the village svikiro for guidance, in the tradition of the rebels of the First Chimurenga, and Chinodya allows this figure her usual numinous trappings, notably the gruff male speaking voice, but he is quick to demystify his medium as she emerges from her trance of possession: "[S]he was a woman again, a quiet old woman waking slowly from sleep" (*HOT,* 223). Moreover, the prophetic warning she gives Benjamin to beware the camouflaged, soot-faced soldier who, a few pages later, will wipe out his fiancée's entire family, is actually nothing remarkable since her description refers to the entire Selous Scouts: He needed no soothsayer to tell him this. It is also true that Benjamin allows the svikiro to give him *nyora,* the traditional incisional rite of protection, thus restoring contact with indigenous practices reviled by his evangelical mother. Yet he appears to do this not out of any profound personal belief but rather as a gesture of solidarity with the people he comes to deliver, and as a way of dissociating himself, as a deacon's son, from his parents' Christianity.

The worldview of Chinodya's novel is in fact a thoroughly skeptical and secular one. Benjamin reassures both his mother and his comrades that he will not be pursued by *ngozis,* the vengeful spirits of the people he has killed in the war, and the author leaves it deliberately unclear whether the dysentery epidemic in the training camp subsides of its own accord or in response to the rural culture's traditional herbal medicines. Chinodya is also vague about whether Benjamin's mother's long-awaited pregnancy is the work of the local healer (the *n'anga*), the Church of the Holy Spirit, or ordinary sexual persistence. This modern secular viewpoint and its effect on guerrilla-peasant relations is the third important point of difference between Chinodya's and Hove's writing.

The Zimbabwean War of Independence was in many important respects a people's war, a popular struggle centered on the reclamation and repossession of lost land, in which all the necessary conditions for the fostering of a popular revolutionary consciousness and the development of a rural cultural nationalism appeared to be present.[6] It was also, however, a guerrilla war, and Chinodya's guerrillas, unlike Hove's, are not based in the peasant culture, which means that their relations and dealings with the rural population are at best problematic. On the one side, the farm foremen, traders, and elders targeted by the guerrillas—many of whom have sons in Ian Smith's army—are still trapped in a colonial consciousness that permits little political awareness. The foreman, trained in habits of self-effacement by his white "Baas," identifies totally with the farm that he is enslaved to; the storekeeper views white people chiefly as the valued providers of black domestic labor; and the old bush woman has never heard of the Chimurenga she lived through as an infant or of its legendary martyrs. On the other side, the guerrillas, though they style themselves "sons of the soil," have no deep-rooted connection with the land, its occupants, or its ancestral traditions, and few of them share the beliefs of the people they come to save. Only one member of the cell believes in the vengeful ngozis of executed sellouts, while two of them reluctantly permit the svikiro to perform nyora on them, and a third insists that "the soil will protect me," giving political mythology priority over religious matters to a degree that is abhorrent to the soil's traditional tillers. The secular pragmatic code of the army of liberation takes no cognizance of ancestral religious customs such as individual funeral rites, the significance of which is effaced by the mass death of war. Military exigencies leave no time for the burial of the dead. The village headman, whose own life is threatened when he pleads for the life of the traitor Mai Tawanda, returns to his village weeping over unburied comrades, "saying what young men they were ... not to cry or flinch or show signs of pain, what young men to bear the weight of death on their own, how sad it was that the dead were just lying there, with nothing said to ease their passage to the other world, how it had never been done, how in the seventy years of his life he had never heard of such a thing" (*HOT,* 194).

Given the sociology of Chinodya's guerrillas, however, this lack of concern for traditional beliefs and sentiments is hardly surprising. Benjamin and his comrades are not in any sense sons of the soil. They are each the politicized products of the sprawling, amorphous townships that lie on the border of the urban and rural worlds and belong properly to neither. This marginal territory is a complex and confused half-and-half world in which goats and donkeys jostle cars and bicycles in the streets, evangelical church groups compete with the *ju-ju* (native medicine) of the local n'anga, and traditional marriage rites require certification from colonial Christianity. It is also a world whose inhabitants, in the post-UDI sixties, are ideologically Westernized and culturally "whitened" (evidenced by the Beatles, miniskirts, and hot pants, wigs, and skin-lightening creams), even as they are politically disinherited and isolated by white power. To the boys from the townships, the bush in which they fight "the people's war" is a world and a cultural time warp away, and Chinodya's gritty, close-grained social realism—which is about the same distance from Hove's more mystical poetic vision—does full justice to their feelings of estrangement and disorientation. These mental gulfs between different parts of the same country have also to be counted among the many fissures opened up by liberation; they are the wounds of a much older, long-standing conflict and will take longer to heal.

Although a wholly imagined work by a noncombatant, *Harvest of Thorns* is one of the most sober and balanced novels to come out of Zimbabwe's War of Independence. There are no patriotic heroes or cynical antiheroes here, no simplistic glorification or disillusionment, and the methods and strategies of both sides in the conflict are held up for dispassionate comparison. The white Rhodesian army terrorizes the rural population with physical brutality, ultimatums (they threaten to shoot Mai Tawanda's policeman son if she does not inform), and with draconian prison sentences for assisting the guerrillas or even failing to report their presence. The guerrillas themselves, meanwhile, resort to terror tactics once cajolement has failed, pressing terrified farm workers into complicity with the murder of their white bosses. The colonial army

A Wounded Nation

wears down peasant resistance with threats and blackmail, the guerrillas with exhausting indoctrination sessions late into the night, capitalizing on the villagers' mental stupor after a hard day's labor, catching them when their defenses are down: "The responsive chants of the villagers will be slurred. Fisted arms will not snap into the sky but will rise feebly over drooping heads; the audience will have to be prodded with song. There'll be a hundred battles with sleep out there" (*HOT,* 163).

The liberation army's midnight raids on rural homesteads, dragging couples from beds to provide food, their "nestling bodies stirred from sleep," recall in their precise details the earlier outrages of predawn police raids on the townships and "the humiliation of being invaded in that naked, marital hour" (*HOT,* 55, 205). In their choice of methods, the nation's liberators appear to have failed to free themselves from its colonial legacy. Moreover, the barbaric excesses and inhumanities of both the colonial and revolutionary armies are portrayed with unflinching accuracy. A white Selous Scout massacres a family of civilians without remorse, and, in the book's most shockingly brutal episode, Benjamin and his comrade Muchapera beat to death the woman Mai Tawanda, accused of collaborating with the colonial forces, while Baas Die coaxes unenthusiastic ululations from the villagers who are forced to watch. It is this single act, among all those in the war, that most haunts Benjamin and takes the heaviest psychological toll upon him. He later reflects that the helpless woman looked like his mother and that, with a son in the colonial police force who could have easily been himself, she could have been anyone's mother. Finally, it is perhaps here, in the traumatized consciousness, the bitter mental harvest of the ex-combatant rather than in the failure of the postindependence society that the nation's unhealed wounds and the thorny legacies of its liberation are most vividly and intensely realized.

Chapter Seven
Regurgitating Colonialism: The Feminist Voice in Tsitsi Dangarembga's *Nervous Conditions*

Discontent with the doubtful legacies of liberation also found expression, albeit more gradually, in Zimbabwean women's writing. The War of Independence saw significant changes in gender roles and relations, but the struggle for national liberation was not matched by any lasting parallel progress in the position of the nation's women. In this entrenchedly patriarchal society, women traditionally had no rights of property ownership or custody over children and were subject to the lifelong guardianship of fathers, brothers, and husbands. During the war they participated equally alongside men, but this was a temporary upheaval that affected only a small part of the population. In the postindependence era inveterate patriarchal attitudes flourished again, female ex-combatants were advised by government media campaigns to return to traditional family roles, and the uncompliant were subjected to blatant intimidation such as the notorious "Operation Clean-Up" of December 1983, in which unattended women were randomly rounded up from the public streets and automatically detained on charges of prostitution.[1]

The dominant patriarchal values behind such actions continued to be reflected in male fiction that emphasized conventional images of the African woman as all-enduring wife, mother, and domestic provider whose self-sacrificing labor in both field and home was taken mostly for granted and so went unvalued and largely unacknowledged. There was little attempt in this fiction to realistically depict the lives of women, little awareness of or interest in their predicament in the new society, and a prevailing tendency to mete out punitive fates to those women who did not conform with received orthodoxies.[2]

Specifically, the Zimbabwean woman writer was hampered not only by lack of information about publishing opportunities and by her meager education (in a 1982 survey 65 percent of the country's unschooled population were women), but, more formidably, by the disapproval or open hostility of husbands who held women's ideas in contempt and by the arrogant sexism of indigenous publishers. The latter adopted standardized, clichéd notions of women as submissive, obedient wives and dutiful mothers and expected women writers to uphold the established male values expressed in these views.[3] Thus it was that the first women authors writing in the indigenous Shona and Ndebele languages in the 1970s tended to take high-mindedly Christian, moralistic stands against "sinful" behavior and metropolitan "loose living" that were still essentially patriarchal in spirit; thus it was, also, that women enrolling in the postindependence literacy campaigns of the early 1980s were trained on texts that still habitually undervalued women, pilloried them for childlessness, and pressed upon them a sense of their general insignificance.[4] In 1987, when 28-year-old Tsitsi Dangarembga submitted her first novel, *Nervous Conditions,* to a Zimbabwean publishing house, only 30 out of a total of 212 published Zimbabwean writers were women, and few of these had shown any signs of incipient radical tendencies.[5] *Nervous Conditions* was, predictably, rejected because of its strong feminist perspective and, upon its international publication in the following year, went on to win the Africa section of the Commonwealth Writers Prize (a Zimbabwean edition finally appeared in 1989).

Set in the colonial Rhodesia of the 1960s, Dangarembga's novel charts the educational odyssey of Tambudzai, or Tambu, out of provincial poverty into the more affluent world of the anglophile professional elite, the coopted middle class of schoolteachers and headmasters who occupy a fragile "honorary space" between the white colonial authorities and their own powerless poor relations. After her elder brother's sudden death, Tambu unapologetically seizes the educational opportunity that was his by right of gender in order that she may do some good "for the family before she goes into her husband's home."[6] She is subsequently transfigured from a lowly peasant girl into a student at her wealthy uncle's mission school and later at a prestigious multiracial convent. Her path to emancipated self-discovery, however, is paved with contradictions, crises, and tribulations, not least of which is her realization and personal experience of the injustices done to women. In her escape from the farm, Tambu exchanges subordination to the will of her shiftless, sycophantic peasant father for domination by her tyrannical headmaster uncle; she learns, as an African woman, to suffer a double "colonization," in which she is a victim to both colonial and indigenous patriarchy. "The message was clear: endure and obey, for there is no other way" (*NC,* 19).

Under the prudish eye of her repressed and repressive Victorian-style uncle and sponsor, she discovers that each new freedom is really a form of alienation that removes her ever further from her indigenous African roots. While she arrives at his mission school expecting to find, under his guidance, "another self, a clean, well-groomed, genteel self who could not have been bred, could not have survived on the homestead" (*NC*, 58–59), she realizes that her earlier life and its traditional values cannot so easily be shed. Tambu's struggle toward selfhood evolves, in fact, into a complexly hybridized and layered identity, a composite personality that is submissive and self-abnegating but also adventurous, rebellious, and reluctant to passively accept the African woman's customary burdens.

Tambu concludes her first-person retrospective narrative thus: "The story I have told here is my own story, the story of four women whom I loved, and our men, this story is how it all began" (*NC*, 204). Two of these women are Tambu's mother, Mainini, who has resigned herself fatalistically to both her poverty and the double burden of black womanhood, and her paternal aunt, Maiguru, a highly educated and prosperous woman who has nevertheless put security before self-fulfillment and accepted domestic subservience to her headmaster husband, Babamukuru (after a short-lived escape from the patriarchal home, she allows him to bring her back and reinstate her in her former role).[7] A third is Tambu's maternal aunt, Lucia, an uneducated but strong and freethinking woman who defies social prejudices to fulfill her own desires and protests against injustice wherever she encounters it. Fourth, and most important for Tambu's growing self-awareness, is her English-educated cousin Nyasha, with whom she develops a close friendship at the mission and who serves in the novel as her rebellious alter ego. Mindful of her need for stable limits and lacking the courage of her convictions, Tambu suppresses her own mutinous instincts, which are acted out in her stead by her defiant cousin. Nyasha rejects her father's conformity to the type of "the good African," the first generation of Christian African elite whom she dismisses as colonial puppets, and rebels against his authority. Under the pressure of Babamukuru's tyranny she suffers a total nervous breakdown, develops anorexia, and is taken into psychiatric care. Tambu survives these trials and traumas, but the conclusion to Dangarembga's female bildungsroman leaves her questioning the true nature of emancipation and the value of the "Englishness" that has come to permeate her own and her country's existence.

Nervous Conditions is a work in the naturalist tradition, but it is remarkable for its high level of imaginative organization and contains some finely judged poetic symbolism. Specifically, there is an unusual and complex treatment of the bodily functions that have to do with the eating and processing of food—of consumption, digestion, and regurgitation—that are made symptomatic of the mental and spiritual health of the larger society and body politic, most especially when they begin to go wrong and break down. Dangarembga devises an intricate network of connections between education and consumption, skillfully using eating as the governing metaphor for Africa's consumption—nutritional, cultural, educational—of secondhand, imitative Western values that destroy its people, a process that removes the book's heroine ever further from her African family, language, and self. On the first page of the novel, Tambu's brother Nhamo, selected by his uncle Babamukuru for education at the colonial mission school, expresses his disgust with the bodily grossness and dirt that he identifies with the African reality: "Moreover, the women smelt of unhealthy reproductive odours, the children were inclined to relieve their upset bowels on the floor, and the men gave off strong aromas of productive labour" (*NC*, 1).

The education with which Nhamo seeks to buy his way out of this physical squalor is envisaged by his family as superior nourishment for a subsequently better fed, healthier body. Nhamo, like his uncle before him, is "a good boy, cultivable, in the way that land is, to yield harvests that sustain the cultivator" (*NC*, 19). His education, paid for by his mother's cultivation of extra crops, is an investment that will return handsome dividends to the family in the form of the foreign food and drinks that it will buy. Appropriately, Nhamo's father, in his homecoming ceremony for Babamukuru, applauds his "benefactor" and "provider" for "having devoured English letters" and "indigestible degrees" with "a ferocious appetite" (*NC*, 36), and Mainini, resentful of the educated sister-in-law who serves meat that she herself cannot provide, accuses her daughter of wanting "to eat the words that come out of her mouth" (*NC*, 140). Thus, although food cultivation translates into education, the latter has a habit of translating back into food: either metaphorically, in the form of a pervasive rhetoric of consumption and digestion, or literally, into luxury foodstuffs that are not locally cultivable (the refrigerated meat brought to the family feast by Babamukuru, and the English breakfasts and tea with biscuits served by his wife).

Nhamo dies, however, and his place at the school is taken by his sister Tambu, for whom food comes to mean a great many things in her educational career. It is a means of survival and an economic mainstay, "the chore of keeping breath in the body" (*NC,* 64). It is also, in its endless cultivation and preparation, a mark of women's servitude and oppression (which even the anglicized Maiguru does not escape), and of male authority. At the meal table Babamukuru manifests his patriarchal power, directing "the ritual dishing out of food" (*NC,* 81), flying into hysterical tantrums when his miniskirted daughter Nyasha stays out late talking to white boys, and, as proof of his absolute authority and her submission to it, forcing her to eat the food that he provides (in Babamukuru's neurotic psychology, "playing with boys" is linked with turning up her nose at his food, identifying puritanism as the principal ingredient of the colonial educational diet that he forces upon his children). As Nyasha comments, "it's more than just . . . a plateful of food"; indeed, it has to do with the prim puritanical code that he has "digested" with his colonial missionary education and made his own— "really it's all the things about boys and men and being decent and indecent and good and bad" (*NC,* 190). At the meal table her copy of *Lady Chatterley's Lover* is confiscated: Lawrence is not yet part of the anglophile cultural diet.

First and foremost, however, food is itself the means by which Tambu breaks free from a life devoted to its cultivation. Long before her brother's death presents her with unexpected educational opportunities, Tambu cultivates her own sale crops to raise money for school fees, growing food in excess of subsistence needs in order to escape from subsistence farming and become one of the (significantly worded) "new crop of educated Africans" (*NC,* 63). This initiates a network of metaphoric connections between education and food that presents neither in a very positive light. The colonial education at issue turns out to be constricting and repressive, with each new freedom a form of alienation. As "food," it proves to be ill nourishing and spiritually deadening rather than healthful and life giving; it is a diet that leaves its devotees stunted and haggard. Significantly, it is tainted at its source, Tambu's school fees being provided by a desiccated, "papery-skinned" old white woman who—because of her fixed colonial view of "the native"—is tricked into compassion for the young vendor of corn.

The motif of misguided nutrition concealing undernourishment is sustained throughout the novel, in which the educated elite's deracinatory Englishness is repeatedly expressed through culinary details and matters of cuisine. Tambu observes of Nahmo, when he returns from his first year at Babamukuru's school, that vitamins have "nourished" his skin and whitened his complexion but have simultaneously induced a language deficiency, causing him to forget his Shona. When he dies, Mainini thinks her husband must have eaten some poisonous shrub to want to send their next child to the same school, "a place of death." Later in the novel, when Babamukuru proposes to send Tambu on from there to the Sacred Heart Convent School, she accuses him of killing her children with "Englishness," taking their tongues (an organ of both taste and speech) and "fattening" them "like cattle are fattened for slaughter," feeding them with English learning that spells the death of their African identity and turns them into white ghosts: "You couldn't expect the ancestors to stomach so much Englishness" (*NC,* 184, 203). Maiguru's spacious table, Tambu muses, speaks volumes about "the amount, the calorie content, the complement of vitamins and minerals, the relative proportions of fat, carbohydrate and protein of the food that would be consumed at it" (*NC,* 69). But she notes also that it exists in an enormous empty room—like its elite owners, in a vacuum. The professional elite's foreign, fragile isolation, sealed off from their indigenous context, is similarly reflected in Maiguru's unused English tea set, in the strainer that filters out Africa to produce a more authentic English flavor, and in her uneaten, indigestible English breakfasts and suppers, in which the white gravy and potatoes obliterate the taste of the African vegetables. Having been flown in from outside, the elite's cultural sustenance draws hardly at all upon indigenous resources. Hence Maiguru's kitchen is symbolically in a state of dilapidation and disrepair; the meat from a traditional local celebration sticks between Babamukuru's teeth, reminding him of traditions that no longer nourish him; and his attempt to refrigerate half an ox, in the domestic English fashion, at the annual extended-family feast is ludicrously inadequate, causing the meat to rot.

If the intake of neocolonial cultural and educational values in *Nervous Conditions* is expressed through the consumption of food, then the rejection of this supply is, conversely, expressed through the inability or refusal to eat. Thus when Tambu is taken off to the mission school in Nhamo's place, Mainini has difficulty swallowing and eats hardly anything. And when, toward the end of the novel, she is informed that Tambu is to go to the College of the Sacred Heart, run by white nuns, she effectively goes on hunger strike, eating less and less and then nothing, withdrawing from her family role into an apathetic stupor (Tambu's own appetite also departs with the news). When Nyasha's prudish parents banish D. H. Lawrence from both dinner-table and educational diet, she declares herself "full" in protest and disobeys her father's command to eat her evening meal; in the same scene Tambu finds that the food "refused to go down my throat in large quantities" (NC, 82).

For Tambu the turning point and culmination of her protest occurs when Babamukuru forces upon her own parents a belated Christian wedding, an action that questions her own legitimacy as well as denying that of traditional African customs. "As if children were meant to be at their parents' wedding!" Nyasha aptly comments (NC, 170). At this point Tambu's body voices its own visceral protest: "I suffered a horrible crawling over my skin, my chest contracted to a breathless tension and even my bowels threatened to let me know their opinion" (NC, 149). On the day of the wedding, Tambu is, preposterously, commanded to attend as a bridesmaid. Her body, deserted by an unwilling spirit, falls into a cataleptic trance, refusing to move, and her subsequent failure to participate in the event incurs severe punishment—15 lashes of Babamukuru's cane and two weeks of menial domestic chores. Similarly, when Maiguru laments her wasted educational opportunities, her body acts of its own accord, her face involuntarily expressing her unhappiness: "The lower half of her face, and only the lower half, because it did not quite reach the eyes, set itself into sullen lines of discontent" (NC, 101). Finally, in the novel's extreme climax, Nyasha revolts against the petty rules and regulations of her father's regime by taking refuge in anorexia and bulimia, either not eating or immediately vomiting what she eats.

Nyasha crams for her exams, with obvious consumer innuendoes, but her overconsumption of Western education does not make her fat because her furious studies are combined with disturbed eating. The longer she stays at school and sits up at night studying, the more suppers and breakfasts she misses: At the literal level, the more she reads, the less she eats. Meanwhile, at the metaphoric level, not only does her neocolonial educational intake leave her culturally and spiritually undernourished but it also makes her critical of the diet of colonial history and literature that she is being fed, so that she digests less and less of what she ostensibly consumes. By an inverse proportion, the more Nyasha chews questioningly over, the less dogma she gratefully ingests. This is expressed at the physical level by her loss of appetite, which is restored for a brief period when exams are over. Her nervous disorder and skeletal appearance return, however, at Babamukuru's next round of petty restrictions. Unable to conceive his daughter's rejection of the value system that he has force-fed her, the father cannot even see her anorexic condition—"Did he not know? Did he not see?" (*NC*, 199). Tambu asks herself. "She does eat her supper when I have time to supervise her properly," he reassures his wife, blinding himself to the fact that as soon as he is gone Nyasha vomits up his food and, with it, his tyrannical supervision and control of her life. It is only when she shreds her colonial history books with her teeth and jabs shards of glass and pottery into her flesh that he calls for the psychiatrist.

Discussing anorexia nervosa, Dangarembga speculates that perhaps "one of the reasons why the girls are so prone to this disease is that if you live a very intellectual life you do become more divorced from the physical aspects of yourself, and it may not be easy to determine what is affecting what."[8] This chimes fairly closely with Tambu's preoccupations in the novel with "questions that had to do with survival of the spirit, the creation of consciousness, rather than mere sustenance of the body" (*NC*, 59). The interview statement, however, is heavily qualified, especially with regard to what causes what, and the narrative perspective on her younger self supplied by Tambu (who is not the anorexic) is largely ironic. Tambu's dissociative opposition of mind and body, spirit and flesh, in which the one develops at the expense of and to the neglect of the other, is in fact against the run of textual evidence. The reading of Nyasha's condition that such a view licenses is perhaps insufficiently psychosomatic to take account of all of the book's symbolic threads. In *Nervous Conditions* the woman's mind and body are not mutually exclusive or inversely proportional but are directly related and act in close concert. What appears to happen is that the body steps in and acts on the mind's behalf, voicing its protest in physical terms, when the mind is unable to speak for itself for the reason that the only language available to it, the language in which its educational diet is encoded, is the patriarchal discourse of the colonial oppressor and his indigenous puppets—a language in which she cannot express what has to be expressed. As Toril Moi puts it, "There simply is no way in which femininity can speak itself within the dominant philosophical discourses: at best it can be traced in the gaps, blanks and silences of the text."[9] In *Nervous Conditions* the women's protests either remain unexpressed or voice themselves nonverbally, outside of language, in "body-talk," the most extreme examples of which are the primal grunts, heaves, and screams of Nyasha's bulimic retchings.

What is being protested, moreover, has essentially to do with mind and spirit rather than with the body and is often of a highly intellectual nature. Heidi Creamer has demonstrated that narrow neurological readings of cases of anorexia and bulimia in Zimbabwean women, published by psychiatrists shortly after the end of the War of Independence, tended to erase the political context and colonial situation in which the patients had been living, thus reducing their disorders to the "nervous conditions" of hysteria-prone personalities.[10] This was but a marginal improvement upon the verdict of the colonial psychiatrists who, unable to believe in the native's cultural rejection of colonial authority, declared the ailment purely imaginary: The fatuous white psychiatrist in Dangarembga's novel pronounces that "Africans did not suffer in the way we had described" and that Nyasha was merely "making a scene" (NC, 201). Either way, the effect was to obscure the exact nature of the sustenance that, in their minds, the patients were refusing or regurgitating. In Nyasha's case, the bulimic consciousness is informed by a highly intellectual awareness of the historical context of political subjugation. When she bites into the colonial history books, she challenges both the official "history," the white lies force-fed to Africans, and the ruling colonial powers who preside over a hierarchy of "groveling," preaching the obedience of Africa's women to her men and of her men to themselves.

Nyasha also rejects the neocolonial definition of herself as a "good African," refusing to be further "cultivated" in the English image, and breaks with authority at all levels: "I'm not one of them but I'm not one of you" (NC, 201). In the portrait of Nyasha, bulimia becomes a vehicle for the indignant regurgitation of a whole neocolonial heritage of obsolete, repressive puritanical values that the indigenous population can no longer stomach. What Mainini in an earlier scene had difficulty "swallowing" and what, symbolically, "lay heavy on her stomach" (NC, 76)— myths about the benefits of Western education—Nyasha now vomits outright. The body, of its own accord, decisively rejects the intellectual diet that the colonized mind has had forced upon it. Clearly, the psychosomatic nature of the illness, translating cultural rejections and disaffiliations into a physical condition, is integrated with the central symbolism of the book that presents neocolonial educational values in terms of food and eating. Earlier, Dangarembga claimed, "Even the history was written in such a way that a child who did not want to accept that had to reject it and have nothing."[11] The revisionary intelligence, faced with the task of rewriting history, has nowhere to begin, no space or terms to express its dissent in; the protesting intellect, as Nyasha puts it, has nowhere "to break out to" (NC, 174).

When Mainini stops eating in protest at her daughter's removal to the convent school, Tambu observes, "Now, unlike a physical ailment of which everyone is told, an illness of this nature is kept quiet and secret" (*NC*, 185). Her mother's psychophysiological condition is virtually a taboo phenomenon, something almost shameful and with a strong hint of foreignness and even unnaturalness in the African context. Yet the crass colonial psychiatrist notwithstanding, the Africans in the novel are no more immune to this "white disease" than to all the others. Commenting routinely in interview on cases of anorexia reported in Zimbabwe, Dangarembga allows for the effects of cultural assimilation that make it almost impossible to say what is authentically "African" any more or what exactly "anorexic" means. Meanwhile, in the more radical vision of the novel, nervous disorders such as hysteria, anorexia, and bulimia are not presented as specifically and peculiarly Western or feminine conditions. The use of food for the purpose of protest is not merely an English affectation indulged in by Nyasha, and her condition is not a solitary but a common and collective one. Mainini, Maiguru, and Tambu all stop eating in spontaneous, unanimous protest against the tyranny of Babamukuru's neocolonial impositions; in their solidarity the author grounds a plea for a more composite African female identity, combining the talents of women of different ages, classes, and educational levels as an alternative to the "extreme, dividing reality" of the status quo (*NC*, 138).

Food, as we have seen, is a symbol in the novel for the African woman's oppression and is linked with alienating colonial educational values and a nutritionless diet of elitist English tastes and manners, all of which feature prominently in this oppression. It is therefore apt that the women should use food to rebel against the neocolonial patriarch's authority—and ironic that when Nyasha, in her bulimic rages, most rejects Englishness, she has attributed to herself a nervous condition thought to be peculiarly English. Thus, far from being marks of Westernization, hunger strikes and eating disorders prove to be very African modes of resistance: They are the means by which African women collectively reject what symbolizes their subservience and seek to create and express a unified identity.

Moreover, Dangarembga devotes a great deal of energy in her novel to deconstructing the conventional binary oppositions and hierarchic categorisms of patriarchal discourse. Each of these hinges on an invisible male/female polarization, with its inevitable positive/negative evaluation: for example, dominance/subservience, intelligence/emotion, rationality/sensuality. In Babamukuru's puritanical missionary ideology, the Manichean antitheses are underlain by moralistic gender dualisms: virtue/sin, good/evil, decency/degeneracy. This patriarchal binarism insists that there is such a thing as an essential femaleness or femininity. In colonial Africa, Maiguru observes, it has led to a prejudice against educated women because of its sexist conception of intelligence as a male preserve, ridiculously equating intellectual prowess with the "unwomanly" or "unfeminine" or even with "indecency" and "looseness." "I was an intelligent girl but I had also to develop into a good woman, he [Babamukuru] said, stressing both qualities equally and not seeing any contradiction in this" (*NC*, 88). Dangarembga subverts these oppositions by reversing the conventional roles.

In *Nervous Conditions* the rational, active challenger is a teenage girl, and the irrational neurotic is the male head of the household. Babamukuru is, of course, the novel's real hysteric and the cause of his daughter's breakdown. He is the center of neurosis in his Western nuclearized family, the sick one who stays well by making the well ones sick, his "bad nerves" expressed in erratic sequences of missed meals and secret, compulsive eating between meals. Babamukuru is a familiar type, a psychological case study in colonial repression. His is the "nervous condition" of the "native" in the Fanonian title, his compensative, domestic power-complex fueled by colonialism's long suppression of traditional male authority in Africa. He is victim to that process identified by Fanon, whereby the protesting energies and "muscular tension" induced by colonial oppression are turned inward and deflected violently back upon the colonized subjects themselves in a "collective auto-destruction" engineered by the colonial authority that is their true target (*WOE*, 43). Unable to voice his frustration with the tiny "honorary space" allotted him in the colonial hierarchy, Babamukuru victimizes his daughter by venting his prurient sexual jealousy of the white boys, the representatives of the white male power to which he must daily fawn and cringe. Dangarembga thus subverts the traditional patriarchal binarisms and, after deconstructing the false essentialisms built into them, is anxious in her use of conventionally "feminine" nervous complaints such as hysteria and bulimia not to fall back into an alternative biological essentialism and to reduce Nyasha's illness to another stereotypical, "female" condition.

Rather than create a new binarism, in fact, Dangarembga deconstructs the ground in which such oppositions reside. Toril Moi, in her essay on feminist literary criticism, argues that, as a result of the dominant and all-pervasive nature of patriarchal power, "there is no pure feminist or female space from which we can speak" and refers to Kristeva's theory of femininity as marginality—that is, as a position rather than a definable quality, and, moreover, a frontier position at the limit of a symbolic order that has habitually defined femininity, patriarchally, as lack, negativity, absence, and nonbeing (Moi, 205). Similarly, Terry Eagleton contends that because women in the male-governed order "are always the negative of that social order, there is always in them something which is left over, superfluous, unrepresentable, which refuses to be figured there."[12] All of this is, of course, doubly true of the twice-colonized African woman, whose marginality as a woman is exacerbated by her cultural uprooting. The colonized African woman, contends Dangarembga, has been written simultaneously out of colonial history books, educational primers, and a public role in society and has subsequently been robbed of her indigenous history, social identity, and self-worth. She writes back from a "void," a "nothing," "a great big gap inside her," since most of what she is has been left unrepresented (Wilkinson, 191, 198). For educated African women like Maiguru, the "honorary space" allotted within the co-opted anglophile elite of colonial puppets is a very small and empty space—really no space at all, says Nayasha, but a series of "loopholes" to be "slipped through" (NC, 179). The primary need of these women is to find a space in which a new historical and social identity can be created and defined. This need dictates the presentation of Nyasha's "anorexic" and "bulimic" conditions, which are not limitingly labeled but are left deliberately open as sites of hitherto unexpressed meaning and spaces for definition.

Thus Nyasha's bulimic voiding of her stomach also represents a verbal void, something outside of and opposed to the prevailing language conventions, and unrepresentable in the Manichean oppositions of a colonial-dominated male value system. It encompasses everything in the female experience that, because it still awaits verbal representation, cannot be said and therefore has to be vocalized in a different way, through the grunts and heaves of the woman gagging on food and retching. It embraces femininity also because its existence has never been admitted, let alone identified, and is open to a plurality of possible explanations—cultural, political, medical, psychological, and so on. The novel's tropology of anorexia and bulimia refers to the uncategorizable in female experience in a patriarchal society and indicates a position (hitherto a marginal one) in which African femininity resides rather than a definition of that femininity, definition having been an exclusively male prerogative up until now.

Much has been said in recent literary theory about patriarchal discourse's monologic and omniscient voices and its phallogocentric closures that presume to penetrate and possess truth through language. Current theory also discusses an opposing *l'écriture féminine* that presents multiple perspectives and opens up language to a challenging plurality of meaning. In keeping with these oppositions, Nyasha can be seen as a force of unvoiced resistance in the novel to the limiting categorisms and closures of the neocolonial order. Her bulimia subsequently embodies a whole complex of issues that are not easily classifiable, embracing everything that is preached at Babamukuru's meal table: the colonial etiquette and cultural politics, the ritualized submission to the father's domestic authority, the mother's infantile sentimentality, the prudery of both parents, and the censorship of everything that offends it. Whereas the father's authoritarianism constantly closes down options and frustrates potential, everything about his daughter speaks of "alternatives and possibilities" that "wreak havoc" with the "concrete and categorical"; her exploring "multi-directional mind" "thrives on inconsistencies" and displays a "passion for transmuting the present into the possible" (*NC*, 75–76, 116, 151, 178). Accordingly, her bulimia is fertile in ambivalence and contradiction and has been seen both as a positive act of self-control and as a despairing, suicidal attempt to efface herself from an alienating environment.[13] Nyasha's refusal of food is at once an assertion and a denial of the body, a complex of oral power and anal repression. The body's vomiting of her parents' foreign food proclaims its punitive rejection of their Englishness, but in its refusal to ingest there is also an implied refusal to excrete, which, it has been argued, signifies the dirt fixation of an arrested anal phase of development and, symbolically, the denial of Africa's dirt and physical squalor (Veit-Wild, 336).

Nyasha's shredding of the history books with her teeth is, at the same time, a parodic reenactment of the colonial subject's hungry devouring of imperial knowledge, eagerly swallowing its falsehoods, and an actual act of demolition that tries to reverse the existing pattern of cultural consumption. "Regurgitation" is, of course, verbally ambiguous, referring to both a literal bringing up of food and, figuratively, to the rote parroting of facts for examinations, and thus contains the possibilities of both rejection and retention. Nyasha's excessive study is in keeping with this paradoxical "logic" since it leads to her critical self-dissociation from what is studied. Thus one commentator on the novel has traced in the pattern of Nyasha's bulimic behavior Irigaray's notion of defiance through overcompliance, of subversion through extreme submission to power discourses that generate hysteria and similar libidinal reactions.[14] Dangarembga's image complex of ingestion-and-regurgitation is thrown open to a variety of possibilities and keeps breaking out into new meaning.

What this process amounts to in real terms for the oppressed women in the novel, however, is fraught with reservations. As Nyasha puts it, "So where do you break out to?" (*NC,* 174). Her mother's desertion of her household role and departure from home is merely a temporary "breaking out," an absence of five days, and Mainini, confronted by Babamukuru's tyrannical demands, can only withdraw into an apathetic stupor. Meanwhile, Nyasha herself, who is unable to answer her own question, arguably breaks out only into another kind of Englishness. Nyasha opposes to her father's prim missionary respectability and Victorian paternalism the 1960s libertarianism to which she has been exposed in London (hence the flaunted copy of *Lady Chatterley's Lover,* on trial in 1963 shortly before her London sojourn). Having experienced the modern mid-twentieth-century white world, she no longer has any use for the genteel puritanism and missionary remnants of Victorianism that still make up such a large part of Babamukuru's ideology.

The deculturation of Maiguru and Babamukuru is not as radical as their daughter's. Belonging to another cultural era, they have failed to update their Englishness. Yet their lives, with their odd mixture of African culinary rituals and Western name diminutives, are neither more nor less hybridized than hers. Therefore, at the crux of the conflict between father and daughter, and only partly perceived by Tambu, is not Western individualism and teenage rebelliousness versus indigenous patriarchal traditions of female subservience but rival modes and manners of Englishness. On the one side, Babamukuru has become almost completely divorced from his traditional Shona culture, and it is no accident that in the part of the narrative devoted to Tambu's stay in his house the sprinkling of Shona words—notably the staple food, *sadza*—disappears from the novel. He has difficulty speaking his people's language and eating their food, he is embarrassed by his brother Jeremiah's traditional welcoming ceremony, and the charade of the retroactive "marriage" that he forces upon Tambu's parents shows him to be painfully out of touch with traditional values. It is not Babamukuru's Africanity that is outraged by Nyasha's behavior but his prim, anglicized missionary sensibility and colonial-legated Christian puritanism, which are as foreign to indigenous African experience as Nyasha's 1960s' liberalism.

On the other side, Nyasha herself, for all her defiant regurgitations, is as anglicized in her own way as her parents and as neocolonial in her thinking. Her attachment to African tradition is entirely theoretical, her interest in her grandparents' ancestral customs more hypothetical than real, and her purely ornamental, decorative interest in clay pots does not express a very African viewpoint. Not surprisingly, Dangarembga describes Nyasha as "a very romantic character, for all that she insists that she is entirely factual and logical and rational" (Wilkinson, 192). In fact, the novel's only concrete link with the ancestral past is Tambu's grandmother, with whom she works in the fields early in the novel and from whom she absorbs scraps of Shona history and learns how to prepare a fine sadza, "so wholesome and earthy, like home-baked cornbread instead of the insubstantial loaves you buy in the shops" (*NC*, 39).

Nervous Conditions is an iconoclastic and at times harrowing indictment of sexual and cultural imperialism in which the stultifying power of colonial assimilation is revealed to be total and inescapable. If there is any way out of the neocolonial elite's terminal Englishness, no directions are given in Tambu's narrative, and what is true for Nyasha is also true, though at a lower level of frustration, for her. At the end of the book Tambu's inner conflict is left unresolved. She returns to her colonial convent to acquire more of the "killing" Englishness that will only deepen her moral dilemmas and exacerbate her country's nervous condition. In the last paragraph she tells us that at that time something in her mind "began to assert itself, to question things and refuse to be brainwashed" but the "long painful process" of "many years" that took her from that initial questioning to the critical position from which she was able to write her story is not described: How she got from there to here, which "would fill another volume," is left unclear (*NC*, 204). Tambu's story is a story of the 1960s. The stories of the 1970s and the 1980s—of the Zimbabwean woman's difficult struggle for freedom and uncertain growth to independence, parallel to the nation's—have yet to be told.

Chapter Eight
Ethnic Voices:
M. G. Vassanji's *The Gunny Sack*

Asians have lived in settled communities in Africa for over a hundred years, and India's commercial contact with Zanzibar and the East African Coast goes back several centuries. Yet until recently the ethnic Asian voice in modern anglophone African literature was, like that of the African woman writer, a minority one that was seldom heard. The novelist M. G. Vassanji has offered, as one possible explanation of this mysterious silence, the closed and closely knit character of Indian communities that makes the detachment necessary for the individual artist extremely difficult.[1] Vassanji, a Tanzanian Asian who left Africa in 1969 at the age of 19, managed to cultivate this detachment only in the second decade of his exile in the United States and Canada. His groundbreaking first novel, *The Gunny Sack* (1989), was not the first Afro-Asian novel. There had been earlier works set in Uganda and Kenya by African-Asian writers, as well as novels with African settings by expatriate writers of Asian descent.[2] Like Vassanji's, these novels dealt at length with Indo-African relations and featured characters with Indian fathers and African mothers, but their focus was on the contemporary generation, living in the aftermath of British colonialism. Vassanji packs much more history and consequently much more of Africa into his book, which is a rich, tumultuous saga covering over a hundred turbulent years and four generations of Indian diaspora in East Africa, from the last quarter of the nineteenth century to the present.

The Gunny Sack is a fictional history of the Ismailis (here called Shamsis), an eclectic, esoteric Muslim Shiite sect of the eighth century that incorporated elements of Hinduism. In the mid-1880s Dhanji Govindji, the great-grandfather of the novel's narrator, Salim, flees poverty and the breakup of the Shamsi community in his native Junapur and sets sail for Zanzibar. He eventually settles in Matamu in German East Africa, where he becomes a small businessman, marries the daughter of a wealthy Indian widow, and, 20 years later, earns the uninvited respect of the local Swahili elders by harboring fugitives during the Maji-Maji rebellion against the German colonial regime. Dhanji, meanwhile, has a grown-up, half-caste son whom he is reluctant to acknowledge: Huseni is the fruit of a liaison with an African slave woman, Bibi Taratibou, purchased cheaply from the local Shamsi headman who helped Dhanji establish his business upon his arrival in Africa. Unable to bear the social degradation attaching to his status, Huseni abandons his own wife and child and disappears into the African interior, whereupon his remorse-stricken father embarks upon a fruitless odyssey—to Mombasa, Nairobi, and beyond—in search of him. Dhanji's quest for his lost African son is financed, however, by money stolen from funds entrusted to him by the local community, and for this misdemeanor he is murdered by his Shamsi brethren on his return, empty handed, to Matamu.

Shortly after Dhanji's death in 1914 the British invade German East Africa, soon to be Tanganyika, and the Dhanji family, informed that they are now "British subjects," relocate to Dar-es-Salaam. Huseni's Indian wife remarries, and his four-year-old son Juma is sent to Kenya to live with his Indian relatives. Though only one-quarter African, Juma, like his father, is forced to live the degraded life of the half-caste, the slave boy running errands and performing menial tasks in the Nairobi household where he grows up. He tries to escape by stowing away on a ship to India but is forbidden entry and, after seeing Bombay only through a porthole, is shipped back to Africa. Back in Nairobi, Juma, now a young man, is married to a lowly Mombasi Indian girl, Kulsum, produces a daughter and two sons (one of them the narrator, Salim), and dies mysteriously after betraying to the British colonial authorities a suspected Mau Mau sympathizer who seeks refuge in his house. Following her husband's death, Kulsum takes her family back to Dar-es-Salaam, where Salim grows up in the heady years of Tanzanian independence and President Julius Nyerere's state-directed socialism, *Ujamaa*. During his traumatic military service at an African training camp in the country's far north, Salim falls in love with a young African intellectual, Amina, and is drawn into her Marxist political circle. Amina, however, proves too radical even for Ujamaa and is detained by the authorities. Faced with his own imminent arrest, the growth of increased anti-Asian feeling in the state, and an impossible domestic situation, in which he is torn between his vibrant African lover and his insipid Indian wife, Salim joins his brother in the United States, where the novel begins.

Into this fictional history of a displaced, dispossessed people and their escapist wanderlust, Vassanji weaves real historical events, opening up novel Asian perspectives on East African history. Here, from the Asian viewpoint, are the Maji-Maji revolt and the end of German rule in East Africa; the Mau Mau insurgency in Kenya; John Okello's pre-Federation putsch in Zanzibar in 1964, in which thousands of Arabs were massacred, and the Tanzanian army mutiny that followed in the same year. Here also are Nyerere's Arusha Declaration, announcing the nationalization of banks and businesses that signaled the economic dispossession of the Asian community; the expulsion of Asians from Uganda by General Idi Amin and the general use of Asians as scapegoats for collapsing African economies, which led to their mass exodus from East and Central Africa in the early 1960s.

The Gunny Sack, however, is anything but the linear historical narrative that the preceding summary suggests. "The stories I tell always begin somewhere else, just like myself," Vassanji has said. "My characters don't mean anything until they have a history."[3] The novel, in fact, begins at the end: Salim returns from the funeral of his great aunt Ji Bai, who is ironically laid to rest in frozen northern ground after completing a return trip from Africa to the India of her girlhood, and, from the distance of a North American hotel, he contemplates the demise of the Shamsi community in East Africa. Ji Bai's beneficent presence in the novel is a crucial, albeit an intermittent and elusive, one. It is she who, when the boy Salim fails to contact his dead father through a spirit medium, takes him to one side and tells him, "Well, listen, son of Juma, you listen to me and I shall give you your father Juma and *his* father Huseni and his father. . . ."[4] Ji Bai's collective family memories are subsequently a constant touchstone for Salim as he moves back and forth in pursuit of his dual ancestry, between the three interlinked generations whose key female figures supply the names of the three parts of the book (Ji Bai, Kulsum, Amina). And it is Ji Bai who bequeaths Salim the all-important gunny sack, the symbol of memory in the novel.

Everything the reader needs to know about the gunny sack is stated on the first page (and again on the last one) of the book:

> Memory, Ji Bai would say, is this old sack here, this poor dear that nobody has any use for any more. Stroking the sagging brown shape with affection she would drag it closer, to sit at her feet like a favourite child. In would plunge her hand through the gaping hole of a mouth, and she would rummage inside. Now you feel this here, you fondle that one, you bring out this naughty little nut and everything else in it rearranges itself. . . . I can put it all back and shake it and churn it and

sift it and start again, re-order memory, draw a new set of lines through the blots, except that each of them is like a black hole, a doorway to a universe. . . . (GS, 3, 266)

The abandoned gunny sack, stuffed with the mementos of a hundred years, is at once a womb and a voice, the generator and the speaker of stories, the stuff and the begetter and (in some cases) the grave of memories. It is, moreover, imaged, analogically, as the favorite child to whom its contents are unfolded. Thus it is fitting that when Salim, the adult version of that child, nicknames the sack "Shehru" and "Shehrbanoo," he conflates Scheherazade and Shehriyar, the respective storyteller and listener in the Arab epic *A Thousand and One Nights*. This is not merely to imply the direct intimacy of narrator and audience in the oral tradition to which both works are indebted but to suggest that the sack both tells and *is* its tale, that the gunny sack itself constitutes the history that it memorializes. Appropriately, on the last page of the novel the sack ends as an image of the lurid, violent history, complete with persecution and pogrom, which it has recounted: "She lies on the floor, crumpled, her throat cut, guts spilled, blood on the floor" (GS, 268).

There is, however, no schematic association or precise synchronization of the sack's contents with events in the narrative. Its "wisps of memory," says Salim, are "asynchronous images projected on multiple cinema screens" (GS, 112). Except for the account book that records the purchase of Salim's African great-grandmother by Dhanji Govindji, the actual items and objects do not specifically evoke or stand for particular memories. As Vassanji puts it, "what happens eventually in the novel is that after a while the gunny sack again becomes a metaphor and objects are no longer that important; it is the memory, the imagination that's important" (Nasta, 19–20). The combination of these two things—memory and imagination—is central to the novel. Ji Bai leaves the sack to Salim, the writer of the family, presumably because its loose reminders of the past are what he needs to trigger his imagination. The gunny sack exists at the point where memory and imagination, history and fiction intersect. It marks the place where the individual storyteller enters into the objective communal world that is the subject of his story; where Scheherazade passes into Shehriyar, narrator into audience. The novel's treasury of tales are in effect told both by and to the sack, for Salim is simultaneously narrator and narrated, being himself a part of the story that he relays from the sack's memories.

The sack is also an important, if rather loose, structuring agent in the novel. "I don't try to fit a story to a structure," Vassanji has said. "What I try to do is fit a structure to a story—or connected stories" (Kanaganayakam, 23). In the novel stories are released by memory, and memory, in its erratic meanderings and capricious associations, keeps remolding the shape of the book so that it assumes the changing contours of the sack whence the remembrances come. As Ji Bai's opening posthumous comments indicate, the selection of a single story may, because of the interconnectedness of all the sack's contents, alter the shape of the entire history; events, like objects rearranging themselves in the sack, are reshaped in the book's narrative vision by memory's shifts of focus and emphasis and are retold in different versions. "You can reconstruct it [the past] only through the paraphernalia it leaves behind in your gunny sack," says Salim. This bric-a-brac, the residue and debris of history, provides no objective testimony in itself, however, but exists only as it is restructured by imagination: "What you manufacture is only a model" (*GS*, 127). It is in fact important for the book's moral vision that the gunny sack should not speak in any single impartial or autonomous narrative voice but with many tongues. In India the gunny sack was traditionally the poor man's suitcase and the means by which small *dukawallahs,* or shopkeepers, transported their entire worldly belongings across the subcontinent or over the sea to Africa. *The Gunny Sack* writes back into history these obscure marginal people who were largely its uncomprehending victims. Salim's "drab Shehrbanoo," whatever relief its marvelous contents offer from the daily tedium, is primarily significant both as the common property and lowest common denominator of the migrant Indian experience and as the trademark and mainstay of the dukawallah's existence. Its influence in the novel is, accordingly, a leveling, equalizing one. The sack spills out, involuntarily and promiscuously, tales of squalor and nobility in which shameful and humiliating memories are mixed with comic nostalgia: Shehrbanoo "has no bourgeois qualms about the quality of her contents" (*GS*, 89). Anonymous voices speak intermittently from inside the sack, taking over the narrative from Salim at critical moments. These include an Indian woman who drowns herself for lack of dowry, a Zanzibari girl whose whole family is slaughtered during the 1964 massacre, and a pluralized dynastic commentator who plays chorus to the economic ruin of the Shamsi community at the fall of Germany's East African empire in 1918. Occasionally the sack adopts a critical, contemptuous tone in opposition to

Salim's, mocking the colonial values that he has absorbed with his English education.

Most importantly and obviously, Ji Bai's sack and its confusing jumble of heirlooms—Muslim rosary and shirt, Swahili cap, account books in Arabic-script—exist at the confluence of racial cultures: "Where Africa opened its womb to India and produced a being who forever stalks the forest in search of himself. It is where Bibi Taratibou, given as a gift for cold nights, was so used and discarded, and then disappeared" (GS, 39–40). The gunny sack wraps in its protective Indian cloth the African part of the Shamsi heritage to prevent it too from disappearing and, following the Yeats and Swahili epigraphs at the entrance to the novel, offers its own defense against transience. Ji Bai laments, "There are those who go to their graves not knowing where they came from" (GS, 134). For the fugitive migrants of a continuing, unending Asian diaspora, Africa is now another of the several places of origin; inevitably, all attempts in the novel to efface African influence and ancestry, to halt hybridization and revert to purist faiths, come to nothing. The attempt by Juma, one-quarter African, to return to an Indian homeland he has never seen ends in farce. The Gujurati missionaries sent out to East Africa to raise the banner against miscegenation never make it beyond the allures of Zanzibar. Salim's part-African ancestry keeps catching up with him and refuses to be denied. Although Salim's family adopts the Indian name Dhanji, his Goan neighbor who takes him to school on his first day puts down on the application form the African name of his grandfather, his "renegade half-caste ancestor," with the result that he becomes "Huseni Salim Juma for ever after." (GS, 108) Years later, when he is selected for national service, he is sent, disastrously, not to the Asian but to the African camp. As Salim puts it, "the name chose me and it chose my future" (GS, 108). Even his first name can be either Indian or African and it is by turns both, as convenience serves. As a child he is, according to his mother's creation folklore, the "overdone" one, left in the oven too long, whereas his lighter brother Sona is the perfect Indian "golden boy" (GS, 73); later, when it is more respectable to be black, he identifies his brother with the yellow of the tricolor Tanzanian flag, which nationalist demagogues link with the Asians, and himself with the black and African.

The multicultural hybridism represented by the sack is best exemplified in the national capital by Kariakoo, the poor African quarter that is in fact only "African" in the generic sense that it contains everything that is in Africa and that is seen by Salim as a zone of total cultural interaction. The "thousand faces of Kariakoo" depicted by "Shehru the Kariakoo hag" include Muslim kanzus, Indian pachedis, Swahili khangas and buibuis, American films, Western pop music, and much more (*GS*, 85, 89). This hybridism is also embodied, in a more mystical and benign way, by the gunny's owner. Ji Bai, who has more Africans than Asians among her friends, proclaims herself at once "Swahili . . . and Indian and Arab . . . and European"—Nyerere, she says, is her "son"—and Amina, who falls instantly in love with her, claims that she speaks better Swahili than the Africans in Nairobi (*GS*, 227–28). Ji Bai's household is "a world of magic and spells . . . of Bantu medicines, Arab djinns and Indian bhuts . . . all under one roof running their nocturnal rounds" (*GS*, 25).

It is one thing, however, for medicines to interact, quite another for people. Ji Bai is less a character in the novel than a concept, quite without dramatic presence, and she exists not at the level of realistic action but at the mythosymbolic level, as a trope for multicultural diversity and interracial harmony. Appropriately, Amina's eulogy reads like an ideological statement, the defense of an idea rather than a real person (she is trying to show that Tanzania is not like Uganda). Ji Bai makes rather large theoretical claims to cross-racial solidarity on the strength of her half-African half-brother, and her idealistic vision is in fact largely belied by the 90 years of racial division, intolerance, and persecution that she lives through. At this point it is relevant to glance at some of the popular image stereotypes of Asians in Africa since Vassanji, though he questions or qualifies many of these, also tests them for what truth they contain. In East Africa the Asians of the colonial diaspora were placed by the ruling whites in privileged but precarious positions of authority over a degraded, indigenous subject race; thus they were divided against rather than united with their fellow imperial victims. According to the popular image, these Asians, though supporting independence movements in the Indian homeland, were indifferent or opposed to African political struggles; in some instances they even acquired a reputation for collusion with the British, which made them ready targets for revenge when the imperial power departed. In addition, according to the stereotype, they were commercially exploitative, socially elitist, and racially exclusive, availing themselves of African women while keeping their own inaccessible. On the economic front, Vassanji writes mainly about poor Indians, so Salim does not measure up to his standard cartoon portrait, drawn by the ideologues of Ujamaa, as "one of the exploiter class, a dukawallah, mere agents of the British" (*GS*, 228).

In other respects, however, the popular images are by turns contested and confirmed. On the subject of politico-racial awareness, Vassanji has commented that, largely as a result of colonial English schooling and contrary to popular notions, there was among African Indians "a strong tendency to look down upon the Indian connection" (Kanaganayakam, 20). Certainly the Shamsis in the novel show little interest in India or Indian independence. But they have equally little interest in local political developments; their sense of specialness as African Indians—neither Indian nor African but superior to both—tends to reinforce their exclusiveness and shut down any sympathy with African aspirations. On the issue of marital exclusiveness, men who are half or three-quarters Indian (Husseni, Juma) are allowed to marry Indian women, and Salim's sister marries an Englishman, but this privilege is not granted to any full-blooded Africans in the novel.

Not surprisingly, therefore, Vassanji's treatment of common causes made between Indians and Africans is a heavily qualified and complex one, and such solidarities are frequently hedged about by qualifications and contradictions that rule out easy moral judgments. Dhanji Govindji's threefold involvement is of a doubtful and troubled nature and exacts a terrible price in suffering. He impregnates an African woman and then, as his racial shame gets the better of his personal guilt, casts her off for a conventional Indian wife and berates his illegitimate half-African son for consorting with his mother. He then violates official Indian policy of noninvolvement in African rebellions by sheltering, at tremendous personal risk, Huseni and other Maji-Maji fugitives from the German authorities, all the while upbraiding them for their superstitious oaths and beliefs. He is subsequently embarrassed by the praise of the Swahili elders (they later give him full African burial honors at his funeral). Finally, consumed by rival guilts, he expropriates communal funds to finance his futile search for his half-caste son and is murdered for repeatedly breaking rank with his own people. Dhanji, his great-grandson speculates, was perhaps finally true to his Taratibou and "risked damnation for their son" (*GS,* 150).

His descendants, however, do not keep faith with his troubled commitments. When the Indian dukawallahs of the next generation protest in 1923 against the colonial government's requirement that accounts be kept in English, they express solidarity with the Swahili elders, whose language many of them speak at the expense of the colonial one. However, they do so partly in order to keep their improbities secret from the British authorities: They close ranks with the African the better to exploit him. Dhanji's grandson Juma, after his abortive Bombay escapade, loses his compassion for Africans and, true to colonial stereotype, ends up betraying Mau Mau insurgents to the British. Juma's widow, Kulsum, though of humble birth and spouse to a man one-fourth African, affects a high-caste exclusivism and a primitivist view of Africa that renders her deaf to Nyerere's overtures on racial equality and causes her to eye her son suspiciously each time he returns from his African lover, as if he "had come with hands soiled by the vilest deed" and has to be purified (*GS*, 229). "Black ancestry was not something you advertised. Kulsum had two girls' marriages to think of. A whiff of African blood from the family tree would be like an Arctic blast, it would bring the mercury of social standing racing down to unacceptable levels" (*GS*, 150). Her African father-in-law (whom she never met) tried in vain to assert solidarity with his Indian half-brother, only to find himself unacknowledged and unwanted, and two generations later, her one-eighth African "Kariakoo boy" son is excluded from the school play by his European and upper-class Indian teachers (meanwhile, on the African side, the schoolgirl Amina is deployed as an auxiliary servant by her English headmistress). Even Salim's (and Vassanji's) enlightened contemporary generation is still partly caught in the colonial racial trap. Vassanji has remarked: "We sent back our British passports and it was a wholehearted embrace of the new political situation that there was. But subconsciously it's possible that the colonial legacy was very strong amongst the Asians because we had certain values which somehow seemed out of place in the emerging political reality" (Nasta, 20). Thus, on a visit to Lake Victoria from the Kaboya army camp, Salim catches himself indulging in Anglo-Indian fantasies of "Burton, Livingstone and Stanley"—"the mind has many sides that do not talk to each other," he explains (*GS*, 201). During his army training he does, for once, refuse local ethnic solidarities, accepting that "an Indian who volunteers for National Service has no-one, no friend, no kin" (*GS*, 217). He starts a relationship with an African girl and refuses to be rumored into marriage to a local Indian one, whereupon he is almost beaten to death by the latter's hysterical brother.

The nerve center of the novel's European-fomented racial divisions is the colonial capital of Dar-es-Salaam, a segregated city zoned into European, Indian, and African quarters. Meaning "Haven of Peace," its portentous name has inauspicious legendary origins in the makeshift settling of a dispute that arose, once more, from the taboo of betrayed racial purity: An African killed an Indian whom he found in bed with his sister. The reconciliatory name-myth is partly eclipsed by the history behind it—"dreams and hopes," comments Salim. The individual quarters of Dar are themselves internally splintered—"Where everyone else saw 'Asian,' the Asians saw Shamsi, Bohra, Ismaili, Hindu, Sikh, Memon, Ithnashri" (*GS*, 146)—and even the transitional zone of Kariakoo, which Salim regards as an area of fruitful interaction, proves in reality to be "a myriad of refracting fragments" where cultures collide rather than combine, meet but do not merge, and coexist rather than interact. Ji Bai's idealistic effusions notwithstanding, the Asians and Africans whose lives cross in this zone appear to have little to say to one another. When Amina is detained by the authorities, a withered old African woman who turns out to be her mother seeks out Salim to request his aid—"Being Asian, she thought, I had access to more influence" (*GS*, 262)—but she leaves before he can find out anything about her and is never seen again. "Shehrbanoo the Kariakoo hag," which stores the assorted keepsakes of the mixed-race quarter, also reflects their disconnectedness: The "dumpy gunny sack" is seen as "enclosing a broken world, the debris of lives lived" (*GS*, 135). In fact, a more suitably ironic image for Indo-African relations in the novel is perhaps Salim's massive black trunk. Upon Salim's arrival at the army camp, a sadistic African sergeant forces him to put the trunk on his head and run up and down a hill with it. The trunk in Indian fiction is traditionally the migrant Indian's storage place for family heirlooms and histories. In this episode it represents the unnecessary weight of possessions and traditions that are locked away and that in turn lock their owners away from the host country, isolating them from the indigenous population. "We Indians have barged into Africa with our big black trunk, and every time it comes in our way," laments Salim. "Do we need it? I should have come with a small bag, a rucksack" (*GS*, 204). Salim is symbolically burdened by the weight of his isolation, his failure to belong. The trunk stands for everything that separates him from Africa, as the gunny sack signifies everything that, albeit in its peculiarly capricious and fragmented way, links him with it.

With the coming of independence Africa has its revenge upon its Indians. An Indian millionaire is slowly reduced to penury, and, at a more sophisticated level of exclusion, Salim the lone Indian is stereotyped into the roles of treasurer and business manager of his university society. But it is in the brutal world of the Kaboya army camp and its local village that the most naked and terrifying expression is given to the racial aggression facing Salim and Amina in the new nation. Here there are no names, only crude racial denominations: "Indian," "Arab," and "African," or, in Amina's version, those who financed the slave trade, those who ran it, and those who supplied it. Here Salim is persecuted, and his ex-classmate Shivji is brutalized and tormented until he in turn becomes a brutal tormentor in his own right, a terrifying figure with a fearful reputation. Neither Salim nor Amina are able to shed their histories and ancestries, which penetrate even into the corners of private relationships. Salim makes brief common cause with Africa through his radical girlfriend but then, like his great-grandfather, settles for a conventional wife of his own race and ends up running away from both.

Running away is a recurring motif in Vassanji's novel and a measure to which each of the four generations resorts. Dhanji flees his Indian homeland for Africa and then pursues his runaway son into the African interior; Juma runs back to India, Salim away to America. In each case, Salim notes, a heavy price is paid: "Dhanji Govindji, his self-respect and sanity. His son, the joys of family life, the security of community life. My father Juma . . . compassion for those of whom he was also a part—if only a quarter" (*GS*, 66). To these might be added Salim's own burden of unexpiated guilt and his separation from his African-born daughter. Each of these men is bedeviled by divided identities, being half one thing and half another; each is confronted by apparently irreconcilable oppositions that he can choose to resign himself to, to resolve, or to run away from. In India Dhanji is troubled by the rival religious fanaticism that finally breaks up the Shamsi community, in Africa by the conflicting impulses of racial shame and sexual guilt. Both Huseni and Juma are torn between their Indian and African selves, as their need for filial and familial acceptance meets with implacable ostracism. Salim's love triangle, exacerbated by the threat of political arrest, is a modified version of his great-grandfather's predicament.

Many of these conflicts and contradictions are, of course, products of the colonial situation. As Vassanji has argued, the protagonists' feelings of hopelessness have not so much to do with any Indian belief in fate as with the sense that everything that happens to them is decided by external agencies that leave them no power of self-determination or independent control (Kanaganayakam, 27). Certainly the attempts by Huseni and Juma to escape the colonially generated contradictions of their lives are largely negative passages, not merely defeatist but also deluded in their regression to false simplistic unities. Huseni vanishes into the continent's interior to become an African pure and simple, Juma to a fantasy India of his imagination (likewise, in the next generation, Salim will become obsessed by his Africanness, Sona by his Indianness). Overwhelmed by the complexities of the present, both men relapse passively into selected ancestral pasts: Unable to forge anything new, they revert to the old. The Indian African, as Vassanji pessimistically states, "is essentially where he came from.... [H]e cannot break with the past" (Nasta, 21). Indeed, *The Gunny Sack* asks important questions about what to do with the past and registers the compelling need to record what is irretrievably passing away in the lives of an uprooted people who, though constrained by their pasts, can never actually go "home" again. Yet there is also an opposing sense in the novel that, though we are indeed where we came from, we are also, in a more practical and immediate sense, where we are now; further, each character's quest therefore is less an ancestral one than a quest for acceptance and identity—albeit a confused identity—in the place that he or she is in. "The past has no end," says Ji Bai (*GS,* 266), but there is a strong counterfeeling in the book that it has to end somewhere if there is to be any practical working with the potential of the present and a commitment to the future. There must be an end to escapes and nostalgic returns to nonexistent pasts, or as Salim puts it: "The running must stop now, Amina. The cycle of escape and rebirth, uprooting and regeneration, must cease in me. Let this be the last runaway, returned, with one last, quixotic dream. Yes, perhaps here lies redemption, a faith in the future, even if it means for now to embrace the banal present, to pick up the pieces of our wounded selves, our wounded dreams" (*GS,* 268). An alternative to running away is to stand one's ground, embrace the contradictions, and find a way of living with them. This is the option posed in different forms by Dhanji Govindji and his great-grandson Salim.

Dhanji's futile odyssey in quest of his lost African son is fraught with contradictions. On the one hand, his flagging commitment to the task evinces his deep sense of racial degradation and his fear of finding Huseni, whom Africa is seen as calling back to itself. Meanwhile, at the symbolic level, Huseni's vanishing without trace into the African interior, never to be seen again, signifies the extent to which the African Indian had, prior to the racial divisions fomented by British colonialism, become indistinguishable from his African setting. When asked about the possible merging of Indian and African traditions, Vassanji replied equivocally: "I don't see any obvious merging, but so what? Our Indianness was already transformed by the Africanness" (Kanaganayakam, 21). In some senses the modern Afro-Indian's Indianness has already, three generations ago, been modified by and absorbed into his birthplace, whereas in other ways it remained unmerged and unmergeable. The symbolism is inevitably tinged with historical ironies. The half-caste was sufficiently African to be merged into the native context; not so the Indian quadroon and octoroon of later generations who, without further intermarriage, become more distinct from their African setting and whose invisibility in it is finally achieved by emigration, not integration.

Even so, there are fruitful countercurrents in this episode that are not qualified by a demurring symbolism. Dhanji is torn by conflicting impulses. His first instinct to disclaim his son—"Tell me, what is my sin, that I should inherit this slave's son with my marriage . . . this junglee who stands out like a wart in this family" (*GS*, 28)—is rapidly overtaken by the equally strong desire to reclaim him and restore him to the bosom of the family. Dhanji's emotional tangle of shame, guilt, and frustrated love precipitates a psychological crisis, and from his unresolved tensions is generated the momentum to pursue the offspring whom he has alienated. In the person of Dhanji Govindji, contradictions are exploded into power, transformed into energy. The exclusive and the eclectic, the purist and the hybrid coexist irreconcilably in the one character, and their creative conflict galvanizes him into action. In this divided state, he raids community funds, symbolically siphoning off part of India in pursuit of the piece of Africa he has engendered, the Africa in himself. Dhanji thus declares a guarded, ambivalent commitment to his new home, running with his contradictions rather than away from them, and the pattern is repeated in the life of his great-grandson.

From the same complex of guilt, shame, and love Salim forges two major new initiatives. The first of these is Amina, the child of a broken Indian marriage who bears the African name of her father's lover and grows up in a new nation where Asians no longer have specially protected, privileged positions and where genuine equality is therefore finally within reach. As Salim says, "from our wounded selves flowers still grow" (*GS*, 269). Through his egalitarian political and sexual commitments, Salim has succeeded in transforming his heritage and subsequently leaves to his daughter in Africa an inheritance different from that left to him. Salim's second initiative is, of course, the book he narrates: *The Gunny Sack* transcends conflicts and contradictions to produce a text that is not Indian or African—or English, though it is written in that language—but something compounded of all of these. "I remember my first view of Shehrbanoo . . . slumped in the inner room beside Ji Bai's bed, her mouth closed with a sisal twine. Ji Bai untied the loose knot, instantly a smile appeared on the gunny where there was a grimace before, and that laughing mouth was never shut again" (*GS*, 135). The gunny sack is the artistic womb that delivers the novel: It represents the transfiguring vision and redeeming power of art, which includes laughter and the comic zest and gusto of narrative composition. Though he runs away, Salim, like Dhanji, demonstrates that the clash of opposites need not be sterile deadlock, a collision of things that fail to connect; rather, out of conflict and division, a new third thing—a genuine synthesis or fusion, which is not merely confusion—may be born.

The symbolism of *The Gunny Sack* is as fertile in contradiction as the dilemmas facing its characters, and the same pattern, involving the transcendence and transformation of oppositions, is at work. Ji Bai's healing powers combine the best of Hindu and Muslim religious cultures in the esoteric Shamsi spirit, collapsing Vishnu into Allah and incorporating Koranic prayers into the Hindu Diwali festival ("sort it all out, you purists," wisecracks Salim). Similarly, the crossbreed Kariakoo boy exists in a transitional zone between cultures, a realm of possibility, and has the potential for realizing the best as well as the worst of both worlds. In the facile ideal image of Ujamaa's official ideology, he may be a "beautiful" child "with the virtues of both races and the prejudices of neither" (*GS*, 185), or his hybridism may be expressed more realistically in his patched-up motley dress and the venomous trilingual obscenity of his speech. Finally, the very material out of which the book's eponymous symbol is made is dual in nature. As a young girl, Ji Bai first uses gunny sacking as a curtain to screen off the African world and then later as a bag in which to gather and transport its motley heirlooms, so that it serves as both a barrier and a bridge between India and Africa. Moreover, even as a curtain the sacking is ambiguous. First, it is a full curtain used to exclude the non-Indian world, then a flimsy half-curtain that provides no real privacy but allows the Kariakoo tenement dwellers to look interactively in upon one another's lives. The world of Habib Mansions where Salim grows up is effectively an expressionistic, exploded stage set through which the narrator acquires intimate knowledge of his neighbors.

In a novel so open to alternatives, it would be unwise to expect anything resembling closure. The gunny is "Shehrazade postponing her eventual demise, spinning out yarns," telling tales that, like the uprooted Asian's quest for identity, "have no beginning or end" (*GS*, 5). Political events—economic dispossession and exodus—provide the book with an artificial closure, but Salim, the last of the runaways, merely removes to a new continent where the African Asian begins a new hybrid existence as a British, American, or Canadian Asian. For we are not only where we came from but also where we are going to next. In that new place the immigrant faces the usual choice of transforming the fugitive self to fit the situation or modifying the milieu to suit the self. But Vassanji is optimistic: "I now see myself as part ... of an invading culture from the Third World which is now helping to transform the cultures that invaded us. ... Anything that is already old and is established needs new infusions; otherwise, it dies. So the mainstream society has no choice but to accept us" (Kanaganayakam, 24). It is not, as Ji Bai claims, that the past never ends; rather, it is always and has never ceased ending. Vassanji's novel reveals that the diasporic Asian identity is an ongoing, evolving thing, constantly opening out to new possibilities, engaged in a process of perpetual transformation in an international world.

In the Heinemann edition *The Gunny Sack* was hailed by the publisher's blurb as "Africa's answer to *Midnight's Children*," but the comparison is misleading. Vassanji's realism is more of the material than the magical kind. Kariakoo's wonders and grotesques—hydrocephalous beggars, two-foot-high dwarfs, inauspicious midday cockatoos that cause football clubs to change their names—are all perfectly at home in their exotic Indo-Arabic-African setting, without any reference to the fabulous or allegoric. Moreover, no special claims are made for the few perfunctory coincidences between international events and episodes in the personal narrative: for example, Dhanji's arrival in Africa at the time of the Berlin Conference and his death at the British conquest of German East Africa; the birth of Salim's sister on 8 May 1945, the day that peace is declared in Europe and Africa instantly delivered from war; and the departure of Salim's English schoolmistress in 1964 at the same time as the British forces' withdrawal from Tanganyika, to be recalled almost immediately to disarm the army mutineers. Salim works his way simultaneously through the contents of the gunny sack and the major events of Tanzania's colonial and postcolonial history, but these are not closely connected, and there are no signs that Salim is developing the comic monomania of Rushdie's paranoid narrator. Neither is there any but the loosest intertextual link between the peripheral Salim-Shivji relationship in *The Gunny Sack* and the more dominant Saleem-Shiva connection, counterpointing the intellectual and the military brute, in *Midnight's Children*.

Vassanji's novel is an uneven achievement, not without weaknesses. The prehistory of Salim's family is compellingly imagined in the first part of the book, which is full of magnificent evocations of Zanzibar and the East African coast at the turn of the century, and the novel regathers intensity in the semiautobiographical narrative of Salim's army and university life that makes up the third part. The writing energy begins to flag and invention to relax, however, during the long middle section on Salim's boyhood and schooldays, in which overindulged childhood nostalgias and juvenile anecdotes are not imaginatively enlivened into fiction; without visionary coloring, the facts by themselves are not enough. Vassanji has claimed that "the narrator is a unifying force" (Nasta, 21), but the narrator acquires an invisible presence, and the novel a diaristic transparency and textural thinness, for much of this middle section, in which the presiding narrative personality is not Salim but his African friend Edward bin Hadith. Hadith's name, literally "Son of Story," is appropriate, for he makes a story of everything, no matter how trivial, and the daily tedium recorded by his anecdotal personalized memory is a negative counter in the novel to the gunny sack's collective memory of significant national and international events. In fact, what Salim calls "the clutter of memory" is too pervasive throughout the book, proliferating characters in the extended family who are often little more than names. One such character is Salim's wife, Zuleika, who is, embarrassingly, married, impregnated, delivered of a daughter, and abandoned all in the space of a few paragraphs. It is simply one of the book's given, unquestioned cultural assumptions that the Indian characters, including those with faint dilutions of African blood, will find Indian wives. It is also assumed that the protagonist, in spite of his African girlfriend, will inevitably, in the author's words, find himself "already committed to someone else in a very Indian way" and in the full knowledge that "Indian relationships are not easy to break" (Kanaganayakam, 26). None of this is artistically worked out in the narrative, however, and Zuleika remains a shadowy presence in the novel.

These blemishes notwithstanding, *The Gunny Sack* is an unusual and exciting work. It charts adventurous new territory, shedding light on a hitherto little known area of African experience and giving voice to a community of people by whom and about whom surprisingly little has been said. The novel is a complex exploration of the African Asian's alternating quests for an ancestral identity and for acceptance by the society he or she is in; it also paints an intricate portrait, by turns moving and funny, of the ways in which Africans and Asians have found themselves involved in one another's lives in the pre- and postindependence eras. "Sure, we too have a history, and old traditions," writes Sona from Europe, "but they are undefined, uncelebrated, and sometimes as confusing as a cauldron of witches' brew" (*GS*, 236). It is a mark of Vassanji's achievement in *The Gunny Sack* that he defines those traditions, celebrates their enduring spirit, and in so doing renders them less confused. It is a sad irony that this neglected part of African history has begun to emerge on the literary map of the continent only in retrospect, at a time when it is almost over. Nevertheless, the novel opens up new, if uncertain, directions in African fiction and occupies an important place in the unceasing hybridization of literary styles and forms in late twentieth-century African writing.

Chapter Nine

Imagined and Other Worlds: Magic History in Kojo Laing's *Search Sweet Country* and Ben Okri's *The Famished Road*

Most of the novels discussed in this book fall broadly within the domain of conventional realism, which presupposes the existence of a solid, well-defined, external reality. Traditionally, this mode of discourse maintains clear ontological boundaries between what, in Western terms, is usually designated as observed and imagined experience, material and magical phenomena, and real and fictional worlds. Toward the end of the 1980s, however, there appeared in African writing a kind of fiction in which these customary lines of demarcation were given more problematic expression or eroded altogether. In these novels different and disparate worlds appear to coexist; there is an indeterminacy with regard to where literal reality ends and metaphor begins, a habitual elision of figurative into narrative space; it is hard to tell in exactly what ways and at what levels human character is constituted. The result was a new, fantastic realism that, in its subversion of dominant realist modes, seemed initially to align itself with other "nonrealist" forms of representation in European postmodernist fiction and recent South American writing. Closer attention, however, revealed its unstable fictional ontology to be grounded in indigenous African worldviews undistorted by Western concepts of reality. The groundbreaking, precursory novel in this school of writing—and a milestone in African fiction—was Kojo Laing's *Search Sweet Country* (1986).

Laing's book is set in Ghana in the mid-1970s during the worst years of Colonel Acheampong's corrupt military dictatorship; its pivotal plot event is the illegal importation of racehorses, under the pretext of government agricultural production policies, by a ruthless academic careerist and political stooge, Dr. Boadi. When the racehorses, which are obviously not farmhorses, break out of their boxes and stampede through the airport, the shocked onlookers are bribed into silence with free beer. The novel then charts the aftermath of the event in the lives of characters grouped around the odious Boadi and his archrival, the scholarly and acerbically idealistic Professor Sackey. These include Sackey's incorruptible protégé Kofi Loww and the principled airport supervisor and reluctant recruit of Boadi's, Okay Pol (both witnesses to the racehorse scandal and thereafter victims of Special Branch intimidation); the curiously named $^{1}/_{2}$-Allotey, a mystical farmer-cum-healer who serves as a focus for Sackey's own thwarted idealism; and a vast array of subsidiary characters and presences.

But the plot, both here and in Laing's subsequent writing, is largely a distracting irrelevance, serving chiefly as a lightweight vehicle for the author's imaginative flights of language and exuberant poetic invention, albeit one through which serious polemical inquiries—into Third World development, Euro-African cultural relations, the psychology of the Ghanaian intellectual—can be read. A synopsis of narrative events gives little indication of the essence of Laing's fiction and its most striking features: namely, its audacious wordplay, eccentrically allusive wit, and intellectual passion; its vividly earthy evocation of the tumultuous life of Accra and popular Ghanaian speech; and its extravagant lyric fantasy, conjured from indigenous animist metaphysics.

Search Sweet Country is, in fact, a book of wonders in which everything—animate and inanimate, natural and supernatural—is endowed with sentient power and energy. "In his [Kofi Loww's] head the buildings, the markets, the streets became alive, became almost passionate with existence."[1] In Laing's universe all things have the power of agency. Buildings dance to the rhythm of human heartbeats, trees exchange roots and hurl down squirrels while their leaves "chatter with profound nonchalance"—"the forests were jealous of sound and were able to create and destroy echoes" (*SSC,* 94)—and the blue-soiled earth dresses itself in hats, churches, and people. One remarkable feature of this surreal undifferentiated flux is the novelist's metaphoric displacement and reallocation of qualities and functions to things to which they are not usually thought to belong. The effect of this is to suspend normal sense-relations and perceptual processes and to produce a kind of behavioral synesthesia in which beards "disagree," smiles detach themselves from their owners and move according to their own momentum, and people "eat" thoughts, gather laughter in cups, and "wear" each other's features: "his eyes . . . contained so much that . . . there had to be more than one human being wearing them" (*SSC,* 17). In one such whimsy the flying witch Adwoa Adde, before embarking upon the "aerial history of Ghana" in which she gathers the complaints and confessions of Accra's downtrodden citizens, borrows a body constituted from dismembered, repositioned human limbs supplied by her spirit mentor. In another scene the same ancestral spirits, by a reverse process, borrow $^1/_2$-Allotey's mouth and nose, leaving him partly disembodied, with a hungry stomach and a squint, as he enters the mystic trance that releases healing energies from his farm.

Much of this, admittedly, is comic invention for its own sake, as in the quirky cameos of the cemetery spirits who borrow the State House and the football stadium for their numinous assemblies, and of Aboagye Hispeed who devises the first do-it-yourself "automatic one-man funeral" and disappears when he stands sideways. But Laing's bizarre figures and conceits cannot simply be dismissed as idle gimmickry. Beneath the rhetoric of fragmentation and disintegration, of borrowed parts and fractured wholes, there is the deeper underlying metaphysic of an animist universe in which, since everything is holistically an aspect of everything else, then nothing is ever wholly either one thing or another. In this hybridic cosmos everything is constituted of halves. As $^1/_2$-Allotey's name indicates, to be allotted only part of everything and to be given everything in parts is what it is to be fully alive. As Professor Sackey tells him, "you either live fragmented and half yourself, half your heart, or you keep slow and whole and die" (*SSC,* 104).

The Ghanaian world of the novel is constituted of antithetical halves that must somehow be reconciled, though they can never be unified into wholes. Hence Sackey, when he contemplates the mind of the contemporary Ghanaian intellectual, is distressed at the absence of a "territory between the supernatural and the purely factual" (*SSC,* 299) because most of his nation's people live in the half-and-half, in-between territory where the numinous and the material liminally coexist. Indeed, most of the novel's action takes place in what Kofi Loww calls "perfect African time—time that existed in any dimension," where the ancestors bring their 50-year-old groundnuts to market alongside the living vendors and where flying witches are still visible "even when . . . vision was blocked by goats, Mercedes Benzes, semi-prostitutes, harmattan or plantain cake" (*SSC,* 38, 150). Thus the Professor warms to $^1/_2$-Allotey's experimental farm venture, with its problematic mixture of subsistence and spirituality, commerce and metaphysics, and applauds his attempts to blend modern therapy with traditional herbal medicines and to infuse new ideas into ancient libation rituals (which outrages the reactionary elders of Allotey's village). Ghanaian Christianity and political morality are represented in the book by similarly complementary but irreconcilable halves—the pragmatic Bishop Budu and his unworldly priest Osofo, the high-principled Kofi Loww and the expediency-serving Okay Pol—and the academic world by Sackey's own quirky mélange of rarefied intellectualism and irrepressible ordinariness.

The "search" of Laing's "sweet country" is therefore the pursuit of wholes by halves, and it is an endeavor that causes the characters' careers to cross in ways that emphasize their interpenetrativeness and simultaneity. This collective search for a more meaningful identity and a more authentic mode of existence during a period of inauthentic political values is symbolized, albeit in partly parodic fashion, by the ancient Beni Baidoo and his quixotic obsession with founding his own village, a dream that he confides to everyone. "Beni Baidoo was Accra," we are informed on the first page. "The search of a fool touches other lives. . . . [He] flowed with his one obsession in and out of the lives he met" (*SSC,* 8). Baidoo is a ubiquitous, choric character who opens and closes more than half of the chapters and makes miraculous comic appearances after a number of key actions—at the airport, in Sackey's car during his visit to $^1/_2$-Allotey's farm, and on the climactic march against the government. He is, moreover, a collective and composite character, a thread of the national fabric who weaves himself, infiltratively, into the book's principal characters, finding something of himself in each of them and answering to their multifarious needs and deservings. Thus Baidoo plays many roles: prophet and clairvoyant, psychologist and political commentator, trickster and fool. Similarly, Kofi Loww, who lends the hue of his eyes to buildings and the sky, feels that "each time [he] took a step he lifted a whole country," and the witch Adwoa Adde discovers on her communal aerial patrols that she is "forced into relationship with everything, and her pulse was the movements of thousands in sleep" (*SSC,* 26, 42). Moreover, although she projects her own spiritual vitality outward onto the urban environment, she is herself a projection of the people's collective imaginings and of popular belief about witches; the relationship between her intrinsic and imparted identities is at times a problematic one.

Apart from Sackey and a few realistically observed minor figures, the characters in *Search Sweet Country* develop much along the lines of these three: That is, they are syncretic rather than unitary creations, poetic concepts and configurations rather than real people (one character, Ebo the Food, is a materialized abstraction). Not surprisingly, there is a price to be paid for this mode of characterization. Laing's Accra is an unapologetically imagined world and language construct, a verbal city self-consciously imposed on an actual one, and although it is presented as a familiar reality in its own right, not as a symbolic extrapolation or allegoric rendering of one, it is nevertheless the result of imaginative projection rather than close observation. In theory, of course, a multiethnic metropolis like Accra is bound to be a visionary concept, an invented place dreamed into existence by a collective imagining, insofar as no single member or ethnic group is able to apprehend its totality or that of its larger microcosm: the nation. To inhabit the city is thus to engage in an act of vision. The problem with this notion in Laing's novel, however, is that the imagined, surreal quality of the narrative does not emanate from the characters themselves, who seem hardly to experience it and to be largely unaware of it. Rather, as Ato Quayson has observed,[2] the visionary element is imparted, often quite arbitrarily, by an oddly displaced narrator and is largely a function of his own idiosyncratic personality and perspective and of the language he describes the novel's inhabitants in. There is thus a curious discrepancy between what the narrator describes and what the characters perceive, and there are occasions (for example, the Sackey-Allotey exchanges) where the interlocutors fail to penetrate the oracular, cryptic register in which the narrator has encoded their dialogue and appear to be understood only by the author, not by each other.

It is most particularly in Laing's language, a language that lives in metaphor, that the willfully attributive quality of his writing becomes a problematic feature of narrative representation. In addition to the book's sheer, utter lyricism, there is a formidable arsenal of exclamations and ideophones, alliterative and onomatopoeic effects, and graphic innovations ($^1/_2$-Allotey is always written numerically), through which the language constantly directs attention to its own physical substance, as well as (by means of ellipses) to its own limitations. Time and again the novel turns self-consciously upon its own peculiar grammar and language—"All flies in bars were commas, for they never fully stopped on one glass"—and in one scene even Baidoo's spindly body becomes alphabetical: "[T]he knees were bent into Vs and Ws and then crossed into Xs, while his mouth formed the vowels" (*SSC*, 223, 277). Sometimes the figurative displacement of bodily organs and functions has a wicked satiric exactness, as when the execrable Boadi fails to win over Kofi Loww: "Dr. Boadi got out of the car after he had put his dazzling smile, for show, out of the window first; but it merely slid unnoticed to

Loww's feet" (*SSC*, 151–52). But when the metaphoric transferences are taken too far they can become irritatingly labored and mechanical, and the tropology takes on a life of its own, running riot with narrative and dramatic integrity. An example is when $^1/_2$-Allotey, a creature constituted entirely of fractions, speaks of his ex-wife by halves (one day good, the next ill), meets her halfway to his hilltop farm, and listens only to exactly half of what she has to say.

The same process is present at the local level of individual metaphor. For example, when Kofi Loww and his father meet "under the shoeshine tree whose breeze polished both souls" (*SSC*, 8), the wordplay on shoe polish and spiritual hygiene (punning on "sole" and "soul") displaces the shiny-leaved mango tree, which virtually disappears. All metaphor is, of course, an act of translation, seeing items and objects in terms of something other than themselves. But in Laing's poetic syntax the figurative signifiers so exuberantly exceed and transcend their material referents that they effectively eclipse them, becoming tropes in their own right; the subsequent removal of tenor from vehicle gives the merely verbal and nominal priority over any sense of an external reality. This deconstruction of the relations between image and object means that the balanced ambiguity of ordinary meaning and allusion that is the key to successful metaphor breaks down, issuing in mannerism, self-delighting whimsy, and some precious, occasionally inept punning: Harassed by the authorities, Sackey lists after his name "degrees of interrogation from the university of the Special Branch"; his amanuensis quips that "a typewriter is only a porcupine with an alphabet on its back"; and Baidoo, in a fit of deathbed lust, questions "the difference between erection and resurrection" (*SSC*, 166, 227, 283). At its worst Laing's conceits lapse into sterile ingenuity, with more dazzle than illumination.

Laing has professed to conceive the ultraestheticized, language-fixated world of his fiction as coterminous with ordinary everyday reality.[3] In practice, however, the author's eccentric verbal attributions confer an arbitrariness and provisionality upon his created world that afford it an equivocal, invisible existence, located somewhere between a real and an imaginary Ghana. It is at once an actual place and an autonomous realm of pure language (a feature taken to further extremes in his second novel, *Woman of the Aeroplanes* [1988]). Thus Beni Baidoo, who spends most of his time "stuck in the oven of words," is really a metaphor for the author. His freedom to go, inexplicably, anywhere and to congregate the whole cast of characters without narrative explanation is the imaginative, obscurantist freedom of the fiction writer. His imaginary village, a thing of words only, is an ironic trope for the novel: "When I have created my village, then you can come and be creative there" (*SSC,* 104).

And yet, if Laing fabulates predominantly imagined worlds, proclaimed through self-regarding images, then these are worlds that themselves toy in unexpectedly serious ways with the very idea of imagined worlds. Societies and nations, like Baidoo and the witch Adwoa, exist both in actuality and notionally in people's minds, as themselves and as they are imagined to be. If the novel's characters are largely unaware of the surreal poetic fiction in which the author has enclosed them, then this is partly because they are themselves deeply immersed in fictions about national values, culture, and language in the country they inhabit. "I only want a little authenticity," the acolyte Osofo protests to his bishop, but Ghanaian public life appears to offer none at all. Instead there are only the National Redemption Council's pompous official fictions of "revolution and self-reliance" and slogans such as "If Ghanaians help the government, the government will help Ghanaians," which mask corrupt collusion and bribery with a facade of moral reciprocity. Equally inauthentic is the belief that materialistic imperatives hold supreme sway in the nation's life; that most Ghanaians, as Sackey puts it, would choose a Mercedes-Benz in preference to a soul and are perfectly content with the gifts of beer and food that in the novel purchase their acquiescence, respectively, in the airport debacle and on the antigovernment march. The truth is that, although they behave as if they are satisfied, they obviously are not: Kofi Loww disdains the free beer; the official who provides it later dissociates himself from the whole affair; and the marchers disperse disgruntled and disillusioned. More fantastically, during the horse stampede, the crowd is asked by the panic-stricken Okay Pol to disbelieve the evidence of its own eyes: "I must warn you all that what you are seeing here is not true . . . you must be interrogated to confirm this . . . the government needs your support . . . these are agricultural horses, to push on Operation Feed Yourself, and they will pull the plough" (*SSC,* 56). Under police pressure, the spectators are persuaded to subscribe to the triple fiction that farm horses are used in Ghana (which they are not);[4] that such horses are imported (again untrue); and that these thoroughbred racehorses are those same drays. The point of such episodes is that what is inauthentic in the popular imagination is not so much the fictions themselves as the cynical belief that charades like these are an accepted, understood part of Ghanaian life. In other words, Ghanaians have come to behave according to an idea of themselves and of how much they are willing, uncritically, to swallow; they have to be reminded that beneath these public falsehoods there are deeper and more genuine human needs and a longing for more authentic values. In the case of Okay Pol, release from the impossible contradiction between fact and official fiction is achieved only by a preposterous piece of bad faith and some disingenuous comic hyperbole: "Pol believed there was some merit in having horses for agriculture . . . and that if a few were racehorses, then you would obviously have faster farms" (*SSC,* 114). By such devices Laing demonstrates that the idea that the populace has to subscribe to fictions is itself a fiction.

According to Sackey, one fiction to which the Ghanaian intelligentsia especially subscribe is the notion that its country's experience can be polarized into the categories of "contemporary" and "traditional," "foreign" and "indigenous," or "Western" and "African." Slyly taking advantage of whatever cultural imperatives are at hand, they then proceed to be "modern" or "traditional" by turns, as convenience and expediency dictate, without making any attempt to confront or reconcile one behavioral mode with the other. By this mental dodge, claims the ebullient professor, the intellectual has internalized the contradiction between spurious alternatives, the distinction between which may be unreal:

> The Ghanaian is indestructible because he has got formed in his head, deep ravines of opposites; if he feels too hot with one being or with one presence, he just hops onto another, thousands of miles away if necessary. And there's something I find very odd: there is no territory between the supernatural and the purely factual. . . . [Y]ou get the factual explanations that do not fit superfactual situations, and you get supernatural answers that fly off at a tangent to the merely factual; and all in the usual polemical stew, with no insight at all for any salt of any worth! . . . [W]e jump, at the opportune times, into the hundreds of little pigeon-holes available in the transcultural carpenter's shop! (*SSC,* 297, 299)

The intellectual psyche thus becomes petrified in paradox and contradiction—"We can't go back, we can't go forward"—resulting in "complete inaction" and "moral abstinence." At the entrenched extremes of this world are, on the one hand, the ultramodern time-serving Dr. Boadis in their Mercedes-Benzes and, on the other, the intransigent elders of $^1/_2$-Allotey's village and Nana Esi who, defiant of Western medicine to her last breath, "turns off her own heartbeat" just before the doctor arrives. Between these rival inauthenticities lies the ordinary everyday Ghana where everything is half one thing, half another, and the foreign is being constantly indigenized, ancient practices modernized and innovations traditionalized.[5] Thus Adwoa's witchflight companion is an English sociology postgraduate; $1/2$-Allotey discovers that he must learn to "live in different centuries at once" and reapprehend traditions in completely original ways if he is to preserve whatever of value is left in them; and the reformist priest Osofo has to explain why, since he "wants so much change," he desires "to introduce so much more tradition" (*SSC,* 73, 261). For Kofi Loww, in his tortured search for authenticity, there is only "the collision of decisions or attitudes, one of which would not vanish but would move into a different relationship, a different collision.... The world was open, no matter how many cultures you shut it in, including your own" (*SSC,* 36). This desire to keep existence hybridically open and fertile with possibility, without subordinating any one alternative to another, is echoed by the village's oldest man—"We must keep that wide wide experience that finds almost nothing odd.... Change everything except the roots that do the changing!"—and by Sackey himself in his call upon the Ghanaian intellectual to "do a little crazy thinking" and exercise "the freedom available to him to create new worlds, new wholes" (*SSC,* 236–37, 300).

How these new edifices are to be built with the only tool that Sackey, a "mason of the mouth," has at his disposal—namely, words—is not altogether clear. It is evident from the demonstrators' fatuous slogan shouting that words do not change the world and are not to be confused with action. To some extent, however, the problem of how to use language to create things beyond language, and thus to fill the elliptic space after the words (presumably, the space for action), is addressed by Laing's own language in the novel. The novelty and originality of this language is not confined to the author's metaphoric adventurousness, his inventive verbal wit, or his use of neologism. *Search Sweet Country* is, as Mary Kropp Dakubu has demonstrated, a fiercely heteroglossic work, employing words from a multiplicity of languages that include Ga, Twi, Ewe, Hausa, Yoruba, Arabic, and pidgin English. Laing's Accra, she says, "is polyglot and multi-ethnic almost to the point of being non-ethnic," its adopted register being the mixed language of "a nation-in-the-making" (Dakubu, 21). The immediate effect of this multilingual rhetoric is to undermine notions of a single unitary body of national values expressed in a national language; further, it makes nonsense of attempts by the National Redemption Council or any other propagandist organ to impose a "national culture." No single character or group in the novel maintains a monopoly over language or even a competence in it (hence the many conversational misunderstandings and communication breakdowns); Laing reinforces this idea by his own added imported words and neologisms, which belong to no African ethnic group. The Ghanaian nation and the continent of which it is a microcosm are perceived to be as protean and unstable as its many imaginers and as the diverse languages and signifying modes in which their imaginings are expressed. Here lies Ghana's and Africa's real authenticity, and the heart of Laing's polemic. His remarkable first novel presents "a nation-in-the-making" through "a language-in-the-making," a medium that is still in flux and in a condition of creative turmoil. *Search Sweet Country* is a hymn to pluralism, a celebration of rampant hybridity, and, in its very openness of form, an implied challenge to the monologic discourse of totalitarian power.

One of Laing's antigovernment demonstrators has "a vision that all the dancers and marchers were tied with one sharp, thin rope, with an infinity of allowance for individual movement, yet holding, invisibly, the entire number together" (*SSC,* 275). The rope might serve as a metaphor for the author's erratic narrative invention that holds together his amorphous cast of characters through the idiosyncratic dance of language. Although this gives the impression that the novel is more tightly organized that it actually is, the novelist's quirky, mercurial personality is a keenly felt presence throughout the book, pulling it under control when it seems least to be so and keeping a shrewd polemical eye on both phony and genuine aspects of the real Ghana in which the book is earthed. By contrast, Ben Okri's *The Famished Road* (1991) is a novel of larger scale and less concentrated power, a more ambitious and diffuse work, and its absolute lyricism makes fewer concessions to social realism, although it is grounded in a worldview not very distant from Laing's.

The narrator of Okri's novel is Azaro, an *abiku,* or spirit child, whose destiny is to die repeatedly in infancy and be reborn to the same mother and who thus exists liminally "somewhere in the interspace between the spirit world and the Living."[6] His is a life that, Okri has said in interview, is "lived simultaneously at different levels of consciousness and in different territories" (Wilkinson, 83), or, as Azaro himself puts it, "Sometimes I seemed to be living several lives at once" (*FR,* 7). Azaro apprehends, communicates with, and draws power from both worlds concurrently, experiencing their rival hungers and deprivations and finding both equally real and grotesque in a bland, naïve, first-person narrative that, structurally and stylistically, refuses to subordinate one to the other. Bestriding the border of life and death in a succession of hallucinated trance states and out-of-body and near-death experiences, the abiku leads a marginal existence that finds its sociological counterpart in the precarious ghetto world. Here, teetering permanently on the edge of extinction, his parents lead lives of daily drudgery and battle for survival against overwhelming odds. In the marketplace of this transitory realm both humans and spirits come—around the time of Nigeria's independence—to transact commercial and political business; Madame Koto's Bar, where Azaro spends much of his time, is a meeting place where the rival faction leaders and their armies of thugs fraternize with animal-headed spirits. The abiku child slips erratically through invisible doorways between these worlds, which elide without warning into each other; in a series of narrative double-exposures, the child maintains a simultaneous dialogue with his earthly and spirit companions, and his biological parents and ancestral guardians.

As in Laing's book, only to a greater and more serious extent, the coterminous nature of the animate and inanimate is taken much for granted in *The Famished Road*. The contiguity of living and unliving, terrestrial and occult worlds, and of observed and dreamed phenomena, all occupying the same geographical space, are also unchallenged givens in Okri's novel, which thus draws less upon the author's own mixed Igbo and Urhobo heritage than the Yoruba worldview, commended by Soyinka for its "integrated essentiality" and "animist interfusion of all matter and consciousness" (*MLAW,* 51, 145). In this worldview, as Azaro's "Mum" puts it, "All things are linked" (*FR,* 483). The interpenetrating elements of this holistic order are not totally assimilated into one another, and neither are the respective realistic and folkloric narrative modes and the literary and oral styles in which they are presented. Yet Okri's accounts of spirit crossings dispense with transitional modifiers and demarcation points to such a degree that the parallel worlds are effectively collapsed into one another; the result is that the reader is never sure which order she or he is in at any given moment (or, indeed, which moment, since the abiku contains within himself all of his past lives and confuses spirits encountered two weeks and 500 years ago).

Azaro's extraordinary spongelike consciousness, although it is the principal focalizing agent in the book, is in fact a radically disunified, uncentered, and diffuse phenomenon; this consciousness is impossible to focus in the way that our knowledge of human beings usually is because it is engaged in a constant interchange with other forms of consciousness in a nebulous metaphysical ecosystem that encompasses human, spirit, animal, and plant life. Azaro, through his supersensory telepathic and clairvoyant powers, enters the minds of others, by turns existing in their dreams and dreaming their existence, and learns the language of animals and the wisdom of flowers. In a process of reciprocal interaction, the abiku's esoteric spirit realm, alternately idyllic and harrowing, encroaches upon and alters the material world and, in turn, takes on elements of the desperate struggle for physical survival in the jungle of the ghetto. Thus Azaro's parents find themselves struggling under the combined oppression of politicians and spirits who use parallel ploys to coerce the starving population; his father, a half-crazed, punch-drunk boxer, fights a three-way epic street battle with his political foes, a professional adversary called the Green Leopard, and the ghost of a late legendary boxing champion. Drawing upon "his curious ability to reach into deep places in his spirit" and release a "ferocious energy," "Dad" turns himself into an elemental, animist spirit (the Black Tyger) in order to fight one (the Yellow Jaguar) (FR, 470). The occult two-way traffic that issues in a regenerative expansion of the spirit for Dad leads, however, to a diminution of shamanic power in the case of Madame Koto, who uses Azaro's numinous presence to siphon off demonic energy from the spirits for the advancement of her political ambitions and materialistic greed. As she enters into corrupt conspiracies with the power-hungry Party for the Rich, her perverted spiritual powers decline in proportion to her increased temporal influence. At the end of the book she gives birth to a trio of the "worst type of spirit-children" whose selfish greed and malevolence reflect her own destructive nature (FR, 465).

The world through which the exiled Azaro trails his visionary abiku-consciousness is a place "where all forms are mutable, where all things exchange their identities" (FR, 457). Indeed, his liminal half-world is a flux of limitless, credibility-defying transformation where everything is really, or is in the process of becoming, something else; the result is that entrances and exits, endings and beginnings, and literal and figurative expression continually blur into one another. In this twilight zone of syncopated realities all Western categorisms are dispensed with. Stones cry, corpses sing, chickens speak, and mythologies do battle; winds and odors, synesthetically, change color; the famished road is forested with talking, human-headed trees; and people, zeugmatically, give off smells, hopes, and "yellow impassivity." Characters are struck blind by flowers, and their heads and limbs mutate constantly into those of animals and reptiles, their thoughts into butterflies. Alongside the customary hybrid grotesques of the Roman grotto tradition—snakes with human heads, girls with fish gills, babies with squirrel faces—there are monstrously deformed creatures with features and limbs fantastically repositioned (breasts on their backs, eyes inside their mouths), strange spirits with borrowed bits of human bodies, three-headed animals, and dwarfs who walk on their fingers. Miraculous reversals and inversions are routine functions of this unceasing metamorphosis. Blindness, Dad discovers, is really insight and illumination, and dead branches living roots; perfidy is really fidelity, disgrace triumph, and despair glory.

The obverse of this epic wonderment, with its strong echoes of folkloric magic, dream-lore, and creation myths, is, however, a harrowing social realism used to present the grinding poverty, squalor, disease, and brutality in which the hapless slum dwellers pass their days. Theirs are lives of backbreaking labor and humiliation, of ruthless exploitation by the racketeer proprietors of rat-infested hovels, and of persecution by rival thug-politicians who coerce voters by intimidation and bribes of poisoned milk and, whether of the Party for the "Rich" or the "Poor," are indistinguishable in their self-interest and indifference to the needs of the population. Azaro's trader-mother, hawking her meager wares in the market, and his laborer-father, quixotically campaigning as boxer and politician to rid the world of suffering and injustice, are Sisyphean figures, staggering under inhuman loads and waging war against unassailable odds. "A man can wander round the planet and still not move an inch," Dad informs Azaro (*FR,* 433) and reveals to him a dream of a millennial road to heaven where the builders, in a spirit of exhilarating futility, progress only two feet in a hundred years. Even then, all of the work has to be done again because each "new generation comes along and begins again from the wreckage," starting with nothing and fated to "make bigger, better mistakes" (*FR,* 330).

The questlike quality of Okri's narrative notwithstanding, these figures lack the epic stature of mythic and folktale heroes because there can be no heroes and no progress in the context of mass deprivation and total victimization that is the novel's anomic postcolonial world. It is, however, to this imperfect, permanently unfinished, world, still struggling to be achieved and always providing reasons to return to the struggle, that the abiku Azaro, in defiance of his spirit guides, compassionately commits himself: "I wanted to taste of this world, to feel it, suffer it, know it, to love it, to make a valuable contribution to it. . . . I wanted to make happy the bruised face of the woman who would become my mother" (*FR,* 5).

The effect thus engineered by Okri's densely figurative style and shifting narrative modes is of two worlds in one, and this crucially informs the ambiguity of the novel's two key motifs, the road and the abiku. The famished road trodden by Azaro is at once mundane and numinous. It is the historical track upon which the new nation-state careers aimlessly forward between a vanishing past and an unprepared future, an image of the uncertain path to independence and a dubious technological progress, and the transitional territory between life and death charted by the spirit child, linking the earthly and supernatural realms. But it is also, more vaguely, the road of imagination and struggle through the chaos and bewilderment of the postcolonial jungle, conveying the hope of transformation that, in an imperfect world, "must always have something to strive towards," even though it can never be fulfilled (*FR*, 329). "They will never finish the road that is their soul," says Dad of the millennial road builders, and later: "All roads lead to death, but some roads lead to things which can never be finished" (*FR*, 330, 498). Perhaps most important, the hungry road marks for Okri the inward visionary quest of the dreaming "soul" or creative imagination that, he has maintained, "opens towards infinity" (Wilkinson, 83): It signifies the artistic and intellectual voyager's personal journey of discovery into the multitudinous variety of existence as conceived in the Yoruba metaphysic.

The abiku who traverses the famished road is a more slippery and, finally perhaps, an aporetic symbol. At the level of political allegory the abiku's ambiguous two-way crossing between unborn and living and between living and dead may suggest the new nation's passage into either life or death. Thus the Half-Child at the end of Soyinka's play *A Dance of the Forests* (1963) may suggest either the unfulfilled promise and unknown potential of Africa's future or its postcolonial entrapment in a cycle of evils inherited from the colonial past. The same author, in his essay "Climates of Art," has posed the rival options of artistic vitality and political oppression, seeing the abiku as both "a metaphor for the phenomenon of creativity" and "an expression of doom" (*ADO*, 258). In other African writing the abiku's cycle of premature, inopportune deaths and failure to reach adulthood has been used as a metaphor for postcolonial Africa's arrested political development, the aborted hopes of nationalism, and the failure of democracy to outlive independence. Thus in Armah's *The Beautyful Ones Are Not Yet Born* Africa's neocolonial regimes are presented as an encycled series of short-lived spirit children who are doomed to repeat the past until they can learn to confront and resist it, therefore preventing their condition from becoming endemic. Certainly there are a number of elements in Okri's novel—the permanently unfinished road and its repeated mistakes, the postponement and nonoccurrence of the much advertised political rally, the vagaries of the period setting—that suggest the infinite deferral of political maturity and true independence. At the end of the book the author at least pays lip service to the idea of the abiku as a trope by which the political paralysis of the new nation-state might be understood. Okri, however, makes some noticeable departures from the conventional model.

First, far from symbolizing the disappointed expectations of human history, Okri's abiku defines himself in opposition to them—"We disliked the rigours of existence, the unfulfilled longings, the enshrined injustices of the world" (FR, 3)—and serves as a yardstick by which the world's failings are measured. Thus Dad's ghetto banquet, where the food shortage and "the betrayed promise of an abundant feast" are images of broken political pledges, is placed against the plenitude of the spirit world "where feasting knows no end" (FR, 44, 48). Nevertheless, although acting as a touchstone for the miseries and misfortunes of the human world, it is his responsibilities toward this world that Azaro, in the teeth of pressure and persecution from his spirit mentors, finally acknowledges and embraces. For this abiku uses what volition he has to choose not death, in the customary manner, but life. Okri's critical reevaluation of the myth results in a reverse-abiku who decides to break the preordained cycle of birth and death and to remain with the earthly parents for whom he has developed a deep affection. Azaro, in fact, has none of the abiku's customary demonic willpower and sadistic delight in maternal torment, as exhibited in Soyinka's poem "Abiku"(although this supernatural malevolence may be the misperception of human eyes);[7] even on the occasions when he slips back into his spirit condition the sense of menace and foreboding usually present at the crossing of numinous thresholds is replaced by exhilaration at access to a magical and marvelous world, an alternative mode of being in which everything is in a constant turmoil of transformation.

Most important, as an alternative to defeatism and despair of the world expressed by the abiku's departure from it, Azaro's commitment to the living seems to Okri to signify a defiant assertion of faith in Africa's material survival and betterment, no matter how difficult the circumstances and how great the suffering. "Africa has an incredible capacity to not die and not be destroyed," he has observed, commending the continent's "great dreaming capacities" and "resilience of spirit" (Wilkinson, 87). Through the device of the spirit child, postcolonial Africa appears to be envisaged as a resilient survivalist, a latter-day Lazarus who keeps coming back from the dead when the modern world has given him up; eventually, by throwing in his lot with humanity, the spirit child outgrows his resurrectionary identity (thus his name is shortened from the original "Lazaro"). Hence, while the traditional abiku, Azaro's friend Ade, takes the "road of our refusal to be," Azaro himself opts for "the liberty of limitations" (FR, 487) and walks the famished road of life, the camino *real*, resolving not to be devoured by its tribulations.

There are, however, problems with reading Azaro as a triumph of willpower and determined optimism. His expression of faith notwithstanding, he is throughout the novel a peculiarly passive and powerless character who performs very few actions, most of them inconsequential, and his shifts from human to spirit realm and back are quite arbitrary and involuntary, dictated by narrative movements that are indifferent to his own desires. Azaro is chiefly, in fact, an awareness and a mode of perception for most of the book, a presence rather than an agent. As Quayson has argued, he exists to convey the dual essence of the abiku, the texture of its fundamental being, "his peculiar condition [being] to see the recurrence of things within the flux of existence"—that is, the extent to which reality is left basically unchanged by events (Quayson, 153). Thus it is not surprising that Azaro is not especially invigorated or regenerated, as in a rite of passage, by his sojourns in the spirit world (it is never clear, in any case, exactly if and when he is in it), and that his ultimate entrapment in the abiku's metaphysical condition of powerless recurrence is explicitly allegorized, at the end of the book, into a fatalistic vision of Africa's abortive postcolonial history:

> Things that are not ready, not willing to be born or to become, things for which adequate preparations have not been made to sustain their momentous births, things that are not resolved, things bound up with failure and with fear of being, they all keep recurring, keep coming back, and in themselves partake of the spirit-child's condition. They keep coming and going till their time is right. History itself fully demonstrates how things of the world partake of the condition of the spirit-child.
>
> It shocked him [Dad] that ours too was an abiku nation, a spirit-child nation, one that keeps being reborn and after each birth come blood and betrayals, and the child of our will refuses to stay till we have made propitious sacrifice. (FR, 487, 494)

This explanatory stiffening into allegory may, perhaps, be a concession by the author to the literal-minded materialists among his readers, but it takes the abiku, problematically, back into familiar tropological territory.

Okri is widely regarded as one of the most multicultural and cosmopolitan of the younger generation of African novelists. His Yoruba paradigm, although culturally encoded, includes interethnically, in its use by a non-Yoruba author, the whole of Africa's and (by implication) the world's people in an ethic of resilient hope and renaissance. Meanwhile, on the stylistic front, his free-floating poetic figurations and free-wheeling narrative invention have been linked with Western postmodernism and South American writers such as Borges and Márquez. These features have not been seen unilaterally as virtues, however, and certainly not by Adewale Maja-Pearce, who narrows Okri's hybrid eclecticism to a matter of literary influence alone and dismisses *The Famished Road* as an inferior imitation of Latin American "magic realism" and "a tedious exercise in the fantastic for its own sake" (Maja-Pearce, 102–3). The response to this kind of criticism, by both the author and his apologists, has been that the spirit world of the novel is not an imaginary mythic, metaphorical, or parabolic construct after the fashion of the magic realists; neither is it a surrealist fantasy, as in the folkloric dream-narratives of Amos Tutuola, where the fantastic events occur only in a hallucinated esoteric realm sharply differentiated from the real world. Rather, it is a reality in its own right, an actuality that is itself fantastical, in which the dead are still alive, the marvelous takes place in the ordinary, and the supernatural is an accepted part of everyday life. In this single, seamless order of being all matter inheres with a spirit potential that manifests itself in erratic shifts of contour, substance, and genus, so that the human figures match the spirits in the bizarre and grotesque. Azaro does not allegorically interpret this paranormal world but simply describes it, and its validity is never questioned. Okri has strenuously denied that he set out to produce strange or fantastical effects: "All I'm trying to do is write about the world from the worldview of that place so that it is true to the characters. . . . It's a kind of realism, but a realism with many more dimensions."[8]

Azaro's narrative is thus intended not as a mythopoetic projection of other or imagined worlds but as a realistic representation of a world that palpably exists, conceived from within an indigenous belief system. His occupancy of the eyes of a "magic animal, looking out for a brief moment into the reality that it saw" (*FR,* 464), is an analogue of the honorary insider's view of the culture given temporarily to the reader. To relocate this spiritual, psychic naturalism in the order of mythopoetics, as some commentators have done,[9] or to displace it into allegoric or symbolic discourse, as the author partly does in the book's finale, is to unhitch the narrative from its realistic moorings and to dilute the strength of its informing indigenous worldview. Maja-Pearce's criticism, however, is based as much on formal as on intellectual grounds. His objection, he explains, is not to "the manifestations of the fantastic as part of everyday reality, but that such manifestations are divorced from the language of the narrative itself," so that there is "no organic connection between language and event" and the fabulous transformations are merely random, unintegrated effects, produced mainly *for* effect (Maja-Pearce, 102). The obvious response to this is that in *The Famished Road* language, supremely, *is* the narrative. "Effects" and "events" form a single register, and the book's verbal momentum derives not from any story element but from its poetic ideas and novelty of incident, neither of which are purely decorative. There is, moreover, ample precedent for this and for Okri's spiral narrative structures and repetitive rhetoric in the African literary sources and influences with which he maintains a highly visible intertextual dialogue in the novel: notably, Tutuola's dream-narratives *The Palm-Wine Drinkard* (1952) and *My Life in the Bush of Ghosts* (1954); Soyinka's *A Dance of the Forests;* and D. O. Fagunwa's *The Forest of a Thousand Daemons* (1968).

Nevertheless, Maja-Pearce's impatience with Okri's novel is partly understandable. *The Famished Road* is bravura experimental writing that errs seriously on the side of excess. Although the stupendous force of its author's poetic imagination and verbal invention and the brilliance of his imagery cannot be denied, it is to be doubted whether his surging lyricism is really suited to the epic form. In the course of a narrative 500 pages long, his surreal tropology, although itself unwearied, begins to weary the reader and, as Maja-Pearce claims, becomes turgid. The problem with the book's endless spectacular mutations is twofold, involving its philosophical vision and aesthetic form. The nature and function of the abiku, as we have seen, is to register the recurrence of things, the essential conditions of being that are not subject to history, and Azaro himself proves powerless to change anything in the order of things. The result is that the unceasing transformations, no matter how sensational, are cyclical in character, emphasizing the ultimate futility of the abiku's progress, and in effect are not transformations at all since, after all the changes, things remain much the same. Meanwhile, in the form of the book, this unavailing change is itself unchanging and is responsible for the note of weary sameness that the novel exudes. Okri explains that to make something good come out of art "you have to liberate it from old kinds of perception" (Wilkinson, 81), and in the novel he repeatedly emphasizes the need to keep the doors of perception ajar. "We must look at the world with new eyes," says Dad, and "KEEP THE ROAD OPEN" (*FR*, 498, 484). The drawback to this, however, is that after a while the constant *re*sensitization of the perceptual apparatus by marvel and wonder leads, through sheer repetition, to a *de*sensitization of vision, a blunting of responsiveness, and the process of renewal, paradoxically, becomes so jaded that it leaves nothing new. Azaro lives permanently at the pitch of transition, where the feelings and sensitivities are highly charged and the mind is illumined by danger, but unrelenting crisis (or novelty, or anything) becomes tiresome, and the monotonous metamorphosis becomes a habit and a mannerism, a literary equivalent of virtual reality, made commonplace by overfamiliarization.

Azaro's simultaneous experience of earthly and supernatural events makes him keenly receptive to the sheer wonderment of existence, enabling him to live "in a state of perpetual astonishment" (*FR*, 327). What is portent and miracle for his rarefied consciousness, however, is often merely bizarre and inconsequential for the reader; hence the inconsequential and merely incidental assume momentous, incongruous proportions in the novel, and it seems at times that Okri is trying to make an artistic virtue out of incoherence. He has, in fact, said that "the novel moves towards infinity" and is written "against the perception of the world as being coherent and therefore readable as a text" (Wilkinson, 83, 85). But what is true for his protagonist at the metaphysical level—that "it may be easier to live with the earth's boundaries than to be free in infinity" (*FR*, 487)—is arguably also true, at the hermeneutical level, for the human reader, who perhaps cannot bear very much infinity or incoherence. Okri has said in another interview that reality can have "a completely different face" when "turned slightly" another way.[10] Accordingly, his characters spend much of their time, in Azaro's phrase, "stepping into distorted mirrors." But the outcome is that their faces, turned too many ways, acquire such a confusing superabundance of features that they are, paradoxically, rendered featureless. In an all-inclusive, holistic universe, where "all things are linked" and everything is really something else, nothing is finally anything. The obverse of total integration and interpenetrative unity is nihilism. The defining contours of identity dissolve, turning the oneness into a sameness, and the links between the book's disparate images—rivers and highways, dreams and hunger, nation and road building, political stasis and abikus—become too tenuous to be meaningful in any interpretative way.

In addition, Okri's political vision is not without its problems. For his generation, too young to have experienced the euphoria of independence, political disillusionment has been much deeper and more grievous than for the older generation of writers. Whereas the latter expressed shock and dismay at the brutality, injustice, and corruption of contemporary Africa, these are regarded, albeit not complacently, as the givens of the postcolonial condition by Okri, who has none of the older writers' faith in remedial political action and improved leadership. Instead, there is in his writing an inward movement away from protest and polemic and toward interior psychic healing; there is also a visionary introjection of the world into the artistic consciousness that places a tremendous emphasis on the redemptive energies of dream, myth, and the imagination. Okri describes myth as "what makes it possible for those who suffer and struggle, whatever the suffering, to live and sleep and carry on" and proceeds to locate a society's "dreams and its myths and its perception of reality" in the "inviolate ... area of the African consciousness" that has remained immune to "the effect of colonialism" (Wilkinson, 85, 86).

Meanwhile, in the novel the renegade abikus take a perverse glory in the imperfections of the world insofar as the latter energize these self-same dreams and myths and foster hopeful imaginings in the mind's pursuit of perfection: "They wanted to know the essence of pain, they wanted to suffer ... and to be imperfect in order to always have something to strive towards" (FR, 329). The more hard-bitten political pragmatists among Okri's critics might reply that what contemporary Africa seeks is in fact not perfection but survival; moreover, it searches for survival not of colonialism and its hangovers but of brutal postcolonial dictatorships, none of which are likely to be much moved by the vague millennial utopianisms of Ade and Dad: "And when people least expect it a great transformation is going to take place in the world. . . . A wonderful change is coming from far away and people will realise the great meaning of struggle and hope. . . . A single thought of ours could change the universe. . . . We can redream this world and make the dream real" (FR, 478, 497, 498). Okri has warned that "one shouldn't offer hope cheaply" (Wilkinson, 88), yet he appears determined in such passages to wrench a desperate last-ditch optimism from the despair of the postcolonial situation by looking for succor and redemption to the "inviolate" part of the African psyche that fosters such dreaming. The result is the notion that the human spirit can somehow reclaim and repossess the world by inwardly "redreaming" it, casually subsuming its horrors and evils in a bland metaphysical idealism; it is the idea that the altered forms of perception and understanding thus engendered can be grounds for radical social transformation and the creation of genuine independence. The logic of this process is not worked out in the text of Okri's narrative, however, and, in the absence of any close political analysis, the victories of Dad (and the African people whom he represents) over corruption and persecution remain at the moral and spiritual level, being little more than ineffectual hopeful gestures.

Azaro's concluding words, "A dream can be the highest point of a life" (FR, 500), are appropriately ambiguous, leaving unclear whether the dream is a heightened form, and the highest point, of perception, or, ironically, the best that we can hope for and all that we are ever likely to have. For Okri, redemptive energy is finally not a political but a purely visionary, imaginative quality, and the reader can be forgiven for seeing Azaro as an image of literary self-absorption, a figure for the romantic artist's solipsistic immersion in a world of his own making. When its problematic political contexts trouble this introversion, the novel falls back too easily on the merely portentous. In the spirit lands, says Mum, "our ancestors ask one another impenetrable riddles all day long," and Dad comments that "life is full of riddles that only the dead can answer" (FR, 480, 40). Using the device of the abiku, who exists in infinity, outside of time, the narrative affects to look on the human world through the eyes of the dead while denying the reader access to their understanding of what they see:

> "From a certain point of view the universe appears to be composed of paradoxes. But everything resolves. That is the function of contradiction."
> "I don't understand."
> "When you see everything from every imaginable point of view you might begin to understand."
> "Can you?"
> "No." (FR, 327)

Faced with the humanly unknowable and impossible, the reader is too often counseled to suspend interpretation of what she or he is reading, and in the ensuing hermeneutical hiatus the novel takes refuge in a facile agnosticism and glib throwaway mysticism in which irritating gimcrack and riddling elements appear to be indulged and cultivated, quite gratuitously, for their own sake.

"In the beginning there was a river," the novel begins. "The river became a road and the road branched out to the whole world. And because the road was once a river it was always hungry" (*FR*, 3). Certainly, the idiosyncratic riverine road through Okri's enchanted forest, never famished of poetic resources, carried the African novel into the 1990s with an inventive exuberance hitherto unknown in the form, albeit along routes that accentuated his status as an eccentric, untypical figure in contemporary Nigerian fiction. The sequel to *The Famished Road,* discussed briefly in the next chapter, indicated no new turning, however, and after some 800 pages of phantasmagoric metamorphosis tempered by hopeful millennial effusions, Okri's superhighway began to look as if it had run itself into a cul-de-sac or was, indeed, more appropriately imaged as a river that goes repetitively, incestuously around upon itself without ever breaking out into the open sea.

Chapter Ten
Prospective: Into the Nineties

The 1990s have seen a number of significant developments in the African novel. There has been an explosion of fiction from the new multicultural South Africa and a continuing flow of novels from Zimbabwe, particularly from younger writers of Chinodya's generation. In this decade the African woman writer has acquired a more prominent profile. The white South African novelist Nadine Gordimer won the Nobel Prize for Literature in 1991, and there have been some groundbreaking works by black African women writers. In *Gwendolen* (1990) the Nigerian Buchi Emecheta tackles taboo themes of child abuse and incest. In her Commonwealth Prize-winning novel *Changes* (1991), the Ghanaian Ama Ata Aidoo deals with the consequences of marital rape, which concept does not exist and for which there are no words in the heroine's indigenous language. She presents in seriocomic form a misconceived attempt to transform a Western-style extramarital affair between autonomous individuals into a traditional polygamous marriage approved by the whole kinship group. In her poetic novel *Nehanda* (1993), the Zimbabwean Yvonne Vera celebrates the ancestral spirit of the land as a source of popular struggle through a life of the legendary martyr of the 1896 Chimurenga. Much recent fiction has broadened links with world literature and international culture; other works have intensified, some narrowly, around specifically African concepts of identity. Continuing developments in the genre—formal, cultural, political—are many and diverse, and it is not my intention in this stocktaking chapter to try to focus what is still in flux but rather to briefly revisit, one or two decades later, some of the writers who have appeared in these pages and to glance at selected significant works by others who have not.[1]

Since *Season of Anomy* (1973), Wole Soyinka's creative prose has included no further fiction, only memoirs and autobiographical faction, and Yambo Ouologuem's long-announced sequel to *Bound to Violence* (1971) has never appeared. After their respective postmodernist experimentation in *Foe* (1986) and *Maps* (1986), both J. M. Coetzee and Nuruddin Farah returned to realism, albeit with a hard symbolic edge. In *Age of Iron* (1990) Coetzee presents the imminent death of white society, allegorically, through the figure of a white Cape Town academic dying of cancer. In Farah's *Gifts* (1992), written under the shadow of the Somali catastrophe of the early 1990s, a love story unfolds against the backdrop of international aid to the famine-struck Horn of Africa, and a symbolic foundling child—Allah's gift—is a locus for the exploration of the complex psychology of donorship and its binding ties and dependencies.[2] M. G. Vassanji left Africa behind to deal with the Asian migrant experience in Canada in his second novel, *No New Land* (1992), but returned to it in *The Book of Secrets* (1995). In this intricate, multilayered novel a British colonial officer's First World War diary of Euro-African relations in Tanganyika, discovered by an Asian in postindependence Tanzania, is a prism through which is refracted East Africa's complex multiracial history and a basis for a philosophical inquiry into what can actually be known about the past.

In the 1990s the Ghanaians Kofi Awoonor and Ayi Kwei Armah returned to fiction after 20-year absences, with mixed results. Awoonor's second novel, *Comes the Voyager At Last* (1992), contains three parallel narratives. The first narrator is a poor black American whose 1950s' experiences fall into the familiar pattern of social deprivation, wrongful arrest, and imprisonment, followed by conversion to Black Islam and a return to Africa. The second narrator is a garrulous and facetious Ghanaian intellectual and poet-broadcaster cloned from Awoonor's own public career. After the American, now called Brother Lumumba, has knifed the African friend of a white expatriate in a nightclub brawl, the unnamed Ghanaian spirits him away to his native village in Eweland where, in a sentimental ending, he is adopted back into the ancestral African fold. In the novel's climactic vision of universal harmony, its twin-narratives of return—the American Negro's to Africa and the Westernized African intellectual's to his native roots—converge in the black American's dream-consciousness and link up with a third narrative, that of a mythic southward journey of a slave caravan from desert to coast, which is interspersed with the primary narratives throughout the book in a series of bardic interludes. The tensions between the Ghanaian's flippant, sophisticated cynicism and the raw racial polemics of the naïve American visitor are too well defined, however, for their sudden assertion of solidarity in the murder scene to be entirely plausible; when Brother Lumumba, during his initiation into village life, discovers in his race-memory a mystic rapport with African ritual behavior and instinctively embraces his lost heritage, the novel lapses into a shallow, simplistic negritude. In the book's conclusion, the personal and mythic narratives, and the nuclear and racial family reunions, coincide too contrivedly, and Awoonor's treatment of race retrieval in the American context, unaided by the visionary poetic lyricism of his earlier *This Earth, My Brother* . . . (1971), is generally disappointing.

Ayi Kwei Armah's *Osiris Rising* (1995) is a richer, more impressive work than Awoonor's and is a more convincing account of a black American returning to African roots. The novel transposes the Osiris myth to modern Africa where Set, the principle of evil, is represented by a state security chief, Osiris's life force by the radical creative challenge of an educational reformer, and Isis, the symbol of restoration and continuity, by a young Afro-American history professor who comes to Africa in search of "creative beginnings" denied her in her own country. In an unnamed West African neocolony the American, Ast, goes in search of Asar, an intellectual leader and former lover from her undergraduate days; he is using his position as a college lecturer to revolutionize the nation's educational curriculum in an attempt to liberate African intelligence from Eurocentric learning systems. In his revised syllabus, colonial history and literature are replaced by their African counterparts, the study of Ancient Egypt is reinstated at the center of African history, and hierarchic models of traditional society are challenged by democratic alternatives such as the classless, antislave, secret societies whose ancient regenerative symbol of the ankh, or looped cross—an egalitarian ellipse opposed to the hierarchic pyramid of power—is a recurring motif in the book. The redesigning of the educational system is underlain by the broad political aims of seeding a long term social revolution in Africa and reunifying the dismembered continent's neocolonial nation-states.

Ast becomes involved with Asar's radical group and is interrogated by his bitter rival, the sinister security director Seth, at his million-dollar high-tech security fortress built on the edge of a city with open sewers, potholed roads, and intermittent electricity and water supplies. Unable to recruit Ast as a spy and also failing to rape her, Seth proceeds to build up a file of faked evidence against Asar; with the aid of an expatriate academic informer and a black American ex-civil-rights activist turned bogus religious leader, he then frames Asar on charges of subversion. Returning from an up-country boat trip, Asar is lured into a trap by the security forces, and as his boat explodes in a hail of bullets, he is literally torn apart, like his mythic prototype, and blown out into the water in "fourteen starry fragments."[3] His nebulous apotheosis as martyr may offer little practical hope for the future, and the book ends bleakly, with the evil Seth hissing another invitation to Ast to come to him. The symbolism of Osiris's unrecovered part (his penis) suggests, however, that Asar's regenerative energy lives posthumously on in Ast and that she, the Isis figure in the fable, will assume the mantle of leadership and thus ensure her beloved's political resurrection. Moreover, the title of the last chapter, "Dwat" ("morning"), encodes a reference to the daily celestial rebirth of Osiris in the constellation of Orion; thus, although its action ends with his death, the novel closes, symbolically, with Osiris rising.

Armah's novel is only partly a personal story. He is concerned here to explore the real, albeit limited, options for change open to Africa's inventive and radical thinkers and the forms that group initiatives might take in a neocolonial world where the power abuses of dictatorial regimes have made moral issues irrelevant to the lives of their people. The abstract communalist rhetoric and cultural polemics of *Two Thousand Seasons* (1973) and *The Healers* (1978) are thus put on a more concrete and personal footing, and the fifth-grove guerrillas and healing conclaves of those works updated to the 1990s. During the ideological debates on new systems and initiatives, however, the dialogue, although spiced with humor, struggles to maintain an authentic conversational idiom, and the novel's handling of the personal risks run by radicals and rebels is curiously lacking in dramatic incident, psychological intensity, and emotional tension. Ast punctures Asar's virtuous altruistic idealism with her personal sorrow only once in the book, bursting into tears when he blithely refuses to let fear of death paralyze his future plans—"It won't matter which of us they kill if we do our work well" (*OR*, 165)—and it is only at the end of the book, as Asar is lured to his expected death, that her cool anxiety finally quickens into real human panic.

Osiris Rising also suffers from its author's continuing polarization of his African elite into mediocre, sterile power-functionaries on the one hand and visionary intellectual bystanders, potent with creative energy, on the other—that is, into those who sell out and those who opt out. It is also handicapped by his simplistic reduction of the complex historical struggle between revolutionary and reactionary forces in postcolonial Africa to the private rivalries of individual personalities. It is clear from what Seth reveals to Ast that he does not take Asar seriously as a political threat: He targets the other man, cynically, because he is jealous of his superior moral and intellectual qualities, none of which he can understand. Asar and Seth, although products of the same social and educational systems, live in separate worlds, free from inner conflicts and in mutual incomprehension of each other's values. The reader looks in vain for either an honest intellectual who flirts with temptation or a member of the power establishment with one touch of regret or remorse. Seth is quite without conscience over his murder of Asar, his sole desire being the acquisition of power over what is still unattainable—the Afro-American woman whom he cannot bully or buy into submission. In fact, neither Asar—with his chronic "lack of self-protective realism" (*OR*, 117) and his foolish faith in his immunity to Seth's machinations—nor Seth, who allows his personal paranoia to override his perception that Asar is no stager of coups but a worker for gradual change, is quite believable. A question mark is also left hanging over Asar's ill-defined conclave of intellectual guerrillas that, like the ancient, secret society of the ankh on which it is based, appears by turns to be a collection of reformers working legitimately within the existing structure, a propaganda-disseminating interest and action group, and an underground political movement with militant connections. The underworld mythology of Osiris leans toward the latter reading, but this is not actualized at the narrative level; here Asar's ignorance of the dynamics of power and his vagueness about what kind of power, if any, is to be exercised in the new order appear somewhat unrealistic in the context of modern Africa. *Osiris Rising* is subtitled "a novel of Africa past, present and future." As the twenty-first century dawns upon Armah's Africa, however, the forces of the future—automation, information technology, computerized surveillance—are all enlisted in the service of reaction and repression, culminating in the cybernetic monstrosities of Seth's Space Age Security labyrinth, whereas the supposedly creative, inventive spirits look for inspiration to the cult societies of the African past.

The novels of the Nigerian Ben Okri and the Ghanaian Kojo Laing inhabit an altogether more hybridized and heterogeneous world, and their portentous, often perplexing, talents have developed apace. In *Songs of Enchantment* (1993), the sequel to *The Famished Road* (1991), Okri continues the story of the abiku Azaro and his hovering, hallucinatory existence "in the middle space between the living and the dead."[4] Once again, the contiguity of spirit and substance, dream and reality, and imagined and perceived phenomena are the accepted givens of the book, requiring no defense or explanation. As the punch-drunk pugilist and prophet "Dad" puts it, "Everything is alive," or, as his abiku son tells him, "All things are linked" (*SOE*, 58, 222).

Songs of Enchantment is, however, a more thematically structured work than its predecessor. In this work the monotonous metamorphosis is periodically relieved by grand controlling images that attract to themselves radial complexes of meaning and nuance. Chief among these crystallizing foci is the figure of the jackal-headed masquerade. This is a creature of many hermeneutical heads, although it appears primarily to signify the naked aggression and brute political will of totalitarian power that, whether it be of the "Party of the Rich" or the "Party of the Poor," spreads itself contagiously through everything with the same intimidating menace. "It was not one mind, but many; a confluence of minds": Even Azaro inhabits the jackal's skull and looks out through its eyes, entering "the universal mind of all evil things" (SOE, 114). Among the book's other intellectual centers is Madame Koto's bar, a haven for both ancestral spirits and slumming political elites and a ready-made allegory of cultural transition. These intellectual hubs include of course Azaro himself, the serial spirit child whose repeated deaths and rebirths gather a number of interpretative threads: ideas of cosmic reincarnation, the doomed colonial-postcolonial cycle of Africa's historical destruction, and the failure of nationalist idealism and democratic ideology to survive political independence.

In his second abiku novel Okri tempers his savage picture of oppression with a number of redemptive, ambitiously hopeful, gestures and resolutions. Azaro explains that his narrative is full of "lives that must be redeemed, sufferings that must be transformed into wonders," and his father waxes prophetic about "the continents of our hidden possibilities, about the parts of us facing inwards in the direction of infinity" (SOE, 289). We need, he says, to bring the visionary into the visible world "and so create a kingdom of serenity and beauty on earth" (SOE, 289). This task, it transpires, falls to "the luminous jugglers of dreams and those who manage to be escape-artists from the hell of our accumulated negative perceptions," the ones who create "realities" with their "thoughts" (SOE, 290). In the last chapter there is a Jungian gathering of these "wise spirits" from all ages who move temporarily from their adventures in infinity to an earthly realm that cries out "for more vision, more transformation, and the birth of a new cycle of world justice" (SOE, 295). All of this, however, begs the question of exactly where, if anywhere, this utopian projection occurs except in the inward-facing consciousness of the appropriately named "escape-artist" and how it translates into present political justice. The artist's visionary ability to inwardly "redream" the world and absorb it into one of his own making seems to have been mistaken for an act of political salvaging, and the essentially sublimatory and consolatory view of art that emerges—that the artist's vision can transcend even the worst sufferings—is pitifully unequal to the world of violent political oppression in which it has to earn its currency.

"Your story isn't going anywhere," Azaro's mother tells his father, who replies: "A story is not a car. It is a road, and before that it was a river, a river that never ends" (SOE, 266). The first indications of a diversion from this circular route are glimpsed in Okri's most recent work, the short novel *Astonishing the Gods* (1995). The book's unnamed protagonist discovers, on learning to read, that he is "invisible," in the sense of being absent from the history books, and journeys to an island where everyone, like himself, is invisible and nameless. But the trope of invisibility for the oral person's absence or marginalization in a literate culture is a deliberately false lead. The hero's pursuit of "the secret of visibility" turns out actually to be a spiritual quest for that supreme invisibility at the heart of which lie the numinous and mysterious, the "something divine" that, for Okri, constitutes the visionary essence of human reality.[5] "The good things," says the narrator, "should be visible, but the best things should be hidden" (*ATG*, 65).

Astonishing the Gods is, in fact, a metaphysical inquiry, by turns playful and abstruse, into the nature of the relations between mental and material phenomena, meaning and being, names and things, word and world. The protagonist's island guide tells him, "names have a way of making things disappear. . . . Things die a little when we name them" (*ATG*, 6). The almost solipsistic sovereignty of mind over matter implied by the style of narration in the abiku novels is here given more explicit philosophical statement. The island's invisible inhabitants simply *think* buildings into construction—magical marble edifices studded with gold, diamonds, and stained glass—and intone landscapes into existence. The awestruck hero is caught up in the usual succession of miraculous metamorphoses; as in Okri's two previous books, the world into which the enchanted pilgrim is projected is a harsh, authoritarian place where justice is severe and the initiate is purgatorially tested by suffering so that, like the perfect "invisibles," he may learn how to transcend it. However, the intellectual extrapolations from the abiku consciousness are stated more boldly here, carrying echoes of Emersonian transcendentalism, Sufism and 1960s' mysticism, and the religious and prophetic material of T. S. Eliot's later poetry and C. S. Lewis's Narnian novels: "He felt the world was telling him to stop looking, for then he would see beyond; to stop thinking, for then he would comprehend . . . then he would find the truest grace" (*ATG*, 39). The originality of *Astonishing the Gods,* however, does not lie in the actual ideas that are advanced. What is new is the spirit of intellectual inquiry itself, the theoretical inquisition at the core of the poetic exotica and the brio with which it is conducted. What most delights, perhaps, in this short work is the occasionally Barthean *jouissance* in the probing of the limits of language, the exposure of the essential unmeaningness and powerful incommunicability of reality: "Things are what they are. That is their power.... If they meant something they would be less.... It is only mystery which keeps things alive" (*ATG*, 11). This new speculative element is a distinctive development in Okri's work and marks at least an interesting turning point, if no major change in direction.

Like Okri, Kojo Laing has continued to mine the fantastical vein of his first two works, and his comic futuristic extravaganza *Major Gentl and the Achimota Wars* (1992) is his most bizarre book to date. In the year 2020 A.D. Europe has retreated into a cyberworld of computerized emblems and virtual reality, in which physical existence and experiential learning have become unnecessary and have been abandoned, along with "language and humanity," to the poorer countries.[6] The cybernetic superpowers, who communicate with each other through exclusive secret codes, have declared Africa to be irrelevant to the modern world and humanly expendable, useful only as storage space, a nuclear sanctuary, a toxic dumping ground, and an experimental germ-and-genetic laboratory. Direct wars, like all direct experience, are now obsolete. Instead, there are computer-coded conflicts with invisible foes and instant replays of simulated, satellite-videoed holocausts. In addition and more traditionally, there are propagandist image wars in which Africa is reduced to a newsreel of famine and primitive degradation by powers who no longer bother to seek knowledge of the continent other than that which they themselves have created. Laing's satiric point is, of course, that for Europe Africa has always existed in a state of virtual reality or, as one character puts it, "the thingness of Africa is the headness of somewhere else" (*MG*, 65).

In one such war, the First War of Existence, the city, country, and continent surrounding the Accra suburb of Achimota have mysteriously disappeared, apparently dematerialized by Western Internet Warriors who, as part of their push to get out of the galaxy, have siphoned off the Achimotans' cerebral energy into cyber- and outer space through brainwave transmissions, erasing place names, cultural traditions, and history. This ingenious trope suggests simultaneously the African brain drain and the continent's omission from the global data network, which means that, informationally, it ceases to exist (the technocratic superpowers who build the information highways also decide where they run). It takes a Second War of Existence for the city to recover its lost country and continent and their missing populations, who were unaware that they had been virtualized, and for that part of the planet that prides itself on never having "ceased to be human" (*MG,* 105) to reassert its right to existence—human, political, artistic—independently of Europe's degrading images of it.

Inevitably, the virtualization of reality rubs off on the Achimotans themselves and opens up rich veins of comic fantasy and wordplay that are the dynamo of the book. In hyperreality "no one is supposed to die very much" (*MG,* 68). The war for Achimota fought by the eponymous hero and his evil archrival, the Italian South African neocolonial agent Torro, is a joke, a fairytale affair in which soldiers move simultaneously forward and sideways, fight on without their heads, and are disciplined for allowing themselves to be killed too easily. Laing's comic phantasmagoria also includes a children's toffee war, horsedrawn helicopters that baffle the enemy by always traveling on the same spot, and a Commander Zero who is a collection of the city's shadows and does nothing except replace his soldiers by thousands of carrot-cultivating rabbits. Laing's whimsical rejoinder to the West's Star Wars and Space Invaders is an army of vegetable cybernauts led by belligerent bananas and pugnacious pineapples. In the climactic, farcical "Wet War," the terrible Torro, who is so virtualized that he needs a computer to map the route of his food from fork to mouth, employs subaqueous cybernetics to bombard Gentl with fruit.

The burlesque sci-fi plot, however, is—like all Laing's plots—a distracting vehicle and figurative device. Laing is really fighting cultural wars in cyberspace. When the fantasy threatens to become too frivolous, it is shored up by serious polemics about spiritually truncated Europeans trapped in "the one-way streets of the universe" (*MG,* 166) and needing aid from the holistic consciousnesses that they are bent on destroying. In *Major Gentl* the Western cybercrats have externalized mind into sheer brain power, bereft of any broad human, moral intelligence capable of perceiving its products. As Africa's standard setters, it is the task of the Achimotans to make intelligence human and consciousness whole again by reestablishing direct contact with organic reality.

Underlying Laing's poetic whimsies of ecologically holistic armies (comprising humans, animals, insects, vegetables, and fruit) are ideas about the whole phenomenon of being, the limits of human consciousness, and the need for a "type of living that had sympathy, power and creation as well as harmony" (*MG*, 165). An important part of Laing's polemic is, as in his first novel, his concern with language. His hybridic interspersal of words from African, European, and invented languages, which results in some mannered, virtuoso word games and polyglot punning, is motivated by a desire "to internationalise the English" and "create one gigantic language" (author's foreword) by opening up parochial parts of the English-speaking world to more expansive possibilities. Surrealist comedy is a daring choice of vehicle for cultural polemic, which sometimes fails to gel with the poetic fantasy. Nevertheless, *Major Gentl* is a witty, provocative work that, in its pioneering importation of cybernetics and hyperreality into African fiction, more than justifies Africa's claim to a place in the modern world that the villains of the tale try desperately to deny.

Before concluding this survey I wish to notice novels by three previously unmentioned writers whose works suggest interesting new directions, starting with the young Nigerian writer 'Biyi Bandele-Thomas. In his first novel, *The Man Who Came In from the Back of Beyond* (1991), Bandele-Thomas presents modern Nigeria as a sprawling, anomic, devastated landscape in which destruction is absolute. After her husband's death from tuberculosis, a mother ends her days as a mad vagrant preying on rubbish heaps, her sons executed criminals and alcoholic suicides, her daughter a prostitute. Corporate responsibility at the state level is as missing as family solidarity at the domestic one. Corpses rot in gutters. Laws that are no respectors of starving citizens are implemented by police who do not care what crimes the indigent resort to to pay their taxes. In one scene of surreal horror, the skeletons of the anonymous poor—victims of road accidents and quack abortionists—are dragged from makeshift congested graves by rabid dogs and trundled to the doors of nearby houses. In this brutish nightmare world anything is possible, nothing surprises—and, in one sense, this is as it should be.

The events in the preceding paragraph are the contents of an autobiographical tale of woe recounted by the character Maria, whose narrative is actually part of the fictional yarn of the extraordinary adventures of the anarchist-robber Bozo Macika (another domestic wreck, whose mother is committed to an asylum for murdering his incestuous father and sister). The lurid, picaresque narrative of Bozo's life and death is itself, in turn, taken from an unpublished novel manuscript ostensibly authored by another solitary survivor of a family annihilation, the eccentric schoolteacher Maude, and perused in the course of the book by Maude's pupil Lakemf on a visit to the teacher's apartment. Thus

Maude's primary narrative forms the enclosing, encompassing frame at the edges of the book. Maude professes to have risen, like his Bozo, from poverty and crime to self-education, and he tells Lakemf that Maria was actually his girlfriend and the real Bozo her former boyfriend. Yet the narrative extravaganza of Bozo's anarchic Bonnie-and-Clyde rampages reads increasingly like pulp fiction, and it comes as no surprise, as the last of the Chinese boxes opens, to learn that the whole thing—Maria, Bozo's life story, and Maude's history of his own privations—is pure invention. It is in fact a grotesque hoax devised by the teacher to cure his pupil of his insatiable juvenile appetite for cheap sensationalism.

In this book the reader is placed in a hermeneutical "back of beyond," at a tremendous distance from events of possibly doubtful authenticity. Thomas has in fact taken the whole of Nigeria's hideous, putrescent, postindependence history—drug-smuggling, government extortion, Bar Beach Show executions—and artfully enclosed it in a sensational Gothic-horror fiction, the form in which it is best expressed. The crowning convoluted irony of Maude's narrative—which, as he says, is "stranger than fiction"[7]—is that so many of its episodes are all too painfully credible and are no less horrifically real for the distancing effects. Bandele-Thomas has written a teasing parable about the relationship that fact and fantasy, reality and fiction, might assume in the literature that addresses the fantastic actuality. At the culmination of the teacher's cautionary tale, these apparent opposites converge in the learning consciousness of the pupil Lakemf, who resolves to renounce his own fledgling criminal career of fraud and petty theft. The author's interpretive maze thus collapses into a succession of old-fashioned moral clichés about art as the conscience of society and the cleansing power of fiction, the lie that makes truth happen.

Bandele-Thomas's simultaneously published *The Sympathetic Undertaker and Other Dreams* (1991) presents the madness of modern Nigeria, once again, with a coarse-grained realism edged with surrealist horror, this time sandwiching the hallucinatory notebook writings of the mad Rayo between the more naturalistic narratives of his unnamed brother. The insane social reality—of private jets and billion-dollar debts, babies born in taxis amid gangwar gunfire, starvation and mindless military terror—is, as in the first book, a hard one for the Western reader to swallow; appropriately, swallowing the unthinkable is a recurring motif in the novel. At the novel's high point of horror, a group of vicious drunken soldiers beats a stationmaster half to death because their train is late; when a naïve young student dares to tend the victim's wounds, the corporal (a future federal minister) draws his pistol and casually blows out the boy's brains, which then fly, gruesomely, into the gaping mouth of a petrified spectator. In one of Rayo's tales within the tale, about the "dream land" of Zowabia where "dream people lived in an endless stream of misery and nightmare,"[8] the ogrish dictator Babagee and his First Lady gulp down their gigantic maws the nation's entire universities, courts, churches, banks, hospitals, and newspapers, replacing them with their own monstrous selves.

The narrative convolutions are again turned to grim ironic effect. From within the dream story, Babagee (really a cartoon version of Nigeria's General Babangida) has his own dream about presiding over an upside-down court where the accused is applauded and rewarded for the size of the bribe he gave to a policeman. To sharpen the local satire, the police force of Zowabia's nearest neighbor, Nigeria, is then singled out as an exemplary model of virtuous entrepreneurial bribe-taking and its military regime lauded for its advanced letter-bomb technology and expertise in kidnapping fugitive diplomats from overseas embassies. Thus, the deeper Bandele-Thomas's fable ventures into "dream" territory, the more preposterously real its world becomes; the more the reader has to swallow, the more sickeningly true it is. At the end of the book, as in his other novel, the convoluted fictional structure is dismantled. The narrator, it transpires, has no brother but is himself the mad Rayo of the dream-notebooks, demented by police torture after leading an idealistic student protest and driven to a suicide attempt. In the novel's final voracious image, the narrator's twin selves are alike dismembered and devoured by vultures. The point is that in a lunatic society, where corruption is endemic, the army is above the law, and a "sympathetic undertaker" offers starving families bulk discounts on coffins, good people are soon driven mad and any distinctions between the sane and insane, the narrator and his crazed alter ego, are meaningless.

The conclusions to Bandele-Thomas's two ambitious fictional tours de force are perhaps too morally pat, but if the deflatory, throwaway finales themselves stick in the reader's throat, this is no doubt intentional. By such means this novelist implicates his own fiction, reflexively, in the trivialization of terror and corruption in modern Nigeria, a country whose surreal reality—like that of Nazi Germany in Günter Grass's *The Tin Drum* or Pakistan in Salman Rushdie's *Shame*—can be presented only at the level of nightmare and delirium and is no longer available to ordinary, everyday perception. *The Man Who Came In from the Back of Beyond* and *The Sympathetic Undertaker* are witty and intelligent experimental fictions, technically sophisticated, verbally and formally inventive, and full of odd, psychological quirks and narrative twists that constantly surprise and subvert the reader. Eclectic and syncretic in their accommodation of influences from contemporary world fiction, they are, moreover, thoroughly modern novels (and indeed postmodern) in their hybrid artistic consciousness.

No less exuberantly inventive and original is the epic first novel, *The Last Harmattan of Alusine Dunbar* (1990), of Sierra Leonian poet Syl Cheney-Coker. This is a fictionalized history of his country (here called Malagueta) from settlement by American-returned slaves in the late eighteenth century through British imperialism and Creole immigration to Arab economic neocolonialism and a failed military coup against a corrupt contemporary dictatorship. Cheney-Coker's sprawling saga is also a magic history whose whole stormy passage—war and occupation, hurricane and flood, malaria and killer bats—is foreseen in the miraculous premonitory mirrors of Sulaiman the Nubian, an itinerant medieval sage, wizard, and mystic occultist. Sulaiman has access to all of Africa's ancient wisdoms and alchemic powers from the Nile to the Zambezi—he cures rheumatism by reciting sage verses and gives pregnant women control over cobras with cassava stalks—and his ageless spirit wanders across the centuries, watching over his people from "the high plateau of the dead"[9] and periodically reincarnating itself in history. Thus, when the returned slave Gustavius and his African wife Isatu are unable to have a child, Sulaiman sends them two of a race of hunchbacked hermaphroditic dwarf children who were abducted from their mothers by an evil djinn and who choose, once every 12 years, to be reborn to a mother who has undergone great suffering. He then endows the resultant child, for whom he has waited 150 years, with his own clairvoyant powers; in the persona of Alusine Dunbar, a vagabond seer with visionary optic lenses in his herniated testicles, he reveals to the 10-year-old boy and future rebel poet the further disasters for which Malagueta is destined, including the final battle for the capital Kasila, in which both the colonial captain and the rebel leader are killed, and the epochal changeover to the colonial order.

Sulaiman has also, on his earthly peregrinations, begotten offspring who are not quite of this world. One such child in time is the Bird-Woman Fatmatta, whose limericks hold back hurricanes and who can converse with animals and open doors by looking at them. Her scorpion look is able to render suddenly impotent any man who forces himself upon her; as prophesied, she is finally seduced by an albino wearing the face and body of another. The message to the Malaguetans is to suspect all white and white-imitative strangers who arrive on their shores. The historical Fatmatta is abducted into slavery in America and dies, an old woman, on her return to Africa. Her spirit, however, visits the wife of the settlement's founder during a difficult childbirth, bequeathing to the woman her magical glass beads, and a quarter of a century later, when the child of that birth, now a rebel leader, falls during the climactic battle for the city, she swoops down to gather his soul and carry it off to eternity. For in Cheney-Coker's magical Malagueta the dead are eternally alive and walk freely among the living as sentient, vigilant presences, visible both in and out of dreams except to those who have been too long in America and have lost the gift of spiritual sight. Even the secular, agnostic founder witnesses the "instant miracle" of a dead man sitting up in his coffin and knows immediately "that all men belonged to another realm of existence . . . that through the present dead, man was alive" (*LHAD*, 143). "Mankind," says a later community leader, "was this contexture of the living and the dead" (*LHAD*, 168).

In this world nothing ever really dies—Sulaiman's ancient learning mysteriously resurfaces a hundred years later in the lives of the pioneers, and the country's indigenous history is revealed to the founder in dreams—and death, because it is seen as a kind of birth, is continually linked with it. The childless mother, on the instructions of the dwarf children, casts her firstborn onto the garbage heap where her father was found dead, whereupon the dead man takes up the new existence into the living world; when the colonial occupation force invades during funeral rites, the spirit of Fatmatta disarms with her scorpion look the colonial captain "who had the temerity to interfere with the dance of the spirits on their journey to a different home" (*LHAD*, 169). What the eponymous hero, on his final wintry visit to the world, is most concerned to preserve from the wreck of history, however, is the African heritage of which he himself is the guardian and protector. In the course of the novel Sulaiman-alias-Alusine comes to embody "the rebelliousness of the land to all things foreign," whether it be white colonists, Arab property speculators, the new commercialism to which the ancient arts and crafts have sold out, or the aristocratic, puritanical, Creole class, the "newly minted black Englishmen" obsessed with status and respectability (*LHAD*, 262, 305). Appropriately, it is Sulaiman-Alusine, the avatar of a time "when the world was a thousand times saner than it is now" (*LHAD*, 295), who launches his protégé on his poetic career by mailing him a library of the continent's mystic cultural treasures. It is also he who, in the book's phantasmagoric climax, strides into the presidential palace of the 1980s, his occult weaponry blazing from his testicles, to inflict a terrible revenge on the despicable dictator Sanka Maru (a version of Sierra Leone's Siaka Stevens) for hanging the one honorable man in his government.

The Last Harmattan of Alusine Dunbar is a harrowing, outraged history, written in fire and blood, telling of stolen freedoms and wrecked families, of loved ones killed and maimed in struggles against overwhelming odds. Yet its historical narrative also has a powerful transcendental, visionary dimension, and it is here that Cheney-Coker's ferocious powers of invention are given free and full play. His forest settlement is a fabulous, enchanted place, and his novel, like those of Okri and Laing, is a book of miracles and wonders. These include flying carpets and a virgin deflowered by a telekinetic statue of a black Christ; a three month's happiness in which the whole community falls asleep and wakes up at exactly the same moment; an elephantine Arab woman whose 10 look-alike daughters multiply geometrically, producing a hundred clones who then produce another thousand, all perfect replicas of herself; and all manner of sympathetic magic in which marvelous, talismanic cures are fashioned from parts of plants and animals. With the aid of magical herbs, Sulaiman's dwarf minions have made the quantum leap that enables them to be in several places at the same time and to represent many alternative lives, whereas the master himself has "conquered the last mystery of how to be alive in the same place where he had died over a hundred years before" (*LHAD*, 289). Cheney-Coker's book is an enigmatic, chimerical work that, in the manner of magic realist writing, contests the borders between reality and illusion, the historical and the fantastical, up to its last page. In its self-referential final sentence, the novel turns problematically upon itself, not in the self-deflatory style of Bandele-Thomas's work but to claim for fiction the power of "eternal public disgrace" over its historical originals, namely the betrayers of the real-life coup in Sierra Leone and that country's apostasy from Sulaiman's heritage.

The Nigerian T. Obinkaram Echewa is an older, longer-established novelist than Bandele-Thomas and Cheney-Coker. His third novel, *I Saw the Sky Catch Fire* (1993), employs more conventional narrative forms such as the colonial reminiscence and the been-to bildungsroman, but it is a remarkable new departure and fills a glaring gap in Nigerian fiction insofar as it is a celebratory paean to the nation's women, sung by a male novelist. At his grandmother Nne-nne's death the narrator Ajuzia, home after five years in America, wonders "again and again what *else* lay buried in her heart, what other wars and secrets had existed in her storehouse of *grief* that she had carried with her into the grave."[10] In this way he reminds us that the rich tapestry of tales unfolded by his grandmother's colonial and precolonial reminiscences have barely opened the door to the treasure trove.

Echewa skillfully encloses the story of Ajuzia's departure for and return from America in a succession of vignettes that movingly commemorate the triumphs, griefs, and solidarities of three generations of Igbo women. Alternating her mood from the dignified to the raucous, the elegiac to the scatological, Nne-nne tells of the adventurous Oyoyo and her comic cross-cultural excursions into the world of urban prostitution, and, on a sadder note, of Ahunze, the village's sole unmarried woman whose strength and independence are resented by the male community and who is subsequently axed to death by a sadistic wife-beating husband for leading a spontaneous collective female protest against his cruelty. Next comes the "Women's War," a more structured mass protest against a colonial census for purposes of taxation, in which the village wives take hostage a white woman, who proceeds to record her comic misunderstandings of Igbo customs in a series of notepad jottings. The spirit of *Oha Ndom*—the Solidarity of Women—is then reenacted at the domestic level in the contemporary narrative when grandmother, mother-in-law, and abandoned wife combine forces to ruthlessly expose Ajuzia's masculine complacency and double standards of sexual morality. Nne-nne dispenses her ripe wisdom, poignantly, to the last breath, staying alive just long enough to persuade Ajuzia's wife, pregnant by another man, to wait for her husband to take her back. She reveals to him, on her last night on earth, that she too took a lover during her husband's imprisonment, reminding him that issues of gender and fidelity know no season or age but have to be lived anew by each generation.

Much of the subject matter of *I Saw the Sky Catch Fire* is, on the surface, the well-traveled territory of colonial conflict and culture collision. What rescues it from the usual banality with which such material is often treated, however, is a sophisticated transcultural awareness. This special understanding makes equal allowance for both the relativities of cultures and their broad underlying universals and permits the author to penetrate imaginatively the inner, subjective lives of persons of another age, sex, or (as in the case of the white woman) race. Nne-nne's commitment extends beyond the confines of her Igbo village to a universal community of women, and Echewa cunningly encodes in her scurrilous sexual banter a whole body of Western feminist theory that opposes the penetrative brevity and closure of patriarchal discourse to the infinite, enduring openness of *l'écriture féminine*: "Men and women are like their organs. A woman's is mostly private, tucked away like a secret purse between her legs, with little to give away how big or deep it really is. A man's, on the other hand . . . swells with pride and longing and waves mightily about. But once inside a woman, it thumps a few times, loses its seed, and soon collapses. . . . A woman endures . . . a woman gets stronger with age" (*ISSCF,* 7).

In *I Saw the Sky Catch Fire* the irreversible cultural hybridization of both author and narrator is a key source of the book's strength, and in this respect Echewa's novel is not alone among contemporary African and postcolonial fiction. In 1990 Salman Rushdie wrote in defense of his novel: "*The Satanic Verses* celebrates hybridity, impurity, intermingling, the transformation that comes of new and unexpected combinations of human beings, cultures, ideas, politics, movies, songs. It rejoices in mongrelization and fears the absolutism of the Pure. *Melange,* hotchpotch, a bit of this and a bit of that is *how newness enters the world.* It is the great possibility that mass migration gives the world."[11] Most of the novelists whose work is touched upon briefly here—Nigerians living in London (Okri, Bandele-Thomas), Ghanaians and Sierra Leonians schooled in Scotland and the United States (Laing, Cheney-Coker)—are the eclectic, syncretic products of this migrant world. Each of them has forged from their irretrievably alloyed experience the complex meaning of what it is to be an African writer at the end of the twentieth century; each has engaged completely with the complex hybridized modernity of the contemporary world that has both formed them and become part of themselves. In Laing's novels the world of cybernetics and computer games mingles multiculturally with African humanism and animist mythology, Scottish words with Ga and Akan. Bandele-Thomas combines an ultra-postmodern reflexiveness with graphic realism; Cheney-Coker interweaves magic and material history. In Okri's abiku epics, chaos theory and science fiction rub shoulders with Yoruba and Ibo folklore, mythology, and oral tradition; the magical metamorphoses of Ovid and Apuleius and the eroded ontologies of modern fantasy fiction (Borges, Márquez, Mervyn Peake) come into contact with the Yoruba world of Tutuola's dream narratives, Fagunwa's novels, and Soyinka's early plays. Whereas some postcolonial critics and theorists have celebrated this syncretism and have accepted the absorption of national and racial cultures into international conglomerates, others have seen hybridism itself as another hallmark of Western, metropolitan influence and as an alternative form of neocolonial hegemony to which the third world is subservient.[12]

The extent to which either the new hybridism or alternative purist exercises in race retrieval and cultural archaeology take their terms of reference from imperial values is beyond the scope of the present work. Suffice it to say that in the 1990s those novels that effect some form of closure around exclusivist and traditionalist models of African identity and notions of a precolonial African sensibility have been in the minority. The latest works of Awoonor and Armah, together with Hove's *Bones* (1990), would appear to fall into this category. Yet even in the Armah and Hove novels the African past is not an excuse for escapism and obsolete nostalgias but serves as a springboard into the future and, in the case of *Osiris Rising,* into a formidably modern world in which the author is completely at home. In the best of these works there is a creative cross-fertilization of the traditional and modern that precludes the absorption of one into the other, a continual rechanneling of old energies into new directions.

Notes and References

Chapter One

1. Kwame Nkrumah, *I Speak of Freedom* (London: Panaf, 1973), xii.
2. Ayi Kwei Armah, *The Beautyful Ones Are Not Yet Born* (Boston: Houghton Mifflin, 1968; London: Heinemann, 1969, reset 1975), 90; the 1975 reset Heinemann edition is cited hereafter in the text as *BONYB*.
3. William Conton, *The African* (London: Heinemann, 1966), 33.
4. Chinua Achebe, *No Longer At Ease* (London: Heinemann, 1960, reset 1975), 94; the 1975 reset Heinemann edition is cited hereafter in the text as *NLAE*.
5. See Martin Meredith, "The Broken Dream," *The Sunday Times Magazine*, 7 March 1982, p. 29; and "What Does Ghana Really Owe?" *West Africa*, 28 January 1972, p. 87.
6. James Booth, *Writers and Politics in Nigeria* (London: Hodder and Stoughton, 1981), 40–56. Booth examines the autobiographical writings of Nnamdi Azikiwe, the first president of the Nigerian Federation, and Alhaji Ahmadu Bello, the first premier of the Northern Region of Nigeria.
7. Ayi Kwei Armah, "A Mystification: African Independence Revalued," *Pan-African Journal* 2, no. 2 (Spring 1969): 145–48.
8. Frantz Fanon, *Les damnés de la terre* (Paris: Maspero, 1961); *The Wretched of the Earth*, trans. Constance Farrington (Harmondsworth, England: Penguin, 1967), 122–23; hereafter cited in the text as *WOE*.
9. P. C. Lloyd, *Africa in Social Change*, 3rd ed. (Harmondsworth: Penguin, 1972), 120.
10. Chinua Achebe, *A Man of the People* (London: Heinemann, 1966, reset 1975), 148; the 1975 reset Heinemann edition is hereafter cited in the text as *MOP*.
11. Ayi Kwei Armah, *Fragments* (Boston: Houghton Mifflin, 1970; London: Heinemann, 1974), 146–47.
12. Wole Soyinka, *The Interpreters* (London: Andre Deutsch, 1965; Heinemann, 1970), 112.
13. Lenrie Peters, *The Second Round* (London: Heinemann, 1965), 42.
14. Neil Lazarus, *Resistance in Postcolonial African Fiction* (New Haven and London: Yale University Press, 1990), 10–24, 30–32; hereafter cited in the text.
15. Wole Soyinka, "The Writer in a Modern African State," in *Art, Dialogue and Outrage: Essays on Literature and Culture* (Ibadan, Nigeria: New Horn

Press, 1988), 20; Chinua Achebe, "The Novelist as Teacher," in *Morning Yet on Creation Day* (London: Heinemann, 1977), 44.

16. Maya Jaggi, "A Combining of Gifts: An Interview with Nuruddin Farah," *Third World Quarterly* 11, no. 3 (July 1989): 186.

17. Chinweizu, Onwuchekwa Jemie, and Ihechukwu Madubuike, *Towards the Decolonization of African Literature* (Enugu, Nigeria: Fourth Dimension, 1980; revised and expanded edition, London: Kegan Paul International, 1985).

18. Adewale Maja-Pearce, *A Mask Dancing: Nigerian Novelists of the Eighties* (London: Hans Zell, 1992), 47, 97–100, 136, 140–44, 171–73; hereafter cited in the text.

Chapter Two

1. Bernth Lindfors, with Ian Munro, Reinhard Sander, and Richard Priebe, "Interview with Kofi Awoonor," in *Palaver: Interviews with Five African Authors*, ed. Bernth Lindfors (Austin: African Research Institute, University of Texas, 1972), 62; hereafter cited in the text.

2. John Goldblatt, "Kofi Awoonor: An Interview," *Transition* 41 (1972): 44.

3. Awoonor seems to have in mind festivals such as the Akan Apo and Afhaye. For details of these, see R. S. Rattray, *Ashanti* (Oxford: Clarendon Press, 1923), 211.

4. See Robin Horton, "New Year in the Delta," *Nigeria Magazine* 67 (1960): 256–74; Louis S. Gates, "Interview with Wole Soyinka," *Black World* 24, no. 10 (August 1975): 40–41; hereafter cited in the text.

5. See Wole Soyinka's two plays, *The Strong Breed* (1964) and *The Bacchae of Euripides* (1973) in *Wole Soyinka: Collected Plays,* vol. 1 (Oxford: Oxford University Press, 1973), 113–46, 233–307.

6. The mystification has been compounded by critics such as Richard Priebe, who writes of Armah's novel *The Beautyful Ones Are Not Yet Born*, "That we never see how regeneration is effected is not important to the integrity of the work, for the tacit assumption of society, and by extension of the artist, is that the ritual process enacted by the hero is the only way society can be rejuvenated." Richard Priebe, "Demonic Imagery and the Apocalyptic Vision in the Novels of Ayi Kwei Armah," *Yale French Studies* 53 (1976): 115; reprinted as "Armah's Mythic Hero: A Man Betwixt and Between," in Richard Priebe, *Myth, Realism, and the West African Writer* (Trenton, N.J.: Africa World Press, 1988), 21–46.

7. Gerald Moore, "Death, Convergence and Rebirth in Two Black Novels," *Nigerian Journal of the Humanities* 2 (1978): 6.

8. Kofi Awoonor, *This Earth, My Brother . . .* (New York: Doubleday, 1971; London: Heinemann, 1972), 148; the Heinemann edition is cited hereafter in the text as *TEMB*.

9. See, for example, the endings of *The Strong Breed* and *The Bacchae of Euripides* in Soyinka, *Collected Plays,* vol. 1.

10. Richard Priebe, "Kofi Awoonor's *This Earth, My Brother* . . . as an African Dirge," *Benin Review* 1 (1974): 97, 99; reprinted in Priebe, *Myth, Realism, and the West African Writer,* 65–78; and in Priebe, ed., *Ghanaian Literatures* (Westport, Conn.: Greenwood Press, 1988), 265–78.

11. Gerald Moore, *Twelve African Writers* (London: Hutchinson, 1980), 248; hereafter cited in the text.

12. Kofi Awoonor, "Voyager and the Earth," *New Letters* 40, no. 1 (1973): 92.

13. Wole Soyinka, *Season of Anomy* (London: Rex Collings, 1973), 6; hereafter cited in the text as *SOA*.

14. In Soyinka's version of Euripides' *The Bacchae* (*Collected Plays,* vol. 1), a communion rite exploited as a tool of oppression by a reactionary regime is mobilized by slaves, under the direction of the god Dionysus, into an instrument of insurrection.

15. Wole Soyinka, *The Man Died: Prison Notes of Wole Soyinka* (Harmondsworth: Penguin, 1975), 189–90.

16. Wole Soyinka, *Myth, Literature and the African World* (Cambridge: Cambridge University Press, 1976), 156; hereafter cited in the text as *MLAW*.

17. Wole Soyinka, Introduction to *The Bacchae of Euripides* (London: Methuen, 1973), xi–xii.

18. Wole Soyinka, "The Critic and Society," in his *Art, Dialogue and Outrage: Essays on Literature and Culture* (Ibadan: New Horn Press, 1988), 166–68; hereafter cited in the text as *ADO*.

Chapter Three

1. Thomas A. Hale, *Scribe, Griot, and Novelist: Narrative Interpreters of the Songhay Empire* (Gainesville: University of Florida Press, 1990), 138–40; hereafter cited in the text.

2. Hale's book includes a translation of *The Epic of Askia Mohammed,* as recounted by the Niger griot Nouhou Malio in 1980; Hale, 178–291.

3. Kenneth Harrow, *Thresholds of Change in African Literature* (Portsmouth, N.H.: Heinemann; London: James Currey, 1994), 174; see also Hale, 154–55.

4. As an example of this view, see Edna Aizenberg, "Historical Subversion and Violence of Representation in García Márquez and Ouologuem," *PMLA* 107 (October 1992): 1244. Wole Soyinka, on the other hand, takes the view that Ouologuem's "method is invariably iconoclastic; nothing survives in it" (*MLAW,* 101).

5. Yambo Ouologuem, *Le Devoir de violence* (Paris: Seuil, 1968); *Bound to Violence,* trans. Ralph Manheim (London: Heinemann, 1971), 3–4; hereafter cited in the text as *BTV*.

6. Christopher Miller, *Blank Darkness* (Chicago: University of Chicago Press, 1985), 231.

7. Walter J. Ong, *Orality and Literacy: The Technologizing of the Word* (London and New York: Methuen, 1982), 151.

8. Isidore Okpewho, "Myth and Modern Fiction: Armah's *Two Thousand Seasons*," *African Literature Today* 13 (1983): 4; hereafter cited in the text.

9. Ayi Kwei Armah, *Two Thousand Seasons* (Nairobi: East African Publishing House, 1973; London: Heinemann, 1979), 3; the Heinemann edition is cited hereafter in the text as *TTS*.

10. A. N. Mensah, "Style and Purpose in Armah's *Two Thousand Seasons*," *African Literature Today* 17 (1991): 6; hereafter cited in the text. Mensah's article contains an excellent analysis of the syntax of orature.

11. See Jack Goody, *The Domestication of the Savage Mind* (Cambridge: Cambridge University Press, 1977), 49–50; D. S. Izevbaye, "Time in the African Novel," *Journal of Commonwealth Literature* 17 (August 1982): 74; and Ong, *Orality and Literacy*, 104.

12. See my own critical study of Armah for a more detailed analysis of the novel's stylistic shortcomings: Derek Wright, *Ayi Kwei Armah's Africa: The Sources of His Fiction* (London and New York: Hans Zell, 1989), 226–33.

13. Ayi Kwei Armah, "African Socialism: Utopian or Scientific?" *Présence Africaine* 64, no. 4 (1967): 15.

14. Kofi Anyidoho, "Historical Realism and the Visionary Ideal: Ayi Kwei Armah's *Two Thousand Seasons*," *Ufahamu* 11, no. 2 (1981–1982): 114.

15. For example, see Ben Okri, *Songs of Enchantment* (London: Vintage, 1994), 157–65.

Chapter Four

1. Adewale Maja-Pearce, "Interview with Kojo Laing," *Wasafiri* 6/7 (Spring/Autumn 1987): 28.

2. Ngugi wa Thiong'o, *Matigari*. Translated from the Gikuyu by Wangui wa Goro (London: Heinemann, 1989), 103, 123; hereafter cited in the text as *M*.

3. See Simon Gikandi, "The Epistemology of Translation: Ngugi, *Matigari*, and the Politics of Language," *Research in African Literatures* 22, no. 4 (Winter 1991): 162; hereafter cited in the text; David Maughan Brown, "*Matigari* and the Rehabilitation of Religion," *Research in African Literatures* 22, no. 4 (Winter 1991): 178–79; and Audrey Wipper, *Rural Rebels: A Study of Two Protest Movements in Kenya* (Nairobi: Oxford University Press, 1977), 156–67.

4. Maya Jaggi, "*Matigari* as Myth and History: An Interview with Ngugi wa Thiong'o," *Third World Quarterly* 11, no. 4 (October 1989): 248; hereafter cited in the text.

5. "Ngugi wa Thiong'o," in *Talking with African Writers*, ed. Jane Wilkinson (London: James Currey, 1992), 133; hereafter cited in the text.

6. Dianne Schwerdt, "Leading the People Home: Matigari as Redeemer in Ngugi wa Thiong'o's Latest Novel," *CRNLE Reviews Journal*, no. 2 (1989): 17.
7. Abdulrazak Gurnah, "Transformative Strategies in the Fiction of Ngugi wa Thiong'o," in *Essays on African Writing: A Re-evaluation*, ed. Abdulrazak Gurnah (Oxford: Heinemann, 1993), 152, 155–56.
8. Mary Langille, "Coming Out of Oral Tradition to Write about Dictatorship: An Interview with Nuruddin Farah," *The Varsity* (University of Toronto), 26 November 1987: 7; hereafter cited in the text.
9. Robert Moss, "Mapping the Psyche: Interview with Nuruddin Farah," *West Africa* 1 (September 1986): 1827.
10. Nuruddin Farah, *Sardines* (London: Allison and Busby, 1981; London: Heinemann, 1982), 170; the Heinemann edition is cited hereafter in the text as *S*.
11. Nuruddin Farah, *A Naked Needle* (London: Heinemann, 1976), 111.
12. Anne Walmsley, "Nuruddin Farah and Somalia," *Index on Censorship* 10, no. 2 (1981): 19.
13. Nuruddin Farah, *Sweet and Sour Milk* (London: Allison and Busby, 1979; London: Heinemann, 1980), 196; the Heinemann edition is cited hereafter in the text as *SSM*.
14. Nuruddin Farah, "Why I Write," *Third World Quarterly* 10, no. 4 (October 1988): 1597.

Chapter Five

1. Breyten Breytenbach, *End Papers* (London: Faber, 1986), 208.
2. J. M. Coetzee, *Life and Times of Michael K* (London: Secker and Warburg, 1983; Harmondsworth: Penguin, 1985), 215; the Penguin edition is cited hereafter in the text as *MK*.
3. Nadine Gordimer, "The Idea of Gardening," *New York Review of Books* 2 (February 1984): 6; hereafter cited in the text.
4. See Kelly Hewson, "Making the Revolutionary Gesture: Nadine Gordimer, J. M. Coetzee and Some Variations on the Writer's Responsibility," *ARIEL* 19, no. 4 (1988): 66–69.
5. See Robert M. Post, "Oppression in the Fiction of J. M. Coetzee," *Critique* 27, no. 2 (1986): 75.
6. On Coetzee's earlier work, see also Paul Rich, "Tradition and Revolt in South African Fiction," *Journal of Southern African Studies* 9, no. 1 (1982): 79; and Michael Vaughan, "Literature and Politics: Currents in South African Writing in the Seventies," *Journal of Southern African Studies* 9, no. 1 (1982): 137.
7. See Susan VanZanten Gallagher, *A Story of South Africa: J. M. Coetzee's Fiction in Context* (Cambridge, Mass.: Harvard University Press, 1991), 168.
8. Folke Rhedin, "J. M. Coetzee: Interview," *Kunapipi* 6, no. 1 (1984): 10.

9. J. M. Coetzee, *Foe* (London: Secker and Warburg, 1986; Harmondsworth: Penguin, 1987), 157.

10. There is an astute analysis of the hermeneutical dilemmas of the narrative voice in *Foe* in Helen Tiffin, "Post-Colonial Literatures and Counter-Discourse," *Kunapipi* 9, no. 3 (1987): 29–30.

Chapter Six

1. See Alec Pongweni, *Songs That Won the Liberation War* (Harare, Zimbabwe: College Press, 1982).

2. Shimmer Chinodya, *Harvest of Thorns* (Harare, Zimbabwe: Baobab Books, 1989; London: Heinemann, 1990), 245; the Heinemann edition is cited hereafter in the text as *HOT*.

3. Chinodya has stated that he meant to show at the end of the novel "a dejected and unemployed ex-combatant, a torn family and a wounded nation." "Forces to be Reckoned With: An Interview with Shimmer Chinodya," *Parade* (11 and 25 October 1990): 25.

4. Flora Veit-Wild, Interview with Shimmer Chinodya in Harare, 1990; quoted in Flora Veit-Wild, *Teachers, Preachers and Non-Believers: A Social History of Zimbabwean Literature* (London: Hans Zell, 1992), 321; Veit-Wild's book is cited hereafter in the text except in multiple references.

5. Chenjerai Hove, *Bones* (Harare: Boabab, 1988), 57.

6. See Liz Gunner, "Power, Popular Consciousness, and the Fictions of War: Hove's *Bones* and Chinodya's *Harvest of Thorns*," *African Languages and Cultures* 4, no. 1 (1991): 77.

Chapter Seven

1. See Flora Veit-Wild, "Creating a New Society: Women's Writing in Zimbabwe," *Journal of Commonwealth Literature* 22, no. 1 (August 1987): 173.

2. See Dieter Riemenschneider, "Short Fiction from Zimbabwe," *Research in African Literatures* 20, no. 3 (Fall 1989): 401–11.

3. See Flora Veit-Wild, *Teachers, Preachers, Non-Believers: A Social History of Zimbabwean Literature* (London: Hans Zell, 1992), 239; *Survey of Zimbabwean Writers: Educational and Literary Careers* (Bayreuth: Bayreuth African Studies, 1992), 91–92, 101–2; and "Creating a New Society," 172–73.

4. See, for example, Veit-Wild's discussion of the work of Joyce Simango and Barbara Makhalisa in *Teachers, Preachers, Non-Believers*, 246–49; and her account of reading matter in schools and literacy campaigns in "Creating a New Society," 172–73.

5. Barbara Makhalisa adopts a more radical stand on fertility and the stigmatization of childless women in her collection *The Underdog and Other Stories* (Gweru, Zimbabwe: Mambo Press, 1984), the first Zimbabwean women's

fiction to be published in English. In the story "Baby-snatcher," a woman who fails to become pregnant is placed under such pressure that she steals another woman's baby. The ironic ending reveals the husband to be infertile.

6. Tsitsi Dangarembga, *Nervous Conditions* (London: The Women's Press, 1988), 56; hereafter cited in the text as *NC*.

7. *Mainini, Maiguru,* and *Babamukuru* are the Shona words for, respectively, *mother, aunt,* and *uncle.* Tambu refers to these three figures by their titular names throughout her narrative.

8. Kirsten Holst Petersen, "Between Gender, Race and History: Interview with Tsitsi Dangarembga," *Kunapipi* 16, no. 1 (1994): 346.

9. Toril Moi, "Feminist Literary Criticism," in *Modern Literary Theory: A Comparative Introduction,* ed. Ann Jefferson and David Robey (London: Batsford, 1982), 218; hereafter cited in the text.

10. Heidi Creamer, "An Apple for the Teacher? Femininity, Coloniality, and Food in *Nervous Conditions,*" *Kunapipi* 16, no. 1 (1994): 359–60.

11. "Tsitsi Dangarembga," in *Talking with African Writers,* ed. Jane Wilkinson (London: James Currey, 1992), 198; hereafter cited in the text.

12. Terry Eagleton, *Literary Theory: An Introduction* (Oxford: Blackwell, 1983), 190.

13. See, respectively, Sally McWilliams, "Tsitsi Dangarembga's *Nervous Conditions*: At the Crossroads of Feminism and Postcolonialism," *World Literature Written in English* 31, no. 1 (Spring 1991): 110; and Miki Flockemann, "Not Quite Insiders and Not Quite Outsiders: The Process of Womanhood in *Beka Lamb, Nervous Conditions* and *Daughters of the Twilight," Journal of Commonwealth Literature* 27, no. 1 (August 1992): 46.

14. Sue Thomas, "Killing the Hysteric in the Colonized's House: Tsitsi Dangarembga's *Nervous Conditions," Journal of Commonwealth Literature* 27, no. 1 (August 1992): 27.

Chapter Eight

1. Susheila Nasta, "Interview: Moyez Vassanji," *Wasafiri* 13 (Spring 1991): 20; hereafter cited in the text.

2. See, for example: Bahadur Tejani, *Day After Tomorrow* (Nairobi: East African Literature Bureau, 1971); Peter Nazareth, *In a Brown Mantle* (Nairobi, Kampala, and Dar es Salaam: East African Literature Bureau, 1972); and, as an example of an expatriate novel, V. S. Naipaul, *A Bend in the River* (London: Andre Deutsch, 1979).

3. Chelva Kanaganayakam, "Broadening the Substrata: An Interview with M. G. Vassanji," *World Literature Written in English* 31, no. 2 (Autumn 1991): 24; hereafter cited in the text.

4. M. G. Vassanji, *The Gunny Sack* (London: Heinemann, 1989), 134; hereafter cited in the text as *GS*.

Chapter Nine

1. B. Kojo Laing, *Search Sweet Country* (London: William Heinemann, 1986; London: Picador, 1987), 56; the Picador edition is cited hereafter in the text as *SSC*.

2. Ato Quayson, "Esoteric Webwork as Nervous System: Reading the Fantastic in Ben Okri's Writing," in *Essays on African Writing 2: Contemporary Literature*, ed. Abdulrazak Gurnah (Oxford: Heinemann, 1995), 147; hereafter cited in the text.

3. Pietro Deandrea quotes Laing in private conversation: "That is the whole impetus behind my language; cubism, expressionism and other aspects of modern art seem to be propounding a world that I feel already exists for me on a day-to-day basis." Pietro Deandrea, "New Worlds, New Wholes: Kojo Laing's Narrative Quest for a Social Renewal," *African Literature Today* 20 (1996): 167.

4. See M. E. Kropp Dakubu, "*Search Sweet Country* and the Language of Authentic Being," *Research in African Literatures* 24, no. 1 (Spring 1993): 30; hereafter cited in the text.

5. Laing cites the example of the Peugeot car that Ghanaians have come to regard as a local, not an imported, product. Adewale Maja-Pearce, "Interview with Kojo Laing," *Wasafiri* 6/7 (Spring/Autumn 1987): 29.

6. Ben Okri, *The Famished Road* (London: Jonathan Cape, 1991; London: Vintage, 1992), 5; the Vintage edition is cited hereafter in the text as *FR*.

7. Wole Soyinka, "Abiku," in *Idanre and Other Poems* (London: Methuen, 1967), 28–30.

8. Jean Ross, "*Contemporary Authors* Interview" (with Ben Okri), in *Contemporary Authors,* vol. 138, ed. Donna Olendorf (Detroit: Gale Research, 1993), 337–38.

9. See, for example: Michiko Kakutani, review of Okri's *Stars of the New Curfew* (short stories) in *New York Times,* 28 July 1989; Alan Riach, "Ben Okri," in *Contemporary Novelists,* (fifth ed.), ed. Lesley Henderson (Chicago: St. James Press, 1991), 707–8; and Tom Wilhelmus, "Time and Distance," *Hudson Review* 46, no. 1 (Spring 1993): 247–52, 254–55.

10. Ben Okri, comment to Diana Giese, quoted in Diana Giese, "And the Winner: Myth and Modernity in Nigeria," *The Weekend Australian* (Sydney), 9–10 November 1991: 5.

Chapter Ten

1. The novels given brief mention in the first three paragraphs of this chapter are as follows, in order of reference: Buchi Emecheta, *Gwendolen* (London: Flamingo, 1990); Ama Ata Aidoo, *Changes* (London: The Women's Press, 1991); Yvonne Vera, *Nehanda* (Harare: Baobab, 1993); J. M. Coetzee, *Age of Iron* (London: Secker and Warburg, 1990); Nuruddin Farah, *Gifts* (Harare:

Baobab; London: Serif, 1992); M. G. Vassanji, *No New Land* (New Delhi: Penguin, 1992); M. G. Vassanji, *The Book of Secrets* (London: Macmillan, 1995); Kofi Awoonor, *Comes the Voyager At Last* (Trenton, N.J.: Africa World Press, 1992).

2. Since completing *Gifts* Farah has been working on a nonfictional book on the experiences of Somali refugees in Europe. See Armando Pajalich, "Nuruddin Farah Interviewed," *Kunapipi* 15, no. 1 (1993): 70.

3. Ayi Kwei Armah, *Osiris Rising* (Popenguine, Senegal: Per Ankh, 1995), 305; hereafter cited in the text as *OR*.

4. Ben Okri, *Songs of Enchantment* (London: Jonathan Cape, 1993; London: Vintage, 1994), 258; the Vintage edition is hereafter cited in the text as *SOE*.

5. Ben Okri, *Astonishing the Gods* (London: Phoenix House, 1995), 4; hereafter cited in the text as *ATG*.

6. Kojo Laing, *Major Gentl and the Achimota Wars* (London: Heinemann, 1992), 2; hereafter cited in the text as *MG*.

7. 'Biyi Bandele-Thomas, *The Man Who Came In from the Back of Beyond* (London: Heinemann, 1991), 25.

8. 'Biyi Bandele-Thomas, *The Sympathetic Undertaker and Other Dreams* (London: Bellew Publishing, 1991; London: Heinemann, 1993), 143.

9. Syl Cheney-Coker, *The Last Harmattan of Alusine Dunbar* (London: Heinemann, 1990), 288; hereafter cited in the text as *LHAD*.

10. T. Obinkaram Echewa, *I Saw the Sky Catch Fire* (New York: Plume, 1993), 290; hereafter cited in the text as *ISSCF*.

11. Salman Rushdie, *Imaginary Homelands: Essays and Criticism 1981–1991* (London: Granta, 1991), 394.

12. In the first category, see Homi Bhabha, "The Commitment to Theory," in *Questions of Third Cinema*, ed. Jim Pines and Paul Willeman (London: BFI, 1989), 111–32; and "DissemiNation: Time, Narrative, and the Margins of the Modern Nation," in *Nation and Narration*, ed. Homi Bhabha (London: Routledge, 1990), 291–322. In the second category, see Anthony Kwame Appiah, "Is the Post in Postmodernism the Post in Postcolonial?" *Critical Inquiry* 17, no. 2 (1991): 336–57; and Michael Lim, "Written Communities: Ghana and the Fiction of Kojo Laing," *New Literatures Review* 28/29 (Winter 1994-Summer 1995): 46–54.

Selected Bibliography

PRIMARY SOURCES

Achebe, Chinua. *Arrow of God*. London: Heinemann, 1964.
———. *A Man of the People*. London: Heinemann, 1966.
———. *No Longer at Ease*. London: Heinemann, 1960.
———. *Things Fall Apart*. London: Heinemann, 1958.
Aidoo, Ama Ata. *Changes*. London: The Women's Press, 1991.
Aluko, T. M. *One Man, One Wife*. Lagos: Nigerian Publishing Co., 1959.
———. *One Man, One Matchet*. London: Heinemann, 1964.
Armah, Ayi Kwei. *The Beautyful Ones Are Not Yet Born*. Boston: Houghton Mifflin, 1968; London: Heinemann, 1969.
———. *Fragments*. Boston: Houghton Mifflin, 1970; London: Heinemann, 1974.
———. *The Healers*. Nairobi: East African Publishing House, 1978; London: Heinemann, 1979.
———. *Osiris Rising*. Popenguine, Senegal: Per Ankh, 1995.
———. *Two Thousand Seasons*. Nairobi: East African Publishing House, 1973; London: Heinemann, 1979.
———. *Why Are We So Blest?* New York: Doubleday, 1972; London: Heinemann, 1974.
Awoonor, Kofi. *Comes the Voyager at Last*. Trenton: Africa World Press, 1992.
———. *This Earth, My Brother . . .* New York: Doubleday, 1971; London: Heinemann, 1972.
Bandele-Thomas, 'Biyi. *The Man Who Came In from the Back of Beyond*. London: Heinemann, 1991.
———. *The Sympathetic Undertaker and Other Dreams*. London: Bellew Publishing, 1991; London: Heinemann, 1993.
Cheney-Coker, Syl. *The Last Harmattan of Alusine Dunbar*. London: Heinemann, 1990.
Chinodya, Shimmer. *Harvest of Thorns*. Harare: Baobab, 1989; London: Heinemann, 1990.
Coetzee, J. M. *Age of Iron*. London: Secker and Warburg, 1990.
———. *Dusklands*. Johannesburg: Ravan Press, 1974; Harmondsworth: Penguin, 1983.
———. *Foe*. London: Secker and Warburg, 1986.
———. *In the Heart of the Country*. London: Secker and Warburg, 1977.
———. *Life and Times of Michael K*. London: Secker and Warburg, 1983; Harmondsworth: Penguin, 1985.

SELECTED BIBLIOGRAPHY

———. *Waiting for the Barbarians*. London: Secker and Warburg, 1980.
Conton, William. *The African*. London: William Heinemann, 1960.
Dangarembga, Tsitsi. *Nervous Conditions*. London: The Women's Press, 1988.
Echewa, T. O. *I Saw the Sky Catch Fire*. New York: Plume, 1993.
Ekwensi, Cyprian. *Beautiful Feathers*. London: Hutchinson, 1963.
Emecheta, Buchi. *Gwendolen*. London: Flamingo, 1990.
Farah, Nuruddin. *Close Sesame*. London: Allison and Busby, 1983.
———. *From a Crooked Rib*. London: Heinemann, 1970.
———. *Gifts*. Harare: Boabab; London: Serif, 1992.
———. *A Naked Needle*. London: Heinemann, 1976.
———. *Maps*. London: Picador, 1986.
———. *Sardines*. London: Allison and Busby, 1981; London: Heinemann, 1982.
———. *Sweet and Sour Milk*. London: Allison and Busby, 1979; London: Heinemann, 1980.
Hove, Chenjerai. *Bones*. Harare: Baobab, 1988.
———. *Shadows*. London: Heinemann, 1992.
Laing, B. Kojo. *Major Gentl and the Achimota Wars*. London: Heinemann, 1992.
———. *Search Sweet Country*. London: William Heinemann, 1986; London: Picador, 1987.
Kanengoni, Alexander. *When the Rainbird Cries*. Harare: Longman Zimbabwe, 1987.
Mungoshi, Charles. *Waiting for the Rain*. London: Heinemann, 1975.
Ngugi wa Thiong'o. *Matigari*. Nairobi: Heinemann Kenya, 1986. Translated from the Gikuyu by Wangi wa Goro. London: Heinemann, 1989.
———. *Petals of Blood*. London: Heinemann, 1977.
Nyamfukudza, Stanley. *The Non-Believer's Journey*. London: Heinemann, 1980.
Okara, Gabriel. *The Voice*. London: Andre Deutsch, 1964; London: Heinemann, 1970.
Okri, Ben. *Astonishing the Gods*. London: Phoenix House, 1995.
———. *The Famished Road*. London: Jonathan Cape, 1991; London: Vintage, 1992.
———. *Songs of Enchantment*. London: Jonathan Cape, 1993; London: Vintage, 1994.
Ouologuem, Yambo. *Le Devoir de violence*. Paris: Seuil, 1968. *Bound to Violence*. Trans. Ralph Manheim. London: Heinemann, 1971.
Peters, Lenrie. *The Second Round*. London: Heinemann, 1965.
Samkange, Stanlake. *Year of the Uprising*. London: Heinemann, 1978.
Samupindi, Charles. *Pawns*. Harare: Baobab, 1992.
Soyinka, Wole. *The Interpreters*. London: Andre Deutsch, 1965; London: Heinemann, 1970.
———. *The Man Died*. London: Rex Collings, 1972; Harmondsworth: Penguin, 1975.
———. *Season of Anomy*. London: Rex Collings, 1973.

Vassanji, M. G. *The Book of Secrets*. London: Macmillan, 1995.
———. *The Gunny Sack*. London: Heinemann, 1989.
———. *No New Land*. New Delhi: Penguin, 1992.
Vera, Yvonne. *Nehanda*. Harare: Baobab, 1993.

SECONDARY SOURCES

Selected Interviews

"Forces to Be Reckoned With: An Interview with Shimmer Chinodya." *Parade*, 11 and 25 October 1990, 25.
Gates, Louis S. "An Interview with Wole Soyinka." *Black World* 24, no. 10 (August 1975): 30–48.
Goldblatt, John. "Kofi Awoonor: An Interview." *Transition* 41 (1972): 42–44.
Igwe, Dimba. "Ayi Kwei Armah's Celebration of Silence." *Sunday Concord* (Lagos, Nigeria), 12 April 1987, pp. 11–12.
Jaggi, Maya. "A Combining of Gifts: An Interview with Nuruddin Farah." *Third World Quarterly* 11, no. 3 (July 1989): 171–87.
———. "*Matigari* as Myth and History: An Interview with Ngugi wa Thiong'o." *Third World Quarterly* 11, no. 4 (October 1989): 241–51.
Kanaganayakam, Chelva. "Broadening the Substrata: An Interview with M. G. Vassanji." *World Literature Written in English* 31, no. 2 (Autumn 1991): 19–35.
Langille, Mary. "Coming Out of Oral Tradition to Write about Dictatorship: An Interview with Nuruddin Farah." *The Varsity* (University of Toronto, 26 November 1987): 7.
Lindfors, Bernth, with Ian Munro, Reinhard Sander, and Richard Priebe. "Interview with Kofi Awoonor." In *Palaver: Interviews with Five African Authors*, ed. Bernth Lindfors, 47–64. Austin: African Research Institute, University of Texas, 1972.
Maja-Pearce, Adewale. "Interview with Kojo Laing." *Wasafiri* 6/7 (Spring-Autumn 1987): 27–29.
Moss, Robert. "Mapping the Psyche: Interview with Nuruddin Farah." *West Africa* (1 September 1986): 1827–28.
Nasta, Susheila. "Interview: Moyez Vassanji." *Wasafiri* 13 (Spring 1991): 19–21.
Osofisan, Femi. "Reflections on a Fading Breed" (Conversation with Ayi Kwei Armah). *Sunday Times* (Lagos, Nigeria), 26 November 1989, p. 5.
Pajalich, Armando. "Nuruddin Farah Interviewed." *Kunapipi* 15, no. 1 (1993): 61–71.
Petersen, Kirsten Holst. "Between Gender, Race and History: Interview with Tsitsi Dangarembga." *Kunapipi* 16, no. 1 (1994): 345–48.
Rhedin, Folke. "J. M. Coetzee: Interview." *Kunapipi* 6, no. 1 (1984): 6–11.

Ross, Jean. "*Contemporary Authors* Interview: Ben Okri." In *Contemporary Authors*, vol. 138, ed. Donna Olendorf, 337–41. Detroit: Gale Research, 1993.

Veit-Wild, Flora. "Interview with Shimmer Chinodya in Harare, 1990." Quoted in Flora Veit-Wild, *Teachers, Preachers and Non-Believers: A Social History of Zimbabwean Literature*, 321–22. London: Hans Zell, 1992.

Wilkinson, Jane. "Kofi Awoonor," "Tsitsi Dangarembga," "Ngugi wa Thiong'o," "Ben Okri," and "Wole Soyinka." In *Talking with African Writers*, ed. Jane Wilkinson, 19–32, 77–110, 123–36, 189–200. London: James Currey, 1992.

Critical Studies and Anthologies, and Journal Special Issues

For reasons of space, uncollected journal articles have not been included here. Most of the articles cited in the chapter notes are published in the journal issues or are reprinted in the critical studies and essay collections listed below.

Achebe, Chinua. *Morning Yet on Creation Day*. London: Heinemann, 1975. Achebe's essays in this and the next listed volume provide lucid insights into the moral and cultural dilemmas besetting the African writer during the political crises of the decolonization period; they also contain sharp criticism of novels by Armah, Awoonor, and others.

———. *Hopes and Impediments*. London: Heinemann, 1988.

Asein, S. O., and A. O. Ashaolu, eds. *Studies in the African Novel*. Ibadan: Ibadan University Press, 1986. A useful introductory volume, with informative and perceptive essays on Armah, Echewa, Mwangi, Ngugi, and others.

Attwell, David. *J. M. Coetzee: South Africa and the Politics of Writing*. Berkeley: University of California Press, 1993. An elegant and incisive account of Coetzee as a writer of complex "situational metafiction" that both reflects and subverts his nation's dominant culture.

Booth, James. *Writers and Politics in Nigeria*. London: Hodder and Stoughton, 1981. Trenchant criticism of Nigerian fiction of the 1960s and 1970s in its political context, together with an informative account of the historical background to federation and illuminating profiles of the nationalist leaders.

Boyce Davies, Carole, and Anne Adams Graves, eds. *Ngambika: Studies of Women in African Literature*. Trenton, N.J.: Africa World Press, 1986. A comprehensive and challenging collection of essays on female portraiture and gender definition in the work of African men and women novelists.

Chinweizu, Onwuchekwa Jemie, and Ihechukwu Madubuike. *Towards the Decolonization of African Literature*. London: Kegan Paul, 1985. An erratic, often ill-informed polemic that has acquired some notoriety for its attack on Soyinka's work as "Euromodernist" and the acerbic replies from Soyinka and others that it occasioned.

Coetzee, J. M. *Doubling the Point: Essays and Interviews*, ed. David Attwell. Cambridge, Mass.: Harvard University Press, 1992. A comprehensive collection of Coetzee's writings and statements on world literatures, popular culture, local censorship, the position of the white writer in his country, and the work of fellow South African novelists.

Cook, David, and Michael Okenimpke. *Ngugi wa Thiong'o: An Exploration of His Writings*. 2d ed. London: Heinemann, 1996. A systematic, in-depth interpretation of Ngugi's fictional and nonfictional writing up to 1993.

CRNLE Reviews Journal no. 2 (1994). "New African Writing and Criticism," ed. Derek Wright. Focuses on African writing and criticism from 1985 onward, with special attention to the younger generation of writers who came to public notice during this period.

Fanon, Frantz. *Les damné de la terre*, 1961. *The Wretched of the Earth*. Trans. Constance Farrington. Harmondsworth, England: Penguin, 1967. The classic analysis of third-world revolution and neocolonialism that deeply influenced African writers and intellectuals, liberals and radicals alike, during the postindependence decade.

Fraser, Robert. *The Novels of Ayi Kwei Armah: A Study in Polemical Fiction*. London: Heinemann, 1980. An introductory monograph that contains lucid thematic and stylistic analysis of the first novel as well as illuminating detective work on the literary ancestry of *Two Thousand Seasons*.

Gakwandi, Shatto Arthur. *The Novel and Contemporary Experience in Africa*. London: Heinemann, 1977. Shrewd and balanced criticism of novels by Achebe, Aluko, Armah, Ngugi, Soyinka, and others that does justice to their stylistic complexities while exposing the simplicities of their political visions.

Gallagher, Susan VanZanten. *A Story of South Africa: J. M. Coetzee's Fiction in Context*. Cambridge, Mass.: Harvard University Press, 1991. The first study of Coetzee's fiction to investigate its national literary and historical contexts in any systematic way, and the best book on the author to date.

Gibbs, James, ed. *Critical Perspectives on Wole Soyinka*. Washington, D.C.: Three Continents Press, 1980; London: Heinemann, 1981. The best critical anthology on Soyinka. Contains lucid lengthy essays on the novels by D. S. Izevbaye and Mark Kinkead-Weekes.

Gikandi, Simon. *Reading the African Novel*. London: James Currey; Portsmouth, N.H.: Heinemann, 1987. Astute analysis of the narrative structure and sociology of a wide range of fiction, including works by Achebe, Amadi, Armah, Ngugi, Ousmane, and Soyinka.

Gurnah, Abdulrazak, ed. *Essays on African Writing 1: A Re-evaluation*. Oxford: Heinemann, 1993. A reappraisal of major figures of the first generation of postcolonial African writing, including Achebe, Armah, Coetzee, Farah, Ngugi, and Soyinka.

———, ed. *Essays on African Writing 2: Contemporary Literature*. Oxford: Heinemann, 1995. This volume, a companion to the preceding item, focuses on the younger generation of writers, offering detailed analyses of novels by Dangarembga, Marechera, Okri, and Vassanji.

Hale, Thomas A. *Scribe, Griot, and Novelist: Narrative Interpreters of the Songhay Empire*. Gainesville: University of Florida Press, 1990. Contains an illuminating chapter on Ouologuem's *Bound to Violence* and its relation to Sahelian oral epic traditions.

Harrow, Kenneth, *Thresholds of Change in African Literature*. London: James Currey; Portsmouth, N.H.: Heinemann, 1994. An incisive study of modern African literary traditions, including chapters on novels by Ouologuem, Laye, and other francophone authors alongside chapters on Achebe and Bessie Head.

Huggan, Graham, and Stephen Watson, eds. *Critical Perspectives on J. M. Coetzee*. London: Macmillan, 1996. A challenging collection of essays on all aspects of Coetzee's fiction. Includes outstanding contributions from Ian Glenn, Benita Parry, and Stephen Watson.

African Literature Today, no. 11 (1980), "Myth and History," ed. Eldred Durosimi Jones. Contains insightful essays on the mythic dimensions of fiction by Achebe, Armah, and Soyinka, including a witty and irreverent essay by Bernth Lindfors on the weaknesses of Armah's historical novels.

African Literature Today, no. 13 (1983), "Recent Trends in the Novel," ed. Eldred Durosimi Jones. Contains searching narrative and stylistic analyses of fiction by Soyinka and Ngugi, together with essays on younger novelists, and a scholarly account by Isidore Okpewho of the oral and mythological backgrounds to Armah's *Two Thousand Seasons*.

Jones, Eldred Durosimi, and Marjorie Jones, eds. *New Trends and Generations in African Literature*. London: James Currey; Trenton: Africa World Press, 1996. A diverse collection of essays on African writing after 1980 from all parts of the continent, including essays on Cheney-Coker, Dangarembga, Laing, radical Nigerian fiction, and Zimbabwean war writing.

Killam, G. D., ed. *The Writing of East and Central Africa*. London: Heinemann, 1984. A wide-ranging critical anthology covering, in addition to East African literature, writing from Zimbabwe and the Horn of Africa. Specific essays are devoted to Farah, Ngugi, Taban lo Liyong, and Meja Mwangi.

Kunapipi 16, no. 1 (1994). Special issue "Post-Colonial Women's Writing," including an interview with Dangarembga and a penetrating analysis of *Nervous Conditions* by Heidi Creamer.

Lazarus, Neil. *Resistance in Postcolonial African Fiction*. New Haven and London: Yale University Press, 1990. A thorough and scholarly study of Ayi Kwei Armah that includes a brilliant deconstruction of the mythology of independence and a penetrating political analysis of the first novel.

Lindfors, Bernth, and Reinhard Sander, eds. *Dictionary of Literary Biography, Vols. 117 and 125: Twentieth-Century Caribbean and Black African Writers*, first and second series. Detroit: Gale Research, 1992 and 1993. An invaluable reference guide containing detailed scholarly essays on all the major African writers.

Maja-Pearce, Adewale. *A Mask Dancing: Nigerian Novelists of the Eighties.* London: Hans Zell, 1992. A pioneering polemic by an iconoclastic Nigerian critic, calling upon Nigeria's novelists to cease purist exercises in racial retrieval and cultural archaeology and instead to fully engage with the complex multicultural modernity of late twentieth-century African experience.

———, ed. *Wole Soyinka: An Appraisal.* Oxford: Heinemann, 1994. Contains astute discussion of the complexities and simplicities of Soyinka's fiction by Abdulrazak Gurnah and of his African worldview by Kwame Anthony Appiah, plus the text of Soyinka's Nobel Prize lecture and a 1993 interview with Soyinka by 'Biyi Bandele-Thomas.

McEwan, Neil. *Africa and the Novel.* Atlantic Highlands, N.J.: Humanities Press, 1983. Perceptive analyses of novels of the independence decade and after, covering works by Achebe, Armah, Farah, and Ngugi, with a particularly lively discussion of satiric form in Soyinka's *The Interpreters.*

Moore, Gerald. *Wole Soyinka.* London: Evans, 1971. Rev. ed., 1978. An excellent condensed study of Soyinka's work up to 1976. Contains astute criticism of the two novels and acerbic comment, in passing, on Armah's *Two Thousand Seasons.*

———. *Twelve African Writers.* London: Hutchinson, 1980. A mixture of sensitive and sharp criticism of postindependence writing, with probing chapters on Achebe, Awoonor, Ngugi, and Soyinka.

Ngara, Emmanuel. *Art and Ideology in the African Novel.* London: Heinemann, 1985. A study of African fiction in the context of Marxist aesthetics with special focus on novels by Armah, Ngugi, and Ousmane.

———, ed. *New Writing from Southern Africa.* London: James Currey, 1996. Has perceptive essays on Chinodya, Dangarembga, Hove, and others.

Ngugi wa Thiong'o. *Decolonizing the Mind.* London: James Currey, 1986. A powerful polemic, by a writer who teaches by example, on the politics of language in African literature.

Nkosi, Lewis. *Tasks and Masks: Themes and Styles of African Literature.* Harlow, England: Longman, 1981. Astute criticism of selected African writings in their sociopolitical contexts by one of Africa's finest literary critics

Obiechina, Emmanuel. *Culture, Tradition and Society in the West African Novel.* Cambridge: Cambridge University Press, 1975. Perceptive analysis of language, characterization, time concepts, and oral influences in selected fiction but weakened by the repetitive, piecemeal approach to the novels under different chapter headings.

Ogungbesan, Kolawole, ed. *New West African Literature.* London: Heinemann, 1979. Good concise criticism of Ouologuem, Peters, and Soyinka.

Omotoso, Kole. *Achebe or Soyinka? A Study in Contrasts*. London: Hans Zell, 1995. A profile of Africa's two best-known writers, exploring their different backgrounds and visions of Nigeria, their respective historical and mythic modes of consciousness, and their responses to their critics.

Palmer, Eustace. *The Growth of the African Novel*. London: Heinemann, 1979. Painstaking descriptive criticism of fiction by the major anglophone and francophone novelists.

Penner, Dick. *Countries of the Mind: The Fiction of J. M. Coetzee*. Westport: Greenwood Press, 1989. An in-depth critique of Coetzee's first five novels in the context of the Western literary tradition, rendered somewhat disjointed by the frequency of subheadings within chapters.

Priebe, Richard, ed. *Ghanaian Literatures*. Westport: Greenwood Press, 1988. Reprints Priebe's essay on Awoonor's *This Earth, My Brother*, together with excellent criticism of Armah's fiction by Gareth Griffiths, D. S. Izevbaye, and Edward Lobb.

———. *Myth, Realism, and the West African Writer*. Trenton: Africa World Press, 1988. A pioneering conceptual, if overly abstract, study of mythic elements and ritual structures in the work of Armah, Awoonor, and Soyinka.

Research in African Literatures 16, no. 2 (Summer 1985). Special Ngugi issue.

Research in African Literatures 20, no. 1 (Spring 1989). Special issue on anglophone fiction, including essays on Armah, Ngugi, and Soyinka.

Research in African Literatures 22, no. 4 (Winter 1991). Includes a "Round Table" on Ngugi's *Matigari*: excellent contributions from Simon Gikandi, Abdulrazak Gurnah, and David Maughan Brown.

Research in African Literatures 26, no. 1 (Spring 1995). Special issue on "New Voices in African Literature," including essays on Dangarembga and Okri.

Rutherford, Anna, ed. *From Commonwealth to Post-Colonial*. Sydney: Dangaroo Press, 1992. Contains two useful short essays on Okri's fiction.

Smith, Angela. *East African Writing in English*. London: Macmillan, 1989. A lucid and knowledgeable introductory study, providing close readings of texts by Farah, Mwangi, and Ngugi.

Soyinka, Wole. *Myth, Literature and the African World*. Cambridge: Cambridge University Press, 1976. Contains subtly sympathetic readings of controversial novels by Ouologuem and Armah.

———. *Art, Dialogue and Outrage: Essays on Literature and Culture*. Ibadan: New Horn Press, 1988. Contains the long essay "The Critic and Society," in which Soyinka responds to Gerald Moore's criticism of the political vision of *Season of Anomy*.

Studies in Twentieth-Century Literature 15, no. 1 (Winter 1991), "Africa: Literature and Politics," ed. Claire L. Dehon. Incisive, in-depth discussion of the political dimensions of key anglophone, francophone, and lusophone texts, including works by Achebe, Aidoo, and Farah.

Veit-Wild, Flora. *Teachers, Preachers and Non-Believers: A Social History of Zimbabwean Literature*. London: Hans Zell, 1992. A meticulous social and ethnographic survey of the production of Zimbabwean literature from the 1950s to the 1980s, strong on cultural history but short on textual analysis.

Wright, Derek. *Ayi Kwei Armah's Africa: The Sources of His Fiction*. London: Hans Zell, 1989. A detailed exploration of the ritual, mythological, and political contexts of Armah's writing.

———, ed. *Critical Perspectives on Ayi Kwei Armah*. Washington, D.C.: Three Continents Press, 1992. A broad selection of responses to Armah's writing, including trenchant criticism by James Booth, Leonard Kibera, and Neil Lazarus, and a subtle account of the novels' phenomenology of perception by D. S. Izevbaye.

———. *Wole Soyinka Revisited*. New York: Twayne, 1993. The only comprehensive account of Soyinka's work in all genres up to 1990.

———. *The Novels of Nuruddin Farah*. Bayreuth: Bayreuth African Studies, 1994. A critical introduction to Farah's seven novels prefaced by a brief account of their complex Somali social and cultural backgrounds.

Zimunya, Musaemura. *Those Years of Drought and Hunger: The Birth of African Fiction in English in Zimbabwe*. Gweru, Zimbabwe: Mambo, 1982. A pioneering study of Zimbabwean fiction of the 1970s by one of the country's major poets.

Bibliographies

Lindfors, Bernth. *Black African Literatures in English* (to 1976). Detroit: Gale Research, 1979. *1977–1981 Supplement*. New York: Africana Publishing, 1986. *1982–1986 Supplement*. London and New York: Hans Zell, 1989.

Zell, Hans, with Carol Bundy and Virginia Coulon. *A New Reader's Guide to African Literature,* rev. and enl. ed. London: Heinemann, 1983.

Index

Achebe, Chinua, 12, 16; *Arrow of God,* 42; *Man of the People, A,* 6, 8, 9–10; *No Longer at Ease,* 1, 9, 10, 14; *Things Fall Apart,* 9, 42
Aidoo, Ama Ata, 19; *Changes,* 162
Algeria, postcolonial independence, 2–3, 11
Aluko, T. M., 5; *One Man, One Matchet,* 1; *One Man, One Wife,* 1
Anyidoho, Kofi, 57
Armah, Ayi Kwei, 9

WORKS

Beautyful Ones Are Not Yet Born, The, 1, 11, 153; hyperbole in, 55; postcolonial corruption and materialism in, 6, 7, 12–13; treatment of intellectuals in, 10
Fragments, 6, 7, 10, 14, 15
Healers, The, 17–18, 58, 165
"Mystification: African Independence Revalued, A," 5, 56
Orisis Rising, 58, 164–66, 179
Two Thousand Seasons, 17–18, 19, 165; orature revisited through, 48–59
Why Are We So Blest?, 15, 16

Arusha Declaration, 125
Awoonor, Kofi: *Comes the Voyager At Last,* 163–64, 179; *This Earth, My Brother,* 12, 19, 23–33

Ba, Mariama, 19
Bandele-Thomas, 'Biyi, 178; *Man Who Came In from the Back of Beyond, The,* 171–72, 173–74; *Sympathetic Undertaker and Other Dreams,* 172–74
Barre, Siyad, 68, 70, 77; fall of, 79
Bella, Ben, 3
Booth, James, 5

Cabral, Amilcar, 18
Cheney-Coker, Syl, 178; *Last Harmattan of Alusine Dunbar, The,* 174–76

Chinodya, Shimmer, *Harvest of Thorns,* 20, 96–107
Chipamaunga, Edmund, *Fighter for Freedom,* 95
Coetzee, J. M.: *Age of Iron,* 81, 162–63; *Dusklands,* 81; *Foe,* 80–81, 94, 162; *In the Heart of the Country,* 81; *Life and Times of Michael K,* 20, 80, 81–94; *Waiting for the Barbarian,* 81
"consciencism," 8
Conton, William, *The African,* 1
Convention People's Party (CPP), 11
Creamer, Heidi, 116

Dakubu, Mary Kropp, 148
Dangarembga, Tsitsi, *Nervous Conditions,* 20, 109–22

Eagleton, Terry, 119
Echewa, T. Obinkaram, *I Saw the Sky Catch Fire,* 176–78
Ekwensi, Cyprian, *Beautiful Feathers,* 2
Emecheta, Buchi, 19, 162

Fagunwa, D. O., 178; *Forest of a Thousand Daemons,* 157
Fall, Aminata Sow, 19
Fanon, Frantz, 8, 11, 17; *The Wretched of the Earth,* 5, 6, 15, 16–17, 118
Farah, Nuruddin, 19–20, 21; *From a Crooked Rib,* 68; *Gifts,* 163; *Maps,* 68, 162; *Naked Needle, A,* 69; *Sardines,* 69, 70–71, 74–75; *Sweet and Sour Milk,* 20, 60, 68–79; *Variations on the Theme of an African Dictatorship,* 68; "Why I Write," 77

Ghana, postcolonial independence, 1, 2, 4, 5–6
Gordimer, Nadine, 88, 162
Grass, Günter, *Tin Drum, The,* 173
Gurnah, Abdulrazak, 67

Hale, Thomas, 43

199

Head, Bessie, 19
Houphouet-Boigny, 3
Hove, Chenjerai, 96, 103, 106; *Bones,* 95, 96, 97, 103, 179; *Shadows,* 96

Ivory Coast, postcolonial independence, 4
Iyayi, Festus, 19

Kanengoni, Alexander, *When the Rainbird Cries,* 96
Katiyo, Wilson, *Son of the Soil,* 95
Kaunda, philosophy of, 8
Keita, Modibo, identification with feudal despots, 47
Kenya, postcolonial independence, 3
Kristeva, Julia, 119

Laing, Kojo, 60, 178; *Major Gentl and the Achimota Wars,* 169–71; *Search Sweet Country,* 140–49; *Woman of the Aeroplanes,* 145
Lazarus, Neil: on Armah's *Beautyful Ones Are Not Yet Born,* 11–12, 13; on authorial disillusionment in postcolonial Africa, 10–11

Machel, Samora, 18
Maja-Pearce, Adewale: *Mask Dancing: Nigerian Novelists of the Eighties, A,* 21–22; on Okri's *The Famished Road,* 156, 157
Marechera, Dambudzo, 95
Masinde, Elijah, 61
Mathenge, Stanley, 61
Mazorodze, Isheunesu, *Silent Journey from the East,* 96
Mensah, A. N., 53, 55
Miller, Christopher, 46
Mohammed, Askia, 43
Moi, Toril, 118–19
Moore, Gerald, 25, 31, 40
Mugabe, Robert, 18
Mungoshi, Charles, 95; *Waiting for the Rain,* 96
Mwangi, Meja, 19

Neto, Agostinho, 18

Ngugi wa Thiong'o, 18; *Devil on the Cross,* 19; *Matigari,* 60–68; *Petals of Blood,* 19
Nigeria, postcolonial independence, 2, 3, 4, 5
Nkrumah, Kwame, 1; fall of, 2, 5–6; philosophy of, 8–9. *See also* Convention People's Party (CPP)
Nwapa, Flora, 19
Nyamfukudza, Stanley, *Non-Believer's Journey, The,* 96
Nyerere, 8, 52, 125

Okara, Gabriel, *The Voice,* 10, 12, 42
Okello, John, 125
Okpewho, Isidore, 50
Okri, Ben, 178; *Astonishing the Gods,* 168–69; *Famished Road, The,* 149–61; *Songs of Enchantment,* 166–68
Ouologuem, Yambo, 162; *Bound to Violence,* 19, 42–48

Peters, Lenrie, *Second Round, The,* 10, 12
Priebe, Richard, 28

Quayson, Ato, 144, 155

Rushdie, Salman: *Midnight's Children,* 137; *Satanic Verses, The,* 178; *Shame,* 173
Rwanda, postcolonial independence, 3

Samkange, Stanlake, *Year of the Uprising,* 95
Samupindi, Charles, *Pawns,* 96
Saro-Wiwa, Ken, 18, 19
Sayyid, 69
Schwartz-Bart, Andre, *Le Dernier des justes,* 47
Schwerdt, Dianne, 66
Sembene, Ousmane, 9
Senegal, postcolonial independence, 4
Senghor, 3, 47; philosophy of, 8–9
Serumaga, Robert, *Return to the Shadows,* 12
Smith, Ian, 96
Soyinka, Wole, 16, 162, 178; on Armah's *Two Thousand Seasons,* 48, 51, 57; on

concept of sacrificial revolutionary, 37–38; response to Moore's criticism, 40

WORKS
"Abiku," 154
"Climates of Art," 153
Dance of the Forests, A, 153, 157
"Fourth Stage, The," 38
Interpreters, The, 7, 12; treatment of intellectuals in, 10, 14–15
Man Died, The, 38
Season of Anomy, 19, 23; history as myth and ritual in, 33–41

Sundjata, 47

Tanzania. See *Ujamaa*

Tarik al-Fetach, 43, 46
Tarik al-Sudan, 43, 46
Tutuola, Amos, 42, 156, 178; *My Life in the Bush of Ghosts,* 157; *Palm-Wine Drinkard, The,* 157

Uganda, postcolonial independence, 3
Ujamaa, 3, 8, 52
Unilateral Declaration of Independence (UDI), 96

Vassanji, M. G.: *Book of Secrets, The,* 163; *Gunny Sack, The,* 20–21, 123–39; *No New Land,* 163
Veit-Wild, Flora, 101
Vera, Yvonne, *Nehanda,* 162

Wiil-Waal, 69

The Author

Derek Wright was until recently associate professor of English at the Northern Territory University, Darwin, Australia, and has previously taught at the University of Queensland and the University of Sierra Leone, West Africa. He is the author of over a hundred articles and essays on world literatures, plus many reviews, and has published six books on African writing. These include *The Novels of Nuruddin Farah, Wole Soyinka Revisited* (an earlier Twayne volume), and *Ayi Kwei Armah's Africa: The Sources of His Fiction,* which was named a CHOICE Outstanding Academic Book in 1991. In addition, he has edited *Extra-Territorial,* an anthology of Australian stories and poems, and *New African Writing and Criticism,* a special issue of the *CRNLE Reviews Journal.*

The Editor

Bernth Lindfors is a professor of English and African literature at the University of Texas at Austin. He has written and edited more than thirty books, including *Black African Literature in English* (1979, 1986, 1989, 1995), *Popular Literatures in Africa* (1991), *Comparative Approaches to African Literatures* (1994), *Long Drums and Canons: Teaching and Researching African Literatures* (1995), *Loaded Vehicles: Studies in African Literary Media* (1996), and (with Reinhard Sander) *Twentieth-Century Caribbean and Black African Writers* (1992, 1993, 1996). From 1970 to 1989 he was editor of *Research in African Literatures*.